DEMOCRACY

DEMOCRACY

BY CARL COHEN

UNIVERSITY OF GEORGIA PRESS
ATHENS

Library of Congress Catalog Card Number: 77–142911
Standard Book Number: 8203–0271–6

The University of Georgia Press, Athens 30601

Printed in the United States of America
by Heritage Printers, Inc.
Charlotte, North Carolina 28202

To
my students and colleagues
at
the University of Michigan

Table of contents

Preface   xiii

PART ONE: THE NATURE OF DEMOCRACY

Chapter   1   What democracy is   1
                  1.1 Some short definitions of democracy   3
                  1.2 The paradox of self-rule   4
                  1.3 The essence of democracy   5

Chapter   2   The dimensions of democracy   8
                  2.1 The measures of participation   8
                  2.2 The breadth of democracy   8
                  2.3 The problem of the unrecognized community   16
                  2.4 The depth of democracy   17
                  2.5 Deep democracy in practice   19
                  2.6 The range of democracy   22
                  2.7 The problem of overlapping communities   25

Chapter   3   Some general observations about democracy   28
                  3.1 Some things democracy is not: common errors   28
                  3.2 On appraising a democracy   33
                  3.3 Democratic forms and democratic processes   36

PART TWO: THE PRESUPPOSITIONS OF DEMOCRACY

Chapter   4   Democracy presupposes community   41
                  4.1 The basic presupposition   41
                  4.2 Political communities and citizenship   42
                  4.3 Non-political communities   45
                  4.4 Community and the rule of the majority   46
                  4.5 On preserving union   47
                  4.6 The breakdown of community   48

TABLE OF CONTENTS

4.7 Marginal community membership   49
4.8 Degrees of community membership   52
4.9 Fraternity   54

Chapter 5   Democracy presupposes rationality   55

PART THREE: DEMOCRACY AND ITS INSTRUMENTS

Chapter 6   Democracy and majority rule   61
   6.1 Decision-making rules   61
   6.2 Appraising decision-making rules in a democracy   62
   6.3 Democratic process and decision-making rules   64
   6.4 Majority rule and its varieties   65
   6.5 Majority rule as the instrument of democracy   68
   6.6 Rule by fluctuating majorities   71
   6.7 On the misuse of majority power   74

Chapter 7   Democracy and representation   76
   7.1 Representation as the instrument of democracy   76
   7.2 Democratic elections in general   78
   7.3 Degrees of representation   79
   7.4 Decision-making rules and representative bodies   80
   7.5 Bases of representation   81
   7.6 Geographical and proportional representation   84
   7.7 Levels of representation   87
   7.8 Representation between elections   88
   7.9 The dilemma of the representative   90
   7.10 The conflict of local and larger interests   93

PART FOUR: THE CONDITIONS OF DEMOCRACY

Chapter 8   Democracy and its conditions   101
   8.1 Relations of democracy to its conditions   101
   8.2 Relations of the conditions of democracy to one another   102
   8.3 Democracy and its conditions distinguished   103
   8.4 The kinds of conditions of democracy   104

Table of contents

Chapter 9   **The material conditions of democracy**   **107**

9.1 The kinds of material conditions   107
9.2 The environmental conditions of democracy   107
9.3 The mechanical conditions of democracy   108
9.4 The economic conditions of democracy   109
9.5 Economic well-being as a condition of democracy   110
9.6 Is "economic democracy" the condition of any genuine democracy?   111
9.7 Democracy and economic systems   115
9.8 Economic equality as a condition of democracy   118

Chapter 10   **The constitutional conditions of democracy**   **120**

10.1 Introductory note on constitutional conditions   120
10.2 Freedoms and rights   120
10.3 Democracy and freedom   122
10.4 Political freedoms   123
10.5 Freedoms of speech   124
10.6 Absolutist defense of free speech   128
10.7 Utilitarian defense of free speech   132
10.8 A conditional defense of free speech   139
10.9 Incitement and advocacy   143
10.10 Free speech and anti-democratic minority   152

Chapter 11   **The intellectual conditions of democracy**   **156**

11.1 Introductory note on intellectual conditions   156
11.2 The provision of information   156
11.3 Democracy and secrecy   161
11.4 The education of citizens   162
11.5 The arts of conferral   166

Chapter 12   **The psychological conditions of democracy**   **170**

12.1 Psychological traits as dispositions   170
12.2 Fallibilistic citizens   172
12.3 Experimentally minded citizens   174
12.4 Critical citizens   176
12.5 Flexible citizens   178
12.6 Realistic citizens   179
12.7 Compromising citizens   180

ix

TABLE OF CONTENTS

	12.8	Tolerant citizens	184
	12.9	Objective citizens	187
	12.10	Confident citizens	188
	12.11	Concluding notes on psychological conditions	189

Chapter 13	**The protective conditions of democracy**		**192**
	13.1	Introductory remarks on protective conditions	192
	13.2	Protection against external threat	192
	13.3	Protection against internal threat	195
	13.4	Undemocratic origins and anti-democratic effects	198

PART FIVE: THE DEFENSE OF DEMOCRACY

Chapter 14	**The vindication of democracy**		**205**
	14.1	General remarks about vindicatory arguments	205
	14.2	Democracy and wise policy	209
	14.3	Democracy and distributive justice	215
	14.4	Democracy and the peaceful resolution of disputes	224
	14.5	Democracy and loyalty	228
	14.6	Democracy promotes freedom of speech	231
	14.7	Democracy promotes intellectual growth	233
	14.8	Democracy promotes its psychological conditions	238

Chapter 15	**The justification of democracy**		**241**
	15.1	Justification and vindication	241
	15.2	The argument outlined	242
	15.3	The justification of democracy in general	242
	15.4	The justification of democracy in the body politic	248
	15.5	Objections and replies	257
	15.6	Equality as an hypothesis	263

x

Table of contents

Chapter 16   The intrinsic values of democracy   268
             16.1   Democracy as autonomy   268
             16.2   Autonomy and heteronomy in government 270
             16.3   Liberty, equality, fraternity   273

PART SIX: THE PROSPECTS OF DEMOCRACY

Chapter 17   Why democracy is not likely to succeed   277
             17.1   A note on political prophecy   277
             17.2   The material prospects of democracy   277
             17.3   The intellectual prospects of democracy 280
             17.4   The fraternal prospects of democracy 284
             17.5   Realism and world democracy   286
             17.6   A concluding note on the future of
                    democracy   287

Index   289

Preface

In this book I present and defend a general theory of democracy. Democracy has become the foremost political ideal in all the world. Praised on every hand, equally by those otherwise in fundamental philosophical disagreement, it is professed by some who understand it little and want it less. As a consequence of careless rhetoric, intellectual confusion, and even some deliberate deception, the term "democracy" has been largely drained of its meaning. Applied to almost everything in the sphere of politics, it has come to mean almost nothing.

The loss is serious. Beneath the confusion and the rhetoric lie principles of highest import. There is a philosophy of government properly called democracy; it deserves to be respected and—in many but not all contexts—to be defended. My object is to provide a theoretical account, coherent and reasonably complete, of what democracy is and how it works.

Of course the same word, democracy, can be used to refer to very different things, and very different words can be used to refer to the same thing. Confusions introduced by this flexibility of language must be guarded against, but it is not words that are my chief concern, and it is neither necessary nor desirable to invent a new name for the philosophy I propose to examine. "Democracy" is a good enough word, and the word will behave itself if we will. The task is to explain this philosophy of democracy, to make it plain, so that it can be fully understood and justly evaluated.

The theory to be developed will address the following questions, here put in bluntest form:

First: What is the *nature* of democracy?

Second: What are the *presuppositions* of democracy?

Third: What are the *instruments* of democracy?

Fourth: What are the *conditions* required for the success of democracy?

Fifth: What arguments are to be given in *defense* of democracy?

Sixth: What are the *prospects* of democracy?

Answers to these six questions appear, respectively, in the six Parts of this book.

Three methodological points deserve mention before development of the theory is begun. *First*: reasonable expectations must be maintained regarding the degree of precision possible in this enterprise. Not political science, but political philosophy is the field of exploration. We may hope for accurate and reliable results, but must be prepared for some degree of vagueness and uncertainty. "It is the mark of an educated man," Aristotle notes in the *Nicomachean Ethics* (I, 3, 1094b) "to look for precision in each class of things just so far as the nature of the subject admits."

Second: in exploring the philosophy of democracy, it is not unreasonable to combine commitment and objectivity. In political affairs, strong feelings of loyalty or aversion are natural and healthy. It is entirely possible to harbor such feelings while undertaking a rational assessment of the governmental system (or other entity) that is the object of affection or repugnance. Unavoidably, bias will distort our judgments. But in the study of political philosophies we are all biased, we necessarily view matters from a particular angle or slant. If now there is a widespread bias favoring democracy, we are challenged to take account of that fact in pursuing its study. The difficulty is not insuperable. Nor should we fear that honest inquiry into the theory of democracy may weaken loyalty to it, or respect for it. A full understanding of democracy and how it operates may prove, in fact, a necessary foundation for enduring loyalty and justified respect. Let us follow the argument where it leads. Strengthened commitment to democracy is not the appropriate aim of an objective study of it, but such commitment may be the natural outcome of that study.

Finally: there is no place for dogmatism in this undertaking. An enormous variety of cultural and philosophic traditions have contributed to the development of democratic theory; that theory is the exclusive property of none of them. It is true that philosophic or religious schools of thought agreeing that democracy ought to be defended do not all agree how it ought to be defended. I aim to provide a defense of it that will prove acceptable to all of its supporters, whatever their religious or metaphysical commitments, and an account of democracy generally acceptable to supporters and critics alike.

In doing this I am allowed no recourse to final authorities; there are none for the resolution of disputes about democracy. No book or document provides the final statement of democracy. No existing scripture is theoretically adequate for the purpose, and even if one were it would be certain to meet with opposition from democrats who deny its authority. No person or persons, living or dead, however great, are entitled to the last word on the subject. As a theory of human government democracy rests upon no ultimate authority, nor is there any single body of doctrine from which it is necessarily derived. As the examination of the democratic process will disclose, that process itself excludes absolute authorities in its own defense. There may be dogmatic democrats; there can be no democratic dogma.

Fallibilism, therefore, is a principle I consciously adopt. Every human being is subject to error even upon those matters closest and most important to him. No conviction—whatever the subjective certainty with which it is held—is exempt from critical review. The principle of fallibilism applies in every intellectual undertaking; in the study of democracy it is cardinal.

While it is true that our judgments are always subject to mistake, however, they need not always be mistaken. Error and uncertainty are common, yet we may have good reason to believe that in some spheres our errors gradually become less numerous and less grave. Knowledge men now possess, where it is most extensive and most secure, has been acquired not by the recognition of absolute truths, but by the laborious correction of mistakes, and the improvement of uncertain theories. So it is likely to be also with regard to our knowledge and our judgments of democracy.

Part One

THE NATURE OF DEMOCRACY

Chapter 1

What democracy is

1.1 Some short definitions of democracy

Democracy is government by the people. This is a definition most dictionaries report and one likely to meet with general approval. It also fits the etymology of the term: *demos*, the people, and *kratein*, to rule, are its Greek roots. Ancient philosophers and statesmen used this concept in a reasonably straightforward way. "We are called a democracy," said Pericles, "because the administration is in the hands of the many and not of the few." Aristotle, after distinguishing several kinds of democracy, says at last, "We may lay it down generally that a system which does not allow every citizen to share is oligarchical (*oligos*, few) and that one which does so is democratic" (*Politics*, IV, 6). In more recent times, Abraham Lincoln's often quoted phrase, "government of the people, by the people, and for the people," suggests the same general idea. Democracy is a system in which the people govern themselves.

Short expressions that purport to define democracy do not explain much, however, even when they meet with general accord, because they seek to put too simply a matter that is not at all simple. Some further examples are: "Government by consent," "Rule by the majority," "Government with equal rights for all," "Sovereignty of the people," and so on. Such epigrammatic definitions are usually not mistaken, but they cannot reach the heart of the matter. When we examine any such expression critically its inadequacy becomes apparent. Government by consent of whom? Consent to what? Equal rights to what? What constitutes consent or equality of right? What is sovereignty, and when do the people possess it? Rule by the majority of whom? Is majority rule always democratic, and do democratic decisions always require majority approval? Surely there is a difference between government *for* the people and government *by* the people; what shall we say of a government that is one and not the other? Where does government *of* the people fit in? Puzzles of this sort abound. It is necessary to begin afresh if we are to understand clearly and thoroughly what is meant by the correct assertion that democracy is government by the people.

1.2 The paradox of self-rule

We say that in a democracy the people rule themselves, that the people are sovereign. This is a figurative mode of speech from at least one point of view. The concepts 'rule' and 'sovereign' are relational: there is no ruler without ruled, no sovereign without subject. Part of what is involved in ruling is the power of over-ruling, of compelling the ruled or of acting against their will. In this important sense the people cannot rule themselves, although one part of the people may rule another part. "It was now perceived," John Stuart Mill wrote in 1859, "that such phrases as 'self-government,' and 'the power of the people over themselves,' do not express the true state of the case. The 'people' who exercise the power are not always the same people with those over whom it is exercised . . ." (*On Liberty*, Chap. 1). Almost a century later this concern had hardened into these assertions by Walter Lippmann: "The people . . . cannot administer the government. They cannot themselves perform. They cannot normally initiate and propose the necessary legislation. A mass cannot govern" (*The Public Philosophy*, 1955, p. 19). No one has put the point more elegantly than Gladstone: "No people of a magnitude to be called a nation has ever, in strictness, governed itself; the utmost which appears to be attainable, under the conditions of human life, is that it should choose its governors, and that it should on select occasions bear directly on their action" (*The Nineteenth Century*, July 1878).

In the world of practical politics it is evident that the people cannot, in the sense indicated, rule themselves. The government obeyed may be of the people's own selection, but the people do not enact or execute the laws. This distinction between rulers and ruled, at least in large communities, is not difficult to draw. Most men are governed but not governors.

Still the notion of self-government is not foolish, and when we use the expression to describe certain states of affairs we seem to make sense. Democratic government *is* self-government, government of the people by themselves. In some contexts such government is a reality. Yet if the earlier objection be taken seriously the people cannot govern themselves. How is this paradox to be resolved?

Consider the use of the expression "self-government" in a non-political context. We speak of an individual as potentially self-governed, governed by himself alone. The usage may be figurative here also, for no single person can over-rule himself, although conceivably his higher

4

faculties may over-rule his lower faculties, if that distinction among faculties can be drawn. Nevertheless, the distinction between governing one's self and being governed by others is of the first importance to every human being. An understanding of self-government on this personal level may serve as the key to the resolution of the paradox of community self-rule.

As an individual I enjoy self-rule when I am not directed, controlled by anyone else. I govern myself when I decide for myself the goals I shall seek, and choose my own means for attaining them. Every man experiences such individual control in at least some of the affairs of his life. Where then is the difficulty? The paradox arises from the fact that the verb "to govern" has a double meaning. In one sense the power to govern includes the power to over-rule, to compel, and therefore implies a bifurcation of governors and governed. This may be called the *administrative* sense of government. In another, deeper sense, to govern is to establish goals or policy, to give direction to the body governed. The latter is the original meaning of the verb "to govern," coming from the Latin *gubernare*, and in turn from the Greek *kybernan*, to steer, or pilot a ship. This may be called the *directive* sense of government.

In any community the government may command, forbid, over-rule; these are its administrative functions experienced directly in daily life, and the ones focused upon by those who argue that a community cannot govern itself. More fundamentally, however, who governs the community guides it, steers it. When this directive function is understood as primary in governing, the paradox of self-rule melts away. Insofar as government is conceived administratively, it involves the conflict of wills and the subordination of some to others, and it must be a portion of the community that governs, not the whole. But insofar as government is conceived directively, involving the determination of policy and the objectives which guide communal life, it may be a few or it may be the many who govern. In principle it is possible for all the members of a community to participate in the establishment of the ends sought in common. If all, or most, do participate in this task, we may fairly describe that community as self-governed.

1.3 The essence of democracy

Democracy is a kind of community government. To specify the nature of democracy, therefore, it is necessary to differentiate this kind of community government from all other kinds. This, in turn, requires an appreciation of the great scope of the concept of community, treated more fully in Chapter 4. There is no practical limit to the number or variety of human communities. The purposes that bind men into community may range from the trivial to the world-shaking; the size of communities may range from very small to very large. The boundaries of a community need by no means be geographical; the principle of its unity may lie in fraternal, charitable, ethnic, religious, or economic concerns. What is held in common by the members of a community may be of passing or secondary concern to them, or it may call forth their most permanent and profound loyalties. In reflecting upon the communities in which democracy can subsist, it is most important that one not focus exclusively upon national states. These are very important communities, and we are understandably very much interested in the way democracy functions in them. But a satisfactory theory of democracy must be applicable to a range of community types and sizes far exceeding that of national states. Communities of greatly different kinds and sizes may be governed democratically.

What does the democratic government of a community entail? The analogy between the life of a community and the life of an individual is again helpful. An individual can be self-governing in choosing his own ends; he can be self-directing, autonomous. Such self-direction or autonomy on an interpersonal scale is democracy [16.1].*

Democracy is government by the people in that it is the system within which the people, the members of the community, participate in the determination of policy for the community as a whole. The directive function of government is central to any account of self-government; it is the fact that this directive function can be widely shared that renders democracy possible.

What is involved in the notion of determining policy for the community as a whole? Clearly that is not a function that the members of a community can perform once and be done with. Policy is constantly being formed and re-formed; the direction of a community requires continual attention. Self-government, therefore, requires a continuing series of decisions, of greater or lesser importance, and it is in the making of these decisions, choices, that participation in policy-making becomes concrete. When the most important decisions of the com-

*Bracketed references indicate chapters and sub-sections found in this book.

munity are reached through the general participation of its members, we may call that community self-governed.

Which decisions are the most important ones, those upon which the entire membership of the community should have some voice? The natural reply is that the membership should have a voice in making decisions that affect them all, or that seriously affect them all. But which decisions are these? This question has no general answer. In many specific contexts it is answered clearly enough by the nature of the community. In other contexts there just may be no agreement upon which issues are rightly dealt with by the membership at large. Conflict on this matter may stem from disagreement over the basic purposes of the community; or (if these be agreed upon) conflict may lie in disagreement over what spheres of activity must be under collective control if those larger purposes are to be realized. Which issues are the proper business of the community is inevitably a controversial question.

Happily this question, however difficult in particular cases, does not have to be answered in order to grasp the essential nature of democracy itself. A statement of that essence, a definition of democracy, I now present with the understanding that it is to receive a good deal of further refinement. *Democracy is that system of community government in which, by and large, the members of a community participate, or may participate, directly or indirectly, in the making of decisions which affect them all.*

Upon this foundation we can build a coherent theory of democracy. A necessary first step is the more careful analysis of *participation* and its dimensions. Two purposes will be served by this. First, democracy itself will be further explicated by such an analysis, since participation is the key notion in its definition. Second, an understanding of what participation concretely involves will make possible a rational estimate of the degree(s) of democracy realized in any actual community.

Chapter 2

The dimensions of democracy

2.1 The measures of participation

Democracy is constituted by participation—the participation of community members affected by decisions in the making of those decisions. But the measures of participation are multiple. Within a given community, and on a given issue, participation may be realized more fully in some ways and less fully in others. Which of these ways is most important may not be clearly decidable; the scale upon which actual democracies are appraised cannot be a single or a simple one. Once having given up the supposition that democracy must be either altogether present or not present at all, it requires only a further adjustment of our expectations to recognize that it may be present in different respects, and to different degrees in each respect. That is the kind of thing democracy is.

I distinguish several *dimensions* of democracy: *(1)** the *breadth* of democracy; *(2)* the *depth* of democracy; *(3)* the *range* of democracy. These dimensions I now proceed to examine in more detail.

2.2 The breadth of democracy

The breadth of a democracy is a quantitative matter, determined by the proportion of those in the community affected by a decision who do or may participate in the making of it. In a perfect democracy all who are thus affected play some part. In most circumstances this can only be an ideal; in communities of any considerable size—say, national communities—it is a virtual impossibility for every full member of the community to play some part in the decision-making process. Even though participation be understood to include many indirect forms of influence upon policy, on any given issue some fraction of the concerned membership will not be exerting influence. That far, the democracy will be less than perfect in breadth. It may nevertheless be very good.

---

*When points made in a discussion are enumerated with italicized alphabetic or arabic characters, they will be discussed in subsequent paragraphs.

The dimensions of democracy

What ratios of participants to total membership deserve the ratings "democracy poor in breadth," "democracy fair in breadth," "democracy excellent in breadth," will never be exactly determinable because certain factual circumstances must be taken into account in any intelligent appraisal of an actual democracy. One of these factual circumstances is the size of the community; a second is the kind of community it is; a third is the character of the specific issues upon which decisions were made when the proportion of participants was measured. Seventy-five percent participation may be high in a national election, but low in the deliberations of a legislative body. Participation of the entire membership may be a reasonable ideal in committees and some clubs, but a wholly unreasonable ideal in communities with thousands or millions of members. Within the same community—say, a legislative body—almost complete participation may be expected on matters of high concern, while it might be anticipated only rarely on issues of more restricted impact.

Crude as numbers are in the evaluation of social institutions, they are a useful measure of relative performance. We can fairly say that, other things being equal, an election in which ninety percent of the citizens vote yields a more democratic result than one in which only sixty percent do so. Communities which regularly elicit participation by a higher proportion of their citizens than other communities of like nature and size are understandably called more democratic, for that reason. Of course, the "other things" may not in fact be equal. Communities with smaller proportions of participating members may be judged healthier democracies in respects other than breadth. To those other respects I turn shortly.

Within the dimension of breadth, further distinctions must be drawn. The essence of breadth in a democracy is the proportion of the community that participates in determining its policies. If we now grant that in most democratically governed communities at least some portion of the membership will not participate on any given issue, it is important to distinguish four categories of non-participants differentiated on the basis of the reasons for their non-participation.

(1) Non-participants who are prohibited from participating by some official provision, some rule or law of the community.
(2) Non-participants who simply do not trouble themselves to participate, although they are entitled to do so.
(3) Non-participants who are in fact prevented from participating by

9

some circumstances within the community, although not officially prohibited from doing so.

(4) Non-participants who deliberately choose not to participate.

If any given democracy is to be correctly appraised, or its breadth improved, these categories, and their applicability to the non-participants in that democracy, must be carefully attended to. *First:* note that of the four, only the first is formally constituted, is de jure; the remaining three result from informal considerations, are de facto. *Second:* note that the non-participants in any large democracy on a given occasion are likely to comprise a mixture of the four cases, and even a single non-participant's motivations may be complex. This means the categorization will often be difficult to apply to particular instances; it remains important nevertheless. *Third:* note that every variety of non-participation is a flaw in a democracy, but the kind and cause of the flaw, and even the seriousness of it, may greatly vary while the superficial results appear the same. A possible exception to the principle that every variety of non-participation is a flaw is presented by category four—non-participation by deliberate choice—which differs from the others in what appear to be fundamental ways. I proceed to examine each of the four categories of non-participation more closely.

(1) Structural Limitations Upon the Breadth of Democracy. When some portion of the community's regular membership is prohibited by rule or law from participating in the making of decisions which concern all, the democracy is structurally imperfect. Obvious examples are England or the United States before women were enfranchised, or communities in which the holding of property is a condition of participating in political processes. In such cases the extension of democracy requires a change in the constitution of the community, written or unwritten. In some instances, as with women's suffrage in the United States, what is required is a specific alteration of a fundamental document. In other instances the constitutional nature of the change is not so obvious; but always it is essential that the fundamental rules governing the structure of the community be modified, if not openly, then at least by reinterpretation.

The seriousness of structural imperfections in a democracy that restrict its breadth will depend upon a number of factors. There is first the question of how strictly the legal limitations are enforced. There is second the question of how large, proportionately, that group is whose participation is prohibited. A third and more difficult question is whether, and to what degree, that reduction of breadth may tend to improve the democracy in other respects. It can be argued, for example, that literacy qualifications for the franchise, although clearly reducing the breadth of a democracy, may tend to improve its average depth [2.4].

Some structural defects can be and have been tolerated for prolonged periods in communities that have been in other respects quite democratic. But structural limitations upon participation have the peculiarity that, however small the group against whom they are directed, they are obviously undemocratic. They are institutionalized interferences with full participation, and evince a deliberate intention on the part of the ruling forces within that community not to trust the people—at least, not to trust all of them.

(2) Non-participation by Default. Non-participation which flows from the neglect or apathy of community members is also an imperfection in democratic process, but its cause is very different and less obvious. Citizens who may vote in an election, but do not take the trouble to do so, reduce the extent of participation in that election and thereby render the results less perfectly democratic. This kind of imperfection is in some ways less serious and in others more serious than constitutionally prohibited participation. It is less serious in that, not being institutionalized, no legal or official action is required to make possible the most general participation. Because it is only de facto, the elimination of such non-participation does not meet with technical or political obstructions of special sorts. The *system* remains essentially democratic, even though the *process* that emerges through the use of that system may degenerate. In the last analysis it is the process that is of greater concern; but it is no small step toward democracy if the system that it employs enforces no abridgment of participation. On the other hand, the fact of non-participation may be symptomatic of a failing far more serious, because more profound, than any structural prohibition. If those who are affected by a decision may participate in the making of it, but do not trouble themselves to do so, it may be that a system of self-government will not prosper in that community because of the character of the citizenry. Significant non-participation by default in a given community may be indicative of the failure, in that community, to realize what I call the psychological or dispositional conditions of democracy [Chapter 12].

Again, the seriousness of this defect will depend upon many factors: the consistency of non-participation; the importance of the issues on which participation drops; and especially, the proportionate size of the non-participating segment of the community. Many modern states generally considered democratic have tolerated and do tolerate very considerable degrees of such non-participation by default. We do not say the democracy fails because of it; however, we may say that because of it the actual process of government (but not the de jure system) is less perfectly democratic.

(3) Non-participation as a Consequence of Social Pressure. The third category of non-participation, although superficially de facto, shares some of the characteristics of the de jure, and frequently combines, from the view-point of the democrat, the worst features of both. Here also, participation is deliberately restricted (as in the first category) although not legally or officially. In this way certain minority groups are effectively barred from (or have their voice diminished in) the political process with regularity and great social force. Such, for example, have been the coordinated pressures by large segments of the American population to keep the Negro from exercising his right to take part in the making of community decisions. The case of the Negro is only one example; other social, ethnic, or religious minorities have experienced similar de facto exclusion. It is extraordinary that, within the great torrent of comment upon racial and religious discrimination in recent years, it is only very occasionally observed that—whatever other injustice such discrimination may involve—it is fundamentally anti-democratic. The case of the Negro in the American South is an excellent example of how social pressure can force non-participation, resulting in the virtual exclusion, in fact if not by law, of a major segment of the community from the process of making decisions which affect the entire community, themselves included [4.6].

Non-participation of this sort, resulting from community pressures not prescribed by the official structure or legitimized by statute, is a most serious imperfection in a democracy. Apart from the manifold injuries to individual citizens and minority groups which result from such pressures, they provide the foundation for the deliberate construction of anti-democratic institutions; they accomplish indirectly what is often unlawful to accomplish directly. Moreover, although these pressures may not take official form, their wide-spread presence weakens the general confidence of community members in their ability to govern themselves. This is a serious blow to democracy, for the confidence of the members, in themselves and in each other, is one of the conditions upon which successful democracy depends [12.10].

(4) Non-participation by Deliberate Choice. Non-participation that is the result of conscious and deliberate choice presents a special case. When the member of the community has what he believes to be good reasons for not participating on some occasion, it is difficult to construe the result that flows from such reasoning as a flaw in the democracy. He may, for example, regard his abstention as a form of protest against an election in which the options on the ballot are so few or so restricted in range that the outcome of the election cannot be at all satisfactory to him. Or, his conscious ignorance about the issues at stake, as compared to that of the remainder who will participate, may be so great, in his judgment, as to render his participation injurious to the quality of the resultant decision.

There are two theoretical ways, both plausible, of dealing with non-participants of this sort. The first is to suppose that the member who consciously refrains from speaking or voting on a given issue has chosen deliberately to have the remaining participants decide that issue for him. In making such a choice, one may argue, he does in fact participate, although indirectly. He allows the remaining participants to be his proxy, dividing his vote equally among them. On this view it is correct to call these cases of abstention, but not, strictly speaking, of non-participation. Hence, there is no need to think them injurious to the democracy.

The consequences of this interpretation, however, render it unsatisfactory. On this view the "democraticity" of an election in which many had refrained from participating as a form of protest would be in no way reduced by these deliberate abstentions. But such an election would in fact be less democratic than one in which abstentions were few. All abstentions are not equivalent to a delivery of proxy, but this interpretation is necessarily blind to the distinctions among them. Deliberate abstention being participation on this account, those who refrain from voting by conscious choice are supposed not thereby to reduce the breadth of a democracy. In practice, however, it is a virtual impossibility to determine what fraction of the non-voters are so by deliberate choice. This fact renders the measurement of the breadth of a democracy, using this interpretation, extremely difficult, and must render it non-quantitative. It would then be necessary to determine why those who did not vote so acted in order to decide which of them were and which were not really participants. Such an approach to the breadth of democracy is theoretically tenable, but practically very cumbersome.

The second account of deliberate non-participation treats it simply as another way in which the breadth of democracy may be reduced whatever the reason for that deliberate refusal. This has the happy consequence of leaving the breadth of democracy an entirely quantitative affair, its measurement requiring no search into the motivations of the non-participants. The apparent fault in this interpretation is that abstentions motivated by a concern for the wisdom of the resulting community decision turn out to be flaws in the democracy. This is no real fault, however, for two reasons: *first:* it is entirely possible that a less democratic procedure will, in some contexts, lead to a wiser result than a more democratic procedure, and it is well if our account of the dimensions of democracy does not exclude that possibility. *Second:* it is entirely plausible to argue that, in some circumstances, the reductions of the breadth of democracy by deliberate choice may still be in the best interests of that democracy, if by that same act, a significant improvement in its depth is also effected. Given the fact, say, that considerable ignorance prevails on a given issue, the overall injury to democracy may be minimized if its breadth is deliberately reduced by the voluntary non-participation of the uninformed citizens. This seems to me the clearest and most satisfactory theoretical account of non-participation by reason of deliberate choice.

On this view, deliberate non-participation is not invariably an injury to the democratic process overall. But the justification of abstention by the democrat is possible only on specific issues before the community. One's refusal to participate on all questions would be, in effect, either a denial of the appropriateness of democracy for him, or (if he does accept democracy in principle) a denial that he is a genuine member of the community in which decisions are being made.

To eliminate non-participation by default or abstention (categories 2 and 4), some democracies have imposed the legal obligation to vote in national elections, thereby compelling participation in some measure. Presumably the reasoning behind such laws is this: in the first place, citizens are, by definition, members of that community. While they may freely abstain from participation on some issues, the election of a national parliament is the concrete exhibition of the democratic structure of the government. Therefore, no citizen of the democracy can be permitted to abstain from the admission of his democratic convictions. In the second place, such participation will be good for every citizen, and for the community as a whole, in encouraging the habits that democracy requires.

The second of these arguments is based upon a factual claim—that legal compulsion develops habits of good citizenship—that appears dubious, but upon which I am not competent to speak. The first of these arguments is more questionable still, for it supposes, but does not show, that a democracy is entitled to force its citizens to accept democracy in principle, whether they like it or not. Such laws, in my judgment, are unwarranted interferences in the personal lives of the citizens. Some will argue that warrant for them can be found in the added strength and security they bring to the democracy. But that such obligatory participation does strengthen the democratic community is very doubtful. Compulsion is more likely to increase resentment and dissension; furthermore, it is likely to reduce the depth of participation, and play into the hands of those who seek to manipulate public participation for selfish ends. And in forcing the participation of all, it reduces the moral and political impact of the voluntary participation of most. All of these consequences aside, the establishment of a legal obligation to vote seems to miss the point of democratic government—that in the long run the health and stability of a democracy must rest ultimately upon the internal desire of the citizens to participate, and cannot rest upon the external imposition of required conduct of any sort.

Concerning all of the four categories of non-participation it should be noted, finally, that there is a tendency to equate participation with voting, and, hence, non-participation with non-voting. This is a mistake; the breadth of democracy ought not be calculated in terms of voting behavior alone. If a community member does cast his ballot freely, that by itself is enough to justify our calling him a participant. There are other important ways, however, in which one may participate in decision-making, some not nearly so obvious or so countable [2.4]. But since it is likely that one who engages in other forms of participation will also vote if he is entitled to do so, it is reasonable to take the voting percentages (at least in large communities) as a rough but imperfect measure of the breadth of democracy in a given community. It is just because voting is only one of the forms of participation that one must, for a full appraisal of a democracy, examine not only its breadth but its depth.

individual participation (if it is called that) is so very thin as to be virtually inconsequential. In the decisions of an absolute ruler the sum of the opinions of all his subjects constitutes but one factor, and that perhaps a negligible one. Where the unanimous agreement of the many may be overruled by one man or by a few, the people clearly do not govern. In a large democracy, on the other hand, while it is true that each citizen's vote is of little consequence, the aggregate vote is of all consequence; it has controlling force. If the members of a large community are to govern themselves, therefore, voting is a practical necessity. The right of suffrage, and its use, is a bench mark in measuring the depth of participation.

Voting is only one of the forms of participation, however, most easily identified, but often superficial. With the casting of his vote the citizen helps to determine the course of action to be taken, but full participation entails much activity prior to that final decision. Effective members of a democracy will be active in deliberations of which voting is only the final stage. They may propose alternative courses of action, attack or defend the proposals of others, investigate and report upon questions of community interest, or in a host of ways influence the opinions of fellow members. At the conclusion of such activities each voice may be counted (if a formal vote is needed) as a proper fraction of the deciding ballot. That vote, clearly, is but one aspect of the participation of the members.

Democratization is most often thought of as the process of broadening participation in community affairs. When the aim is to introduce democracy into communities in which it has not yet developed, this is reasonable, for until some breadth of participation is achieved there can be no democracy. The democratization most imperative for political communities of the present day, however, is increase in the depth of participation. Universality of suffrage, if not realized in fact at least permitted in law, is now closer to the rule than the exception. Most sorely needed now is enrichment of the quality, the fullness of the participation that does take place. The ideal democracy is one in which the citizen takes part in government not merely by helping to choose between Tom and Harry (or between Harry and no one at all) but by doing what is reasonably within his power to identify issues, formulate proposals, weigh evidence and argument on all sides, express convictions and explain their grounds, help to nominate party candidates —and in general to foster and to strengthen deliberation. A community that not only permits generalized participation, but beyond that encourages participation that is informed, continuing, vigorous, and effective, and that realizes such participation in fact, with ultimate power retained by the participants—that community manifests democracy of depth as well as breadth.

2.5 Deep democracy in practice

How practical is the deep democracy just described? The degree to which this ideal can be approximated in concrete contexts is a matter ultimately decidable only by experience in those contexts. But whether democracy both broad and deep is ever substantially realizable in human communities is a question clearly answerable now. It is. What is actual must be possible. The clearest proof of the practicality of full democracy is the actual existence and success of such government in some of the communities in which many of us participate every day. In club rooms and committee rooms, in homes and offices, the decisions governing community life are often—I do not say usually, but often— reached through participation that is universal (or nearly so), informed, active, and effective, that is, through democracy of breadth and depth.*

Two objections to the ideal of deep democracy, on grounds of alleged impracticality, I answer here. *First*: the critic may grant that the ideal can be realized in small communities—in clubs or towns—but deny that it is realizable in large communities, nations especially. We ought not admit (what this criticism might suggest) that the realization of deep democracy in small communities is unimportant; but we may readily agree that fullness of participation is in many ways more difficult to achieve when the community is large. When the community is one of millions, universal participation in depth is a practical impossibility.

Nevertheless it is significant that many national democracies do permit and encourage participation in depth. More than that, intelligent, intense participation is in fact realized, not uncommonly, in many democracies as large and cumbersome as our own. In most Western democracies of the present day the opportunities to participate fully and effectively are abundant. The channels of participation are not always clear, and on some issues they may be few, but they are real.

*Said the academic man, when first shown an exceedingly intricate machine, all its parts working away: "Yes, I see that it works in practice. But does it work in theory?"

There is hardly any question of community concern upon which the citizen of a large Western democracy cannot make his voice heard if he is willing to expend the necessary effort. Of course he may not win the day—but it is not a reasonable demand to make of democracy, or of any system of government, that every citizen always have his way.

We may demand of a democracy, whatever its size, that any member have the chance to participate in decision making if he is prepared to devote energy to the task. Such opportunities are generally open to citizens in large democracies, through political organizations on many levels, and especially through political parties. The avenues of participation, the parties in particular, are under-used by the mass of citizens in most democracies, with the result that parties often do not represent, as fully or fairly as they might, the interests even of their own nominal members. But thorough-going democracy is time-consuming and troublesome for all; that is part of the price that must be paid for it. If the greater part of the community will not pay the full price, they will not get the genuine article.

Second: "It is not the fact of participation in depth by some individuals that I doubt," the critic may rejoin, "but the possibility of a large democracy that exhibits significant depth overall. It is not an accident, but a consequence of the laws of human behavior [he may continue] that every large democracy must remain generally shallow." This criticism makes a factual claim about the nature of human communities requiring much empirical support. The critical claim is exceedingly strong, applying not only to all actual but to all possible large human communities. Extraordinary evidence would seem to be required to establish it; it is not clear what kind of evidence or argument would do that. The task of appraising evidence and argument so directed belongs properly to the sphere of political science; for the present, controversy over what is possible leaves the question moot.

But suppose—what I do not grant—that we did have reasonable warrant for the belief that large human communities can never exhibit deep democracy overall. What follows from that? We would have then to recognize that the earlier account of democracy both deep and broad must remain no more than an ideal when the community is very large. But that it is an ideal never fully realizable in large communities does not even tend to show that it is an inappropriate ideal. It may be a goal never completely attainable—like full employment or the eradication of disease—but that does not speak against the practicality of retaining it as a goal toward which we may move. The depth of democracy, like most affairs in the political sphere, is a matter of degree. There is, after all, an enormous difference between a system in which the citizen does little more than vote, and one in which the many other channels of participation are ever more widely and more fully used. Probably it never will be the case that all the citizens of a national democracy will participate in depth in their common government. But surely more may do so than do so now—and then we may rightly say that, although still deficient, that democracy is better than it was, deeper than it was. Should the critic wish to argue that deep democracy is an improper ideal for large human communities, that it is an ideal toward which they ought not move, he cannot defend that claim by showing that it is never perfectly attainable. He would then be obliged to deny outright the justifiability of the democratic ideal, at least in that context. The arguments concerning the justification of democracy I treat later [Chapter 15].

The critic may conclude by pointing out that, at least at present, all large democracies are in fact rather shallow. This too is an empirical claim, although it may indeed be true. Again, what follows from it? Surely it does not follow from the fact that a democracy is not now deep that it could never become so. Even if it be granted that every existing national democracy is gravely lacking in depth, that does not even tend to show either that that depth cannot be increased, or that it ought not be increased. I submit that it is a serious error to suppose that human government can never be any different, or any better, than it is or has been. And we may be reasonably confident that democratic ideals will not be best realized by those who scorn them as utopian.

Concerning the practicality of deep democracy, then, I conclude that important human communities exemplifying democracy both broad and deep are actual, and more are possible. Participation in depth in community affairs, for many citizens of large national democracies, is an accomplished fact, and within existing structures opportunities abound for the greater generalization of participation in depth. The claim that large democracies can never exhibit overall depth is dubious as a matter of fact, and irrelevant to the wisdom of retaining deep democracy as a national ideal. The claim, even if true, that all existing national democracies lack overall depth, is still less relevant to the appropriateness of the ideal of full participation, and would reflect only upon our accomplishments to date in developing democracy in these contexts.

There is no a priori limit upon the fullness of each citizen's participation in community affairs. Hence there is no a priori limit upon the overall improvement of democracy along the depth dimension. The obvious shortcomings of contemporary national democracies in this dimension indicate mainly that the potentialities for growth in this direction have been very little explored. Mistakenly supposing that democracy rests only in universality of suffrage, it has been generally concluded that, such universality achieved or nearly achieved, the democracy is mature. In fact, most national democracies in the twentieth century are very far from mature. So far are they (including our own) from democratic maturity that the ways in which we fall short are just beginning to be recognized.

2.6 The range of democracy

Within a particular community participation may be virtually universal, relatively deep, and effective in deciding some issues of general concern, while on other issues popular participation may be quite without effect. We would then be inclined to say that the democracy is genuine as far as it goes. But how far it goes is a vital question in appraising the overall democracy in that community. The kinds of questions upon which the voice of the people rules, and the restrictions upon the authority of that voice, if any—these determine the *range* of democracy in any community. The wider that range (so long as the issues are of common concern) the more fully is democracy realized.

The range of democracy is a subtle affair, for it is often exceedingly difficult in a given community to determine which issues the voice of the people genuinely decides. In making this determination, it will be helpful to recall the distinction, earlier drawn [1.3] between the directive and the administrative senses of government. In the former sense the governors steer the community, choose the direction in which it shall go; in the latter, the governors implement these larger directives by the enactment of legislation and the administration of particular affairs. It is in the former, directive sense that the members of a community may possibly govern themselves; in the latter, administrative sense we can almost invariably distinguish between governors and governed. Corresponding to this distinction, there are two levels upon which the range of a democracy may be appraised. The first is the range of sovereign power, the second the range of effective power, actually in the hands of the members of the community. So I distinguish the *sovereign range* from the *effective range* of a given democracy.

The sovereign range of democracy in any community is determined by those matters over which the affected public have, truly, ultimate authority. It is quite possible, indeed highly probable, that the members of a community will knowingly and voluntarily adopt a decision-making procedure which involves their relinquishing direct or immediate control over some affairs. This happens often (but not always) because of the difficulties created by sheer size. It is impossible, in very large communities, for all to participate directly in every decision (or even most decisions) of public concern. So a democracy often faces the practical necessity of devising machinery for the intelligent resolution of complex or technical issues that cannot be adequately dealt with by the members at large.

This machinery may be of two sorts. It may be purely *representative*, the people selecting deputies who act for them in certain affairs. The relations of democracy and representation I discuss in Chapter Seven. It is enough to point out here that a representative system does not necessarily restrict the sovereign range of a democracy; a representative government may be genuinely democratic if participation in the selection of the representatives is broad and deep, and if the representatives remain responsive to the needs of their constituents.

Alternatively, the community may employ decision-making machinery for complex affairs in some spheres that is not representative, but *private*. Decisions affecting the entire community may then be made by independent commercial or educational or religious institutions whose authority rests, ultimately, on the people's wish that decision-making power be so dispersed. In such cases also there need be no restriction of the sovereign range of the democracy if the people retain the authority to set limits upon, and otherwise regulate, private decision-making bodies.

In short, it is a virtual necessity for a large democracy that it develop systems of indirect control over different spheres of decision-making within its own jurisdiction. The systems chosen may vary. So long as the system in force is freely chosen and freely retained by the community, and so long as it remains within the legitimate authority of that community to alter or abolish any indirect system in any sphere, in an orderly fashion, it is correct to say that the affairs thus disposed remain within the sovereign range of that democracy.

The *effective range* of democracy in any community is determined by two factors: *(1)* how numerous and important the issues are upon which the community at large actually participates in deciding; *(2)*

how effectively the members of the community may influence or alter decisions, normally made through systems of indirect control, if it is their pleasure to do so.

Except in the smallest of communities, the effective range of a democracy requires some limitation. In large communities it will be sharply limited; the brute necessity for indirect decision-making renders that unavoidable. Indeed, the institution of representative machinery is a deliberate reduction of the effective range of the democracy. That such machinery is often essential and highly desirable is proof that it is not always in the interests of a democracy to extend its effective range without limit. What its proper extent should be depends very largely upon the size and nature of the community, and the kinds of problems it is likely to confront.

Because there is a tendency for the members of a democracy to suppose that the effective range of that democracy ought to be expanded where possible, and because representative institutions do reduce that effective range, there has been a countervailing tendency in some democracies to remove certain issues from the jurisdiction of the representatives and return them to the realm of direct popular control, or at least to make it possible to effect such a removal. This tendency may have happy consequences for the democracy in causing representatives to be more sensitive to the needs of the citizenry. It may, however, prove to be injurious in two ways. First, in further draining the energies of the electorate it can result in the enlargement of effective range at the price of serious loss in depth of participation. Second, in removing (or threatening to remove) certain questions from the control of the representatives, this tendency may interfere with the proper fulfillment of the duties with which the representatives are charged, thereby damaging the effectiveness and success of the representative machinery over the long run. These issues arise inevitably in any theoretical examination of representative democracy [7.8].

It must be frankly admitted, then, that most large democracies—and all modern national democracies—have severely restricted effective range. That fact will prove dismaying if the range of a democracy is identified with its effective range, and the vital distinction between effective and sovereign range is ignored. But there is an enormous difference between (a) the removal of issues from the range of all public control in principle, and (b) the removal, *by* the people, of certain issues from the scope of direct public action, because of their delicacy or complexity, although such issues remain subject in principle to the wishes of the citizenry. The latter is common in democracies, being a reduction of effective but not sovereign range; the former is a reduction of the sovereign (and hence, a fortiori of the effective) range, and is therefore a direct impairment of the democraticity of the community.

How wide the sovereign range of a given democracy really is will be in every case a serious empirical question. But to determine, within the flux of political affairs, how many or how important are the public issues really excluded from the sovereign power of the people will often prove a most difficult question. It may have no definitive answers. Marxists and others frequently argue that the democracy claimed by Western governments is fraudulent because what they (the critics) believe to be the most fundamental issues—to wit, economic issues—are not truly under the control of the members of the community. This is a serious criticism and must be met; I deal with it in discussing the economic conditions of democracy [9.6]. In like manner the claim of some socialist countries to be fully democratic is contested by some on the ground that many crucial directive decisions rest not in the hands of the citizens but, in reality, within the power of a self-selecting elite. Again, in some countries of Latin America, the cluster of perpetually ruling families is often referred to as the *oligarchía*, not because voting is restricted to a few (it may even be obligatory for all) but because in spite of generalized participation in national "democratic" elections the people do not seem to be able to make their will felt on major issues. Sometimes the machinery of participation is kept from its proper effect, and policy questions of importance to the entire community are decided against the interests and will of the masses, behind the scenes and in ways difficult to specify. Where such criticism is justified democracy is frustrated not by the limitation of the breadth or depth of participation (which may be adequate) but by the de facto restriction of its sovereign range. The scope of ultimate popular control in the decision-making process remains always a central question for every democracy.

2.7 The problem of overlapping communities

A special problem concerning the range of democracy is encountered in situations in which it is possible to identify two communities, both of which are genuinely concerned in the outcome of a given question, but only one of which has the authority actually to decide the question—and where the deciding community is a subgroup of the other. Here tension arises not from the failure to recognize a larger community [as described in 2.3] but from the fact that the concern of the smaller community in the issue at hand is believed so much more intense that its members alone, rather than the larger group, are given a voice in the resolution of the issue. An example of this is the system used by many local communities when presenting changes in real property taxation for approval or disapproval by ballot. The procedure frequently adopted permits only the owners of real property to vote on such questions, presumably on the grounds that it is they above all who are affected by the proposed change, since they pay the taxes being decided upon. The non-owner of property in that community may reply, however, that any action regarding such tax changes seriously affects the entire community, not only because taxes affect rents, but also because the tax rate bears directly upon the schools or other services offered by the community to all of its members. Since all in the community are concerned (he may continue), all, freeholders and non-freeholders alike, should have some say in the matter.

Our understanding of democracy will be deepened by reflection upon the considerations which render such conflicts puzzling. In the example given there are two distinctly identifiable communities—the community consisting of residents in that district otherwise qualified to vote, and the community consisting of that sub-group of such residents who are also freeholders. Does the decision to allow only the freeholders the right to participate on questions involving property taxes support democracy in that community? The answer is: It depends upon which community one has in mind. And which community one has in mind will very likely be determined by the kinds of interest he believes are deserving of protection in deciding the issue at hand. Where only freeholders are allowed to vote on such questions, there certainly is democracy among the community of property owners who are being taxed; but the non-freeholder may complain that, in depriving many citizens of a voice on important local affairs, the range of democracy in the community at large is seriously impaired.* If all residents are permitted to vote on the tax question without regard to their ownership of property, the larger community is certainly experiencing democracy; but the property owners may complain that many are being permitted

---

*Note, however, that the non-freeholder's opportunity to participate in ways other than by voting is not denied. This may be small satisfaction to him, but it does tend to mitigate his exclusion from the decision-making process on such issues.

to participate in deciding questions that do not affect them directly, since they do not have to pay the taxes they approve. Thus democracy in the smaller community suffers, they may say, not from the exclusion of those who ought to participate, but from the inclusion of those who ought not, with a resultant dilution of the effectiveness of the votes of the members really concerned in the outcome.

The lesson for democratic theory is important. Whether the range of democracy has been inappropriately restricted by some procedure depends upon which community that question has been raised about. Where there is uncertainty regarding which of two overlapping communities ought to have decisive control over a given issue, there will be an apparent disagreement over the range of democracy. Determining what questions are really subject to the will of the people requires that we determine first who, in that context, "the people" are. So a given outcome may appear to have been reached very democratically from the perspective of one community, but very much less so from the perspective of another, much smaller or much larger.

So long as the disagreements or uncertainties regarding community context have not been resolved, problems arising from the overlap of communities may be viewed either as issues of breadth or of range. Consider once again the example of tension between a larger community of residents and a smaller community of resident-freeholders within it. Where the non-freeholders are excluded from voting on property taxes we could describe the situation, from their perspective, as one in which the breadth of democracy is restricted, structurally impaired (with respect to some issues), by this exclusion. Or we could describe the same situation as one in which the breadth of democracy is not impaired, but its range is limited so as to exclude from genuinely popular control issues of just that sort.

Problems created by the fact that communities overlap, and sometimes conflict, can only be resolved by determining explicitly which issues should be decided by which communities. Such determinations ought to be made upon the merits of particular cases; in each case a judgment is presupposed concerning the specific community within which democratic rule on those matters is most important. In general, the question of what issues are subject to the control of the people in a given community is one concerning not the breadth of a democracy, but its range.

Chapter 3

Some general observations about democracy

3.1 Some things democracy is not: common errors

A democratically governed community is one in which the members of the community genuinely govern themselves, in which the governed participate in making the directive decisions which affect them all. Although not new, this approach to democracy has not usually been accompanied by much refinement in the analysis of that participation which is the heart of the matter. As a result, the account of democracy as government by the participation of the governed has sometimes been held naive, unrealistic. It need not be so. It would be naive and unrealistic to suppose that participation in government must take the form of a town meeting or something much like it. This crude model of participatory government is what the critic of democracy as participation frequently means to reject. Government by town meeting being usually impractical in the world of political affairs, and being rarely employed, an account of democracy as government through participation is discarded in favor of a theory that fastens upon some other characteristics.

Such alternative accounts of democracy are often superficially plausible. Their plausibility stems from their emphases upon certain real and important consequences of democracy, or facets of it, while its essential core has been missed. The preceding discussion of the essence of democracy, and of its dimensions, makes it now possible to identify some common errors of this kind. Rather than criticize alternative accounts of democracy individually, I shall specify the kinds of oversight or mistake that have often led to the rejection of a participatory theory of democracy, and to the construction of another.

(1) The failure to appreciate the complexity of participation, or to distinguish the several dimensions along which it may take place, has been an almost universal deficiency. This failure has made it very difficult to deal intelligently with the problems these differing dimensions create for democratic theory and practice. It has been a leading cause of the identification of participatory government with the crudest and most obvious forms of direct democracy. Moreover, when participation

in real communities proves defective in some respect, the failure to make these basic distinctions has rendered it practically impossible to specify clearly what features of the government of that community are not fully democratic. In a word, the participatory account of democracy has been often rejected because the analytic tools needed for the application of that account to actual communities had not been devised.

(2) There has been a tendency to think of democracy as a system of government found only or primarily in national communities. The result has been a grossly narrowed view of the forms and institutions democracy may employ. So one finds some theorists identifying democracy with certain representative systems, or defining democracy in terms of the conduct of political parties, or the freedom of elections, or the provisions of written constitutions, and so on. Once having focused attention upon such institutions—which are indeed the valued instruments of very large democracies—it is possible to overlook the participatory foundation, for one has thereby already excluded from attention other self-governing communities that may not need the particular devices of a national democracy. The recognition that democracy is a way in which the members of any community, large or small, may govern themselves points clearly to the need for a theoretical account that does not rely upon institutional or other features present only in communities of special kinds.

(3) Particularly regarding the dimension of range there have been unfortunate and erroneous conclusions drawn concerning what is entailed by a participatory account of democracy. Having said that democraticity is a function of the participation of the community members in their government, it is concluded wrongly that such participation must be specifiable in every important decision-making process where the democracy is genuine. There has been a common failure to distinguish sovereign from effective range, and a consequent tendency to identify the range of participatory democracy only with its effective range. Now the effective range in large democracies, as noted earlier, must be quite limited. This fact, combined with the inability of some theories to make the needed distinction, has led many political theorists to assert that democracy cannot be understood in terms of participation. For (they argue) if any actual country really is a democracy, and if in that country the vast run of decisions of public concern are not made by the public at large, it appears that that country's being a democracy must result from something else—from the presence of certain balancing tensions,

or certain rights-protecting institutions. Thus do we get definitions of democracy as a system in which the major community interests are in rough equilibrium; or as a system in which the leaders must compete for the support of the members; or as a system in which constitutional guarantees of basic freedom are actually in force.

Such accounts of democracy mistake effects for causes. In a healthy national democracy a rough equilibrium of internal interests, and competition for votes among those seeking to be leaders, will very likely come to pass. But these conditions arise, when they do, as the consequence of participation by the citizens who are, basically, the constituents of the several internal interest groups. In such a community parties are likely to form, constitutional guarantees are likely to be developed. But they are not the democracy; that they are not is demonstrated by the fact that it is possible to imagine (and even at times identify in fact) democratic communities in which any one of these features is absent. In subsequent discussions of the principle of majority rule in a democracy [Chapter 6], and of the problems of representation in a democracy [Chapter 7], I shall explain how these several organizational features, so often praised, may function as the instruments of a large democracy. It is a common and unfortunate error to confuse these instruments with the system of self-government they are designed to serve.

(4) Some inadequate accounts of democracy are greatly reinforced by an overly narrow "realism" in which their proponents take pride. Such theorists argue, in effect, that if national democracy is to be taken seriously there must *be* perfect examples of it in the real world. They do take democracy seriously, but deny that it has the nature I have claimed for it, because the multi-dimensional ideal here described is never fully realized on a national scale. Then democracy must be understood as something else. What does seem common to the nations we call democratic? Parties, and elections, and competition for support, and so forth. These then—in the effort to be "realistic"—are chosen as its identifying and essential features. This course is triply mistaken.

(a) It misapprehends the functions of political realism and political ideals. An honest and clear-headed look at the way things really are in the world of politics is always in order, but the results of that inspection are misused when treated as theoretical ideals. Democracy is unavoidably imperfect in practice; ideal democracy—broad and deep and wide in range—may be unrealized, or even unrealizable, but functions nevertheless as a theoretical model after which actual communities may try to pattern themselves. Of course one can, if he wishes, call what he finds in some particular communities, "democracy." This may bend the common usage of that term, but there is nothing wrong with the procedure so long as one knows what he is doing. The name "democracy," however, has an emotive attractiveness that cannot be ignored. Applying this name arbitrarily has the effect of elevating certain actual practices —in this or that actual country—to the status of ideals for national government. Every existing democracy falls short of the ideal, however, and can stand improvement. The procedure of the so-called realist makes it impossible to know how to effect such improvement. Once identified as models of democracy how can specific governments be made more democratic? In what direction are they to go next? No doubt a new set of ideals will have to be constructed for them. It would be more candid, and more theoretically helpful, to admit openly that democracy is an ideal all nations are far from achieving perfectly— although, in this or that country, certain institutions may clearly help (or hinder) the realization of that ideal. The task of the political realist is to tell us honestly and accurately where we are, but not where we want to go.

(b) The identification of democracy with particular governments, or particular sets of existing national institutions, serves only to becloud the issues that arise among competing nations over the degree to which each of them does or does not realize democracy. To claim that democracy is what certain countries are is to resolve such issues arbitrarily. The question is begged. What had been at issue was whether this or that set of national institutions was more (or less) democratic. The reasonableness of the question—indeed, the seriousness of it—is an indication of how inadequate any account of democracy must be which is based upon particular existing governments.

(c) Finally, the proclivity of "realists" to focus their attention upon national institutions, upon party structures, and upon the competition for support among leaders, etc., tends to promote the same narrowness of theory earlier mentioned: the development of an account of democracy that is applicable to nations but inapplicable to the important small communities of everyday life that surely may be said to be, in no derivative or secondary sense, democratic or undemocratic.

(5) It is very commonly said that democratic government is government based upon the consent of the governed. This claim is correct in

one important sense, but it cannot serve as an adequate definition of democracy. The consent of the governed does not by itself *constitute* democracy, even though such consent may be *necessary* for democracy. The happy and proud acceptance by a people of the absolute dominion of their monarch has been frequent enough in history, even very recent history, to assure us of that. The governments of Japan and Germany in the years just prior to the Second World War could not be called democratic by any stretch of the imagination—but that they received the vigorous consent of their citizens cannot be seriously doubted. Without consent of the citizenry there can be no democracy; that is not at all to say that democracy is equivalent to government by consent. Consent is a necessary condition of democracy, but not its sufficient condition.

The role of consent in democratic theory cannot be dispensed with quite so shortly, however. Those who treat democracy as equivalent to government by consent are not likely to be making so elementary a mistake as that of confusing a necessary and a sufficient condition. What then have they in mind? It must be that the consent of the governed which they identify with democracy is something more than mere acquiescence or acceptance. And there is in the root of the word consent some support for an enlargement of its meaning. To "con-sent" is to "feel together"—to be of the same feeling, at least for the purposes of action in the case at hand. It is some such commonality of feeling, underlying joint action, that is probably intended in this extended concept of consent. How does this concept come to be identified with democracy? Perhaps it happens like this. It is very clear that in a democracy one must recognize the legitimacy of a great many governmental acts, some of which he does not approve of in substance. In its particular nature he may think a certain act most unwise, even though he recognizes an obligation to acquiesce in its implementation. The legitimacy of the act, in such circumstances, seems to arise from the general consent given to it. This analysis is correct as far as it goes, but it does not go far enough. It is not consent alone that establishes the legitimacy of governmental acts in a democracy. The source of that legitimacy is rather the political process which gives rise to that general consent. Consent is given in these cases (even by him who objects to the substance of the act) *because* the decision so to act was reached democratically. Consent of the governed is wrongly identified with democracy; but it is an identification easy to slip into, since general consent is a natural consequence of the use of a decision-making procedure in which all may take part, and to which, therefore, all are committed. Thus one may consent to the implementation of a given decision even though he opposed it vigorously during its consideration. This does not mean that he must change his mind about the wisdom of the act at the moment of its passage; he may still think it wrongheaded and ill-advised. But his consent to that act of government may be genuine, nevertheless, for he has (or could have) himself taken part in the resolution of that matter. To that participatory system of decision-making he may be fully committed.

Of course, this is an account of consent by the governed *to government by themselves*. Not all or even most cases in which peoples have consented to the acts of their leaders can be analyzed in this way. This is the central point. Where general consent has such a foundation it is a democratic consent; where it does not it may be consent to the decisions of a dictator or an oligarchy. That is to say, once again, that the consent of the governed is not peculiar to democracy, although such consent will be a natural consequence of it.

In short, "the consent of the governed" can have the profound importance often attributed to it only when it flows from the adoption of certain governmental procedures. These procedures necessarily involve positive action or deliberate forbearance on the part of citizenry at large. That is why theories of democracy which rely heavily upon "consent" generally involve (although obscurely) much more than consent. These further, essential elements are the participatory processes here being explored.

To show that these mistakes and limitations may be consistently avoided with an account of democracy as government by participation —where the complexities of such participation are more fully recognized—is the burden of the present work. Only such an account, I argue, can do full justice to democracy as a governmental ideal and as a practical form of government realized to some degree in communities of many kinds and sizes, while at the same time providing a coherent explanation of the role of elections, political parties, constitutionally protected rights, and other highly-prized institutions of national democracies.

3.2 On appraising a democracy

The degree to which democracy has been realized in any community depends upon a number of factors: the breadth of participation in determining community policy, the depth of that participation, and the range of issues upon which such participation is or can be genuinely effective. There are no formulas by which achievement on the distinct dimensions of democracy can be cross-compared, or the total complex of achievement graded. Only one of these factors is even roughly quantitative, and the other two are essentially incommensurable. All of which goes to show what a sticky business we are about. It is not only that the appropriate depth and breadth will vary with the size of the community, and with its purpose, but that differing possible combinations of breadth, depth, and range may result in governments quite different, yet all essentially democratic. Is it more democratic for all to participate to some degree on most questions of general concern, or for a smaller percentage to participate more fully on not so many of the important issues? Of course the answer is: it depends. It depends upon how much smaller the "smaller percentage" is, upon how fully is "more fully," and upon which questions may be cut out of the range of public participation. It also depends upon whether the communities concerned are large or small, and upon what the principle is which unites the membership into one community. How genuine the democracy is, in short, depends upon a host of considerations that relate in various ways to the participation of the membership of that community in its public business.

So democracy, like most other affairs in the world of human society, is a matter of degree, and a matter of degree on many levels. The crucial questions to be answered in appraising democracy are not, 'where is it?' and 'where is it not?'—but, where democracy is the professed aim and ideal, 'how broad and deep is it?' and, 'upon what issues is it really operative?'

One is likely to appraise a democracy because of his desire to improve it, or at least to find out how it might be improved. But the question 'how may democracy in this community be improved?' harbors a serious ambiguity. Two very different kinds of things may be meant by "improvement." One may be asking how democracy can be extended, or deepened, or in some way perfected in its kind. This is essentially the question of how a community professing democracy may realize that ideal more fully, may become more democratic. However widely the democratic ideal is accepted, it can rarely if ever be completely realized in all of its dimensions. The task of making democracy more perfect of its kind is one that concerns its enlargement, in breadth, depth, and range, within the given community. Insofar as we do take democracy as an ideal, our understanding of its dimensions will enable us better to direct our efforts toward its more perfect realization. But the practical implementation of that ideal depends also upon an understanding of the conditions of the success of democratic government, and upon the development and control of these conditions [Part Four].

On the other hand, one asking how a democracy can be improved may be chiefly interested in changing (as he believes) for the better the policies of that democratic community. He may seek to make the laws it enacts juster, and its policies wiser. Such goals will involve judgments about the justice of law or the wisdom of policy in the light of some value or values—say progress, or power, or peacefulness— which are not implicit in democracy, but may or may not be realized by it. Ultimately improvement of this kind is likely to take place in a democracy only when its members are improved—that is, when there is change for the better in the beliefs and attitudes of those whose participation determines policy, or the selection of policymakers. Where people govern themselves, it is likely that the government will be better if the people are better. It is reasonable to suppose that, in the long run, wiser decisions will be made by wiser decision-makers. But specific changes of policy—toward enlargement or retrenchment, toward peace or war, and so on, are never entailed by democracy as a philosophy of government. Any changes of policy or program may be sought by the members of a democracy; only if these changes bear directly on the ability of the members to participate may they be sought in the name of democracy. So Ernest Barker has wisely written that the way of democracy "is not a solution, but a way of seeking solutions—not a form of State devoted to this or that particular end . . . but a form of State devoted, whatever its end may be, to a single means and method of determining that end. The core of democracy is choice, and not something chosen; choice among a number of ideas, and choice, too, of the scheme on which those ideas are eventually composed" (*Principles of Social and Political Theory*, 1951, p. 207). Improvement in this second sense, therefore, is very much the concern of the citizen of democracy, in his capacity as evaluator and participant—but it is not necessarily the concern of democracy itself. Nor is it my concern in discussing the principles that underlie democratic process. It is at once disturbing and reassuring to realize that, in a genuine democracy, the people will probably get the leaders and the laws they deserve.

3.3 Democratic forms and democratic processes

The degree to which democracy is actual in a community is not determined by its formal structure. That structure may or may not be instrumental in realizing *processes* of decision-making that are genuinely participatory. Processes are goings-on, and democratic processes are a certain sort of goings-on. This is why democracy is never complete, never accomplished. It is a way of doing things, and that way is more or less fully actualized in the doing. One profound truth about democracy is that we never simply have it, or establish it, but continually realize it in action and live it.

It follows that the democracy of any community cannot be static. Participation of the membership will vary constantly, from day to day and year to year, from decision to decision, and possibly in differing directions during the same period along its several dimensions. One advantage in recognizing these distinct dimensions is the greater insight they permit into the changeableness of democracy. The verb, participate, literally means to take part (*L., partis, capere*). How universally, how deeply, and upon what issues the members of a community are taking part in their common business are not questions regarding what has been done, but what is being done now. Democracy is always in a state of being achieved, but the achievement of a democracy is never completed.

Here is the point of the commonly made distinction between the spirit of democracy and its forms. It is the distinction between the dynamics of democratic process, and the relatively stable character of institutions that may or may not embody that process. Often we may wish to attend to the character of the decision-making processes actually taking place, rather than to the formal instruments these processes employ. Genuine participation may be effected through a great variety of institutional devices; democracies are of all sizes and kinds, parliamentary and presidential, formal and informal. But the presence of any particular political device, or set of devices, is no guarantee of genuine democracy in the community in which such devices are established. Electors may be coerced, elections controlled, courts corrupted. The most noble and "democratic" of constitutions may be at once flaunted and flouted. This is not to make little of formal democratic institutions, or to disregard their important role in making participation effective. Elections and courts and constitutions can function as the invaluable instruments of democracy, still they cannot *be* democracy. To take them as democracy is to become so absorbed in the forms as to miss the spirit of the process they serve.

In this respect we are often deceived, not only by false democracies in countries and communities of which we are not members, but sometimes, too, by the formal but superficial character of the democracy in communities of which we are ourselves members. We must remember always that the reality or unreality of democracy is determined not by any set of institutional arrangements, but the character of the actual decision-making process, whatever the formal arrangements may be.

The spirit of democracy is of far greater import than its forms. In a working democracy, the forms will provide the framework within which constant political activity goes on. But that activity is likely to overflow, perhaps outrun its forms. If the spirit of democracy pervades the community it is improbable that any set of forms will fully encompass it. Indeed, one of the marks of a healthy democracy is that it will be constantly experimenting with its forms, creating new instruments with the aim of promoting ever more general and more genuine participation.

Part Two

THE PRESUPPOSITIONS OF DEMOCRACY

Chapter 4

Democracy presupposes community

4.1 The basic presupposition

Having given an account of what democracy is, I turn to the question of what it presupposes. What is it that government by the participation of the governed requires always and everywhere, and would be inconceivable without? As widespread efforts are now being made to establish democratic government in lands where it has not been known before, the answer to this question is of fundamental interest. If democracy presupposes circumstances realized only rarely in human history, we should be quite pessimistic about its future. If it presupposes circumstances never yet met with, we should conclude that democracy is an unrealizable ideal, unless there were some reason to expect the future realization of those presently nonexistent circumstances. If, on the other hand, democracy presupposes circumstances commonly or universally met with in human society, we have reason to believe it feasible and to expect its occasional occurrence.

The mere presence of that which it presupposes does not, of course, guarantee the success of democracy; its successful practice requires that a number of further *conditions* be met. These operational conditions I treat at length in Part Four; the *presuppositions* of democracy are logically prior to them.

The most basic presupposition of democracy is *the existence of a community within which it may be operative.* Rational discourse about any particular democracy presupposes some understanding of the community in which that democracy is (or could be) realized. The process of democracy is the process of group participation in common government. For that process to go on there must be, implicitly or explicitly realized, a body with some common concerns and some roughly identifiable membership. Only when some community of interest exists is it conceivable that its members can resolve to deal jointly with common affairs through general participation. It is not even possible to say clearly what democracy is without using the concept of community; the earlier account of the nature of democracy necessarily employed that concept. It is now time to expand that account by explaining further the place of community in democratic theory.

The varieties of community in which democracy can operate are limitless. They may range in size from the family or club at one extreme, to the nation or international community at the other. The duration as well as the size of democratic communities may greatly vary. A religious community may pursue its temporal and eternal ideals democratically over a period of millenia; a band of individuals having no other interests in common than the need to overcome a common obstacle may pursue that end democratically over a period of days or hours. Communities in which democracy functions may or may not be geographically delineated; their requirements for membership may be formal or informal, exact or inexact. Any combination of size, duration, location and formality may characterize a democratic community. What is absolutely essential in every case is that there be some common interests or problems, some concerns which bind them, however loosely or briefly into a self-conscious unit. Only within some community can self-government go on.

4.2 Political communities and citizenship

Of communities in general we may distinguish two kinds, *political* and *non-political*. Examples of the former are the township, the city, the nation-state. Examples of the latter are the family, the fraternal organization, the religious congregation. Both kinds are important, neither is intrinsically preferable. Democracy may (but need not) be practiced in communities both political and non-political; in either case its implementation requires that the members of that community know themselves (or be generally known as) members of it, for it must be practically determinable who, in fact, may participate in the affairs of a given democracy.

Political communities are distinguished by the universality of membership in them, within a specified geographic domain. There will be, of course, some marginal cases—persons resident in a given domain who are not full members of the body politic there [4.7]. In general, however, the political community includes everyone—all the inhabitants of the city or country in question. Not every political community is sovereign; the city, for example, may govern its affairs only within certain limits set by the sovereign state of which it is a part. Even where not sovereign, however, the political community is of enormous importance to each of its members as determining in large part the laws he must obey, and the conditions under which he lives.

By "state" is normally meant the sovereign political community. The formal recognition of great and sovereign political communities, whose members share common concerns of large scale and long duration, effects the division of the planet into nation-states. Whatever may be said for or against the nation-state as a human institution, the reality of such communities, past and present, is a stubborn fact.

There are other great communities, too—ethnic, linguistic, religious, and so on. They may not need government; when they do they may or may not be governed democratically. The fact that an individual may know himself to be a member of two or more great communities having inconsistent methods or goals is a common source of personal anxiety, sometimes the cause of moral agony.

Among all the communities of men the political community occupies a very special place. Aristotle says that it is "the highest of all communities" and that it "embraces all the rest." Even if one does not agree that the political community is *the* highest, embracing *all* others, he is likely to admit that most of the communities in which he enjoys membership owe their security and perhaps their existence to the larger community of civil society. In the present age, for good or ill, the political community of leading importance is the national community, the nation-state.

Membership in a political community is citizenship. We may speak of citizenship in a school or family, but such expressions are metaphorical, derivative. Strictly, the citizen is he who is, by law and custom, a fully accepted member of the political community. It is therefore correct to speak of one as a citizen of Paris, or a citizen of Michigan; but the political communities of chief importance being national, citizenship most usually refers to membership in nation-states. I am a citizen of the United States of America; he is a citizen of France.

The objectives, crass or noble, professed by a nation are of high importance to every citizen of that nation because, by virtue of his citizenship, he must in some measure share those objectives. Citizenship in a national community identifies a man. It identifies him legally in any case; when citizenship is deliberate and proud it identifies him, in part, morally as well, in indicating the great community whose objectives are his. Citizenship in a democratic nation is particularly important because in it, though his voice is only one among many, the objectives of the nation arise from the participation of the citizens.

The act of becoming a citizen—or of reaffirming one's citizenship—is and ought to be, therefore, an act of great solemnity. The ceremony of "naturalization," signalizing with formality the changed nature of the new citizen, is the public proclamation of the new and overriding loyalty to the political community being joined, and his renunciation of all conflicting loyalties to other such communities.

Most citizens of every nation, being "native born," do not experience the formal joining of the community, and have only rare opportunity to make conscious acknowledgement of their membership in it. When a citizen does so—reciting (if an American) "I pledge allegiance to the flag of the United States of America and to the Republic for which it stands . . ."—in school or elsewhere, his acknowledgement is likely to be superficial, without full understanding of the consequences of citizenship in that community. Perhaps a ceremony for the native born, like that experienced by the naturalized, in which loyalty is solemnly pledged and full citizenship announced, ought to be instituted. It might be called, "citization," being a formal recognition of citizenship; or better, "civization," being the formal confirmation of membership in the civil community.

Here lies the deep wisdom of those who have held that political society begins with social contract or compact. Whether civil communities were actually formed at some point in time by contractual arrangement is not fundamental. Whatever the historical process of formation, civil communities once formed have a quasi-contractual character, and that character is a presupposition of democratic practice. With or without ceremony, tacitly or explicitly, the citizens of every democracy must "put on the bonds of civil society," in Locke's eloquent phrase, by "join[ing] and unit[ing] into a community for their comfortable, safe, and peacable living one amongst another, in a secure enjoyment of their properties and a greater security against any that are not of it" (*Second Treatise of Government,* #95).

No such community can be based upon force. By force a collection of persons may be coerced or cowed into obedience; by force they may be frightened into seeking community for protection. But the nature of genuine civil community is such that force cannot be the principle of its unity. That unity must be founded on consent, and that consent is the logical, if not the temporal beginning of any democratic political society—where, as Locke says, "men have so consented to make one community or government, and are thereby presently incorporated and make one body politic."

4.3 Non-political communities

Important as political communities are, they constitute only one of the kinds of communities to which men belong; citizenship, associated chiefly with them, is only one of the ways in which membership in a community is formally recognized. In other communities, of smaller scale, shorter duration, and perhaps lesser import, membership may still be a matter of concern. In almost any sphere of human life common affairs may be managed democratically, but in every case such management presupposes some known community in which participation can go on.

The college club or fraternity may serve as a homely but suitable illustration. Whatever the consequences of a fraternity system for the larger democratic community, the process of decision-making within college fraternities is usually exceedingly democratic. Discriminatory selection of members by social groups may not be conducive to democracy in the large; such groups, each exacting intense loyalty from its members, may adversely affect the spirit of democracy in that larger society. But features of the fraternity system that may conceivably interfere with democracy on the larger scale serve the development of democracy on the smaller scale. Consciousness of active membership in any community is a presupposition—although not a guarantee—of democracy in that community. It is noteworthy that, in American college vernacular, full members of a fraternity are called "actives." They acquire that status only after a relatively long probationary period as "pledges" during which their loyalty to the group has been pledged, publicly announced, and tested, but their full membership not yet won. Members of college fraternities do participate in fraternity affairs almost universally with enthusiasm and sincerity. The breadth and depth of the democracy developing within such communities is due in part to the consciousness of community that is first stimulated by striving after membership, and then reinforced by the process of studying, playing, and living together. Entrance into the fraternal community is celebrated, by old members and new, in the ceremony of "initiation"—a ceremony that may be more frolicsome than that of naturalization, but which functions in its own context in quite the same way. As the purposes that bind the group into a brotherhood may be laudable and serious, the initiation may be serious too. At some point in it the new member will be called upon solemnly to avow his loyal commitment to the ideals of the fraternal order. This initiates his active participation in that social community.

Some such initiation (although involving little if any ceremony in many non-political communities) is a pre-condition of every operative democracy. Those religious congregations that are governed democratically may serve as yet another example, the operation of their self-government similarly requiring that the community members be identified as clearly as possible, the community demarcated. Formal recognition of membership is likely to be celebrated by a ceremony of confirmation, with which youths are brought to full membership in the congregation. In Judaism the Bar Mitzvah has precisely that function, permitting the boy for the first time to participate in certain ways in the observances of the community, and in publicly admitting him to full standing in the synagogue. The heart of some Christian observances is the ceremony called *communion*; it occupies a central place in worship not only because it symbolizes the close relations sought with higher beings, but also because it concretely manifests community among the worshippers themselves, their common acceptance of certain beliefs and ideals, one with another and with God. The first communion in which the young Christian may participate fully is normally that celebrated just subsequent to his confirmation as a full member of the religious community. And the punishment of *excommunication* is awful not merely because of the ostracism entailed, but because one banished from the religious community has no opportunity to participate with the community in certain forms of worship believed essential.

The fact that any community—political, fraternal, or religious—distinguishes clearly between members and non-members is no evidence of its democracy. Tight communities may be highly autocratic. But any community that does practice democracy presupposes by that practice a community of some kind. Only within it can the right to participate be recognized and a system of general participation made effective.

4.4 Community and the rule of the majority

The principle of majority rule is a common and powerful instrument of democracy [Chapter 6]. The application of that principle supposes a social unity; there can be no rule of the larger part unless the larger part and the smaller part are indeed parts of one whole.

This is clearest in cases where the community has not developed sufficiently to support democracy, even though democratic ideals are sincerely professed. The present state of Pan-American relations is a case in point. Although the twenty-odd nations of the Western Hemisphere recognize many common concerns, and act jointly on many affairs, they do not form a community sufficiently cohesive to make democracy possible in the Pan-American community as a whole. Any nation in the hemisphere happening to find itself in a small minority on an issue of vital concern to it, but voted on by all, would simply not recognize the opposing majority as legitimately decisive. "Our opponents constitute a numerically larger group," the spokesman of that nation might say, "but the principle of majority rule does not apply in this case." Why not? Suppose that the opponents do indeed constitute the larger number, both of countries and of persons. Still they would not be, in the crucial sense, a larger part. Part of what? Part of a self-conscious whole, a community within which minorities may be distinguished and the majority may legitimately claim to rule.

4.5 On preserving union

The community democracy presupposes cannot be formed once for all, but must constantly be re-formed, and will always be waxing or waning. The growth and endurance of any democratic community will much depend upon certain intangibles—the spirit of union, the feeling of the members that their common membership is somehow deeper and more important than any issue over which disputes may arise among them. The more pervasive and gripping is this spirit of union, the more durable is the democracy likely to be, perhaps proving able to withstand the most bitter internal conflict. As consciousness of community is less intense and less profound, democracy in that community must be less secure, more likely to encounter internal issues with which it cannot cope. The commitment to union largely explains why compromise can prevail among widely divergent views within a democracy, but often does not prevail between democracies [12.7].

Here is the root of much traditional worry, by democrats, about factionalism, and the divisive import of certain issues. In the history of the United States, especially, there has been strong and widespread feeling that, though the cost be very great, the Union must be preserved. Our Civil War, beyond its economic and moral causes, was above all a struggle to protect that without which there could be no continental democracy—the unity within which differences, however bitter, might be discussed and in time resolved.

The founders of the American nation clearly expressed this concern. There was a need for strength through mutual support, and a desire for the economic advantages of a federated republic. But fundamentally it was to make possible the amicable resolution of differences among the American states that union was first urged, then prized. The first President, addressing his countrymen on leaving office, said of union:

> . . . it is a main Pillar in the Edifice of your real independence; the support of your tranquility at home; your peace abroad; of your safety; of your prosperity in every shape; of that very Liberty which you so highly prize. . . . [I]t is of infinite moment, that you should properly estimate the immense value of your national Union to your collective and individual happiness;—that you should cherish a cordial, habitual, and immoveable attachment to it; accustoming yourselves to think and speak of it as the Palladium of your political safety and prosperity; watching for its preservation with jealous anxiety; discountenancing whatever may suggest even a suspicion, that it can in any event be abandoned, and indignantly frowning upon the first dawning of every attempt to alienate any portion of our Country from the rest, or to enfeeble the sacred ties which now link together the various parts. . . . [Y]our union ought to be considered as a main prop to your liberty, and . . . the love of the one ought to endear to you the preservation of the other.

Not for nothing is George Washington called the father of his country.

Quite deliberately the originators of this experiment in democracy chose, as the name of this republic, the *United* States of America. It is fitting, too, that the great seal of that republic should have inscribed upon it the motto whose application makes democracy possible: E pluribus unum; Out of many, one.

4.6 *The breakdown of community*

The community presupposed by democracy deteriorates when minorities within it are arbitrarily excluded, by law or in fact, from participation in the life of the whole. Beginning only as imperfections in a democracy, such exclusions may end by destroying it.

John Dewey has argued that "the very fact of exclusion from participation is a subtle form of suppression" or coercion ("Democracy and Educational Administration," 1937). Principles of exclusion that do not openly intimidate or oppress those excluded often have that result indirectly, sometimes without even the awareness of the victims. As exclusion becomes more deeply embedded in the structure of a society, part of the social habits of excluded and non-excluded alike, it comes to be accepted by all as the natural and proper state of affairs. The result, Dewey points out, is that the experience of the masses becomes so restricted that they are no longer conscious of their own restriction. He concludes: "It is part of the democratic conception that they [the masses] are not the only sufferers, but that the whole social body is deprived of the potential resources that should be at its service." Exclusion within a purportedly democratic community—even when effected by the express will of the majority—tends to be disastrously self-defeating.

Ironically, while principles of exclusion have destructive consequences for a democracy, they tend to serve the excluding majority as self-justifying. In restricting the public experience of some minority the education of that minority is damaged. Informal education is narrowed by the very fact of exclusion from political life. Formal educational opportunities inevitably suffer also as a result of the under-representation of the excluded minority in governing assemblies. The upshot is a minority whose members are far less able to contribute what potentially they might. The inferiority of their contribution to the public process, itself a consequence of exclusion from that process, thus appears to justify their continued or extended exclusion from the same political process. But the very spiral of social oppression that may be travelled to the detriment of democracy may also be travelled in reverse. Increasing *in*clusion, no less than exclusion, can demonstrate its own worth. When minorities previously oppressed are brought into the processes of participation, their experiences are broadened, their education both formal and informal improved. Any man's immediate experience of democracy tends to raise the quality of his contribution to the common weal.

In sum, democracy depends vitally upon its communal foundation; its more perfect realization requires a community that is inclusive, self-conscious, and united.

4.7 Marginal community membership

Some groups are normally and properly excluded from full participation in democratic politics. Chief among these are *minors, convicts, aliens,* and *the insane.* These cases of marginal community membership pose no serious problem for democratic theory.

The presumption in a democratic society is that all may participate. Exclusion of any sub-group can be justified, therefore, only by showing that its members, although in the community, are not fully members of it, in some sense that establishes the inappropriateness of their full participation in its affairs. The hardship of such marginal membership is usually the denial only of the right to vote, though other restrictions may be imposed. Since participation takes many forms, of which voting is but one, persons holding such marginal memberships, although suffering a real deprivation, are not fully excluded, and may enjoy considerable influence upon the community through other channels.

Either of two different principles may legitimize the denial of the franchise, both relating to the special nature of the sub-groups marked off. The burden of proving their applicability in any case, however, rests upon the excluding body; individual instances of exclusion may prove highly controversial.

The first principle concerns the *capacity* to participate fully. Some elements within a political community—minor children and the insane are the outstanding examples—fail to qualify for full participation because of some clearly established incapacity on their part. Being what they are, of tender years or unsound mind, they cannot do what full members of the community must be able to do in exercising the franchise. No doubt many who are accepted as full members of every democracy behave childishly or irrationally; but they are capable of not doing so, while that expectation is unwarranted in the case of minors and the insane. Full membership in the community is denied such individuals on the implicit ground that they are not yet, and perhaps may never be, fully developed persons. It is not merely that they are not wise enough (for who will decide that?) but that something necessary for the completion of personality—reasonable maturity or rationality—is just missing. The level of maturity or rationality that full membership requires is difficult to determine, and a matter always open to review. Complete psychotics we do not allow to vote; neurotics on the other hand are very many indeed, and we do not dream of disenfranchising them, even if they could be accurately identified. But the line between neurosis and psychosis is neither clear nor generally agreed upon. In like manner, we are uncertain of the age at which maturity sufficient for voting rights is to be presumed. Is it twenty-one years, or eighteen, or as some have suggested, nineteen? There is no magic in a number, and everyone realizes that a person's chronological age is an unreliable index of the maturity of his judgment. Still, children of twelve must not be given the vote, as adults of thirty (other qualifications aside) must be. Although we cannot say with certainty where the lines are rightly drawn, we muddle through as best we can, making such distinctions as reasonable men can in the light of their present knowledge. This uncertain and flexible application of principles clear in the abstract is a common feature of a working democracy.

Exclusion principles based upon the incapacity of certain groups to participate have often been employed illegitimately and cruelly. Those without property were long excluded from participation on the ground that their propertylessness proved their inability to direct their own affairs, and a fortiori, their inability to help direct the affairs of all. Second-class citizenship for Negroes was long defended, as slavery had been defended for centuries previously, on the ground that Negroes were not fully human. However absurd such suppositions may be, many are still misled; we are well warned to accept no claim concerning any group's incapacities until they have been firmly and empirically established. It bears repeating that in a democracy the presumption must always be against exclusion; upon those who propose to disenfranchise must rest the burden of proof.

A second kind of exclusion principle justifiably employed in some circumstances concerns not incapacity but *some deliberate act or acts* which establish the non-membership (or restricted membership) of those who have so acted. Felons, for example, are presumed to have put themselves against the community in such a way as to nullify their rights to participate fully in its affairs. We say that they are "outlaws" —having put themselves outside the rule of law they forfeit part of their right to help frame the laws.

Similarly—but with no supposition of wrongfulness or crime— aliens are also persons whose deliberate acts exclude them from full membership. They reside in one political community but consciously and publicly retain primary allegiance to another. An alien is of course subject to the laws of the land in which he resides, and his interests there may be carefully protected; but his right to participate fully in the government of that community must await his full membership in it. Until by deliberate act that citizenship is sought and awarded, and earlier loyalties disclaimed, at least a formal allegiance is owed to foreign bodies. Only by explicit renunciation of that allegiance, and formal

51

acceptance of the new one, does an alien become a citizen, fully enfranchised [4.2].

We cannot say absolutely, then, that every exclusion from participation is inconsistent with democracy. We can say that no persons who are full members of the democratic community may be justly disenfranchised. The only factors that may conceivably justify denial of franchise in a political community are those based upon the nature of the membership enjoyed by those in question in the community within which the democracy subsists. To the extent that any are excluded, by any means, on any other bases—race, political persuasion, religion, or the like—the community permitting such exclusion is, if a democracy at all, an imperfect one.

4.8 Degrees of community membership

Ought membership in a community be treated as a matter of degree? The child, the felon, the psychotic, are members of the community after all, and in some cases very important members. If each suffers some disability, permanent or temporary, believed to justify disenfranchisement, we might say that persons in these categories are simply members in different degree from the standard. Such an approach has some theoretical plausibility; one could argue that it is implicit in any account supposing some members not to be "full" members of a community.

Moreover, once degrees of membership are explicitly recognized, they might apply not only to cases like those of minors or felons, but to a host of other categories, distinguished, perhaps, by the quality of contributions made by the several members of each. To effect this it would be necessary only to apply some system of plural or fractional voting, so as to be able to weigh more heavily the participation of those who are members of higher degree, while giving at least some voice to all who are members in some degree. Under plural voting specified members of the community are given two or more votes, the rest one or less; under fractional voting specified members of the community are given some portion of a vote, the rest one or more. The two schemes are identical in principle, the former aiming to increase the influence of a few, the latter aiming to reduce the influence of a few. They could be combined, or more complicated systems for the award of voting power might be devised.

Plural voting is no new idea. It has arisen, historically, in partial democracies designed to favor the wealthy, and operates there by awarding extra votes to members of certain elite sub-groups, graduates of certain universities, and the like. Such distinctions cannot be tolerated in a full democracy.

Some varieties of plural voting might be justifiable in a healthy democracy, however, under certain special circumstances. When, for example, it can be shown that although all deserve a voice, some in the community are measurably more concerned in the outcome of certain decisions, all members might be awarded votes proportionate in number to their concern. Such systems are commonly employed in private commercial organizations, the number of votes cast by each shareholder being exactly proportionate to the number of shares he owns in that corporation. A somewhat similar device might be instituted where communities overlap [2.7]. In voting upon local tax levies, for example, every regular member of the community, freeholder or not, might hold at least one vote, while every freeholder might be awarded (say) one additional vote for every so many thousand dollars of assessed property valuation owned by him, upon which the tax in question is to be levied. Thus, viewing the entire community as one, of which the community of freeholders is a clearly identifiable sub-set, the more intense interests of that sub-group could be recognized concretely, while the right to participate is enjoyed to some degree by all.

Such systems are dangerous, because the criteria for determining intensity of interest are usually impossible to determine justly. Even where great differences of concern are identifiable, the appropriate recognition of those differences in terms of voting power is forever arguable. In the tax example, is it each five thousand dollars of assessed valuation that deserves an additional vote? Or ten? Or two? Who could fairly say? Any such system in a political democracy must prove arbitrary in its operation. It lends itself to abuse; and even when administered conscientiously it is sure to lead to injustice.

Systems of plural voting are also generally impractical. Except in special cases the degree of intensity of concern has no clear measure at all. Membership in most democratic communities is very unlike holding shares in a private corporation. But since such measures are absolutely presupposed by any system of the sort here entertained, the unavailability of the measures renders any such system wholly inoperable—unless, of course, entirely arbitrary measures are imposed.

While it is in principle possible, therefore, to distinguish several degrees of membership in a community, that is a system generally and wisely rejected in almost all democracies. It is simpler, and in the end fairer, to develop and apply clear criteria for deciding who are voters and who are not. It is to sharpen these criteria that formal rites of initiation, confirmation, or naturalization are devised. Intensely affected minorities may find this hard, at times, but they are likely to have other devices upon which to rely in protecting their interests. If the matter is of gravest concern, they may even resort to the threat of separation from the community. Short of that, the decision-making machinery is likely to afford them other weapons. In any event, the effort to protect them through a system of plural voting is likely to produce more inequities than it averts.

Finally, there is a special and very important reason why differentiation of members by category, for the purpose of awarding votes, is unjust when the democracy is that of a political community. Membership in that community—as I shall later argue [15.4]—is of such a kind that (with some special exceptions) no distinctions among the members *can* be made on the basis of differing intensities of concern or degrees of membership. All who are members are members equally, each having the highest stake in the security and general well-being of the political community in which he lives.

4.9 Fraternity

The ideal condition, in which many individuals are bound one to another, and into one community, we call *fraternity*. Fraternal bonds arise from the explicit recognition of common purposes and common commitments. That recognition being rarely as deep or as widespread as it might be, its further development is the perennial goal of those who seek to establish or to improve democracy. Fraternity and community refer in different ways to the same state of affairs; they are expressions of the same fundamental interpersonal relations from different perspectives. The concept of community is the expression of these relations as viewed from without; the foregoing account of community is that of a presupposition of democracy, objectively considered. Fraternity is a specifically moral concept, prescribing these same interpersonal relations for persons hoping to govern themselves. Fraternity is the ideal expression of community, therefore also the presupposition of democracy, subjectively considered.

Chapter 5

Democracy presupposes rationality

The second presupposition of democracy is *rationality*. Community, the first presupposition, concerns the relations between persons; rationality concerns the nature of the persons thus related. Democracy is inconceivable without both. The community is the essential context of the democratic process; within that context the members must be supposed to have at least the fundamental capacities that general participation in common affairs requires. These fundamental capacities are summed up in the concept of rationality.

What rationality involves, precisely, is not easy to specify. In general we may accept the criteria classically laid down. A rational man possesses, at the minimum, two faculties: *(1)* the faculty of forming a plan or grasping a rule for judgment or action, and *(2)* the faculty of using that rule, by applying it to particular cases, or following the plan of action. Because the rules and plans that must function in a democracy are interpersonal, we may add to these a third, *(3)* the faculty of intellectual communication, of reasoning with one another.

To treat rationality in terms of faculties may seem old-fashioned. The terminology is indeed old, and can be replaced. What is essential are not the words, but the facts—the members of a democracy must be able to do certain kinds of things. They must be able to formulate principles (in some contexts called "rules," in others "laws") for their common governance. They must be able to apply these general principles in action, to decide what does and what does not accord with the rule. And if rules or laws are to govern the community, the members of that community must be able to communicate effectively, to understand one another's reasons and purposes, and to codify at least some of their collective judgments. If rationality be understood as the capacity to do these things, democracy presupposes that its members are rational; if they are not rational, self-government through participation is out of the question.

Democracy does not presuppose, however, that its members employ these capacities constantly, or even most of the time. Rational faculties must, of course, be developed and used if the democracy is to operate successfully. The degree of development required will vary with context; the bearing of that development on the practice of democracy will be examined more fully in discussing the intellectual conditions of democracy [Chapter 11]. That development, however, *pre*supposes a community membership at least possessing the basic faculties of reason.

Some hold that democracy is a utopian and unrealizable ideal in that, requiring rational members, it presupposes what never can be. This criticism has two variants, each resting upon different false premises. The first variant overstates the requirements; the second variant understates the facts. On the former account it is suggested that democracy cannot work unless reason rules universally in human life, as it surely does not. On the latter account it is suggested that democracy cannot work because, although its demands for rationality are moderate, humans are so thoroughly irrational and stupid as not to be able to fulfill them. Both accounts are refuted by the practical success of democratic governments in many contexts. Democracy is a human institution, having requirements that render it not always successful, but essentially operable by human beings as they are.

There is an important truth in one aspect of the second variant of this criticism. *If* it were a practical impossibility for men to formulate rules jointly and abide by them; *if* it were impossible (or nearly so) for men to reason with and understand one another, *then* it could be argued that democracy is utopian because its practice presupposes what never is the case. The antecedent of this hypothetical proposition is false, but the hypothetical as a whole is true. Democracy does presuppose fundamental rational capacity; the absence of the latter in a community would entail the absence of the former.

That democracy presupposes the inherent goodness of men is another claim about it that is both common and mistaken. Of course it is true that the wide presence of certain moral virtues among the members of a community is likely to render its democratic government more successful in practice—but that can probably be said with equal truth of every governmental form. That men are inherently good, or inherently bad, is doubtful in any case; but there is no more reason to believe that democracy presupposes the one than the other. In principle democracy is entirely feasible even among a community of selfish or evil men. Indeed, part of its value lies in the fact that it enables men in whom goodness and badness are well mixed to live decently with one another.

I conclude that the presuppositions of democracy are very commonly realized in fact. *Communities,* large and small, are among the most ubiquitous features of human existence, and play a vital role in the life of every civilized man. *Rationality* is the universal (or almost universal) capacity of human beings, and has even been viewed, in some philosophical traditions, as the distinctly human characteristic, differentiating man from all lower animals. I certainly do not suggest that the presuppositions of democracy are realized everywhere, or in any single place at all times. When and where they are realized, moreover, I would insist that by themselves they provide no assurance whatever that democratic government will work smoothly, or that it is the best of the available alternatives. That its presuppositions are frequently realized, however, is beyond reasonable doubt.

It remains to account for the fact that, even where its presuppositions are realized, democracy may not develop, or may develop and then fail, or may continue meeting with only limited success. For such an explanation one must go beyond what democracy presupposes, inquiring carefully into the conditions of its operational success. Before this inquiry (the substance of Part Four) the account of democracy must be deepened, clarified, and made more concrete by explaining the relations between democracy itself and certain instrumental principles with which it is closely and rightly associated. This explanation will be the object of Part Three.

Part Three

DEMOCRACY AND ITS INSTRUMENTS

Chapter 6

Democracy and majority rule

6.1 Decision-making rules

Self-government must frequently be culminated; decisions must be made. Ideally, decisions in a democratic community will be the outcome of continuing, vigorous discussion; in each process of general participation having many stages, taking action will be the final stage. However much or little this ideal is realized, community life requires that some decisions be reached, some specific courses of action chosen. Centrally important, therefore, are the rules according to which particular decisions are made; if the community is or wants to be democratic, it is through these decision-making rules that the will of the membership is given concrete effect.

There are many decision-making rules consistent with democratic government. Their kinds need to be distinguished, their respective merits and limitations understood. In reviewing them, I shall argue that democracy is not logically tied to any single decision-making rule. Depending upon the nature of the community and its problems, different rules may serve as the valuable instruments of democracy.

A given democratic community need not employ the same rule in reaching all decisions; different kinds of issues render different kinds of decision-making rules appropriate. The rule for establishing everyday regulations, statutes or bylaws, may greatly differ from the rule for amending the fundamental law, the constitution, of the community. Successful democracy requires intelligence in the choice of its operating rules.

A paradox arises from the fact that any decision-making rule for ordinary legislation seems to suppose another, possibly different rule, at a more fundamental level, for deciding upon the day-to-day rules. That more fundamental rule seems to suppose yet another beneath it, and so on. As a practical matter, however, we do not normally build a democracy from nothing, but work *in medias res*, with the rules already in effect. Some constitutional rules, written or unwritten, are generally supposed, and they are likely to specify procedures for their own revision. Building upon these we seek to construct and improve a democratic decision-making system.

6.2 Appraising decision-making rules in a democracy

Connections between the decision-making rules of a democracy and its breadth are complicated and need to be sorted out. Some rules, giving to one person or one small group of persons the power of directive decision, are clearly anti-democratic and may be put aside. Of the rules consistent with democracy, all permit, but most do not require, great breadth of participation to legitimize decisions. In most cases, therefore, actual breadth of participation may vary greatly from decision to decision, while the same rule is in effect. It is also possible for the rule to vary while the breadth of participation remains constant.

Democratic rules almost invariably will specify what percentage of those who do participate are needed to decide the matter at hand. But it is not the case that an increase in the percentage of participants required for decision necessarily yields a correlative increase in democraticity. Democracy may be frustrated if either too few, or too many, of those participating are required to agree to make decisions binding. Choosing the best decision-making rule for a given context is a complex matter.

Appraisal of any decision-making rule in a democracy must be made in view of the total consequences of its employment. Of these consequences there are two major kinds. The first is the tendency of a rule to provide protection to each member of the community, protection against decisions that somehow injure him, or affect him adversely. The second is the tendency of a rule to make the will of the community effective, by making it possible to reach decisions and to reach them efficiently. In appraising a democratic decision-making rule, therefore, one must weigh both its *protectiveness* and its *efficiency*. Unfortunately, between these two large objectives there is considerable tension.

Greater protection will flow from decision-making rules as they become more *inclusive*, that is, as they require the explicit agreement of a greater percentage of the deciding body for positive action. The more inclusive the rule, the less likely any individual (of unspecified interest) will be to find himself in the minority, and the easier it will be for an adversely affected minority to gather the votes needed to block action.

Inclusiveness may be absolute or relative. A rule is inclusive in the absolute sense (to whatever degree) when the agreeing percentage required is a percentage of the entire membership—e.g., when a majority of all the members of some committee, or two-thirds of all the members of some senate, are required for action. Inclusiveness is relative when the percentage required is a percentage of some fluctuating body, those actually voting, or those actually present. Absolute inclusiveness is more cumbersome than relative inclusiveness, and is employed only in special cases; it has the merit, however, of encouraging democraticity by requiring for action a breadth of participation that might not have been otherwise attained. Less inclusive, or only relatively inclusive rules do not entail that the number of actual participants will be fewer, but they permit decisions with fewer participants. That is a danger as well as a convenience. To limit this danger quorum rules are effective in some contexts, insuring that no formal action may be taken without a fixed minimum of participation, or at least presence, by the membership.

Greater efficiency, on the other hand, will tend to flow from rules that are less inclusive, a small percentage of the deciding body being required for action. This is true whether the requirements be imposed absolutely or relatively, but the former category may be put aside as exceptional. Among normal rules, framed in terms of those voting (or occasionally those present) the less demanding the requirement for agreement, the more readily will agreement be achieved. Of two rules, one requiring agreement of three-fourths of those voting, the other a bare majority, the latter will obviously permit positive action to be taken more quickly, and supported more stably than will the former. The less inclusive rule permits more immediate response to needs felt in the community. It is likely to prove more effective, too, in making possible some action (say, with majority support) where no proposal whatever could be enacted if the support of three-fourths were required. The cost of this efficiency and effectiveness is risk. Any citizen not knowing at a given time what issues will be decided by a rule about to be chosen should certainly expect to be more frequently in the losing minority under the rule of the majority than under the rule of three-fourths.

Because the objectives of protection and efficiency necessarily conflict, no rule can fully maximize both. At one extreme, the rule giving power of directive decision to one man, the autocrat, may avoid haggling and delay, but gives everyone else no protection whatever against the autocrat's use or abuse of his power. At the other extreme, the rule permitting action only when the community is in unanimous agreement gives complete protection to every member against positive decisions adverse to his interests, but is likely to impose intolerable burdens on all by rendering it virtually impossible to take any community action whatever. Every other decision-making rule occupies some point between these extremes. Ideally, we seek that intermediate point which effects the best available compromise, assuring democraticity and reasonable protection, while imposing the lightest practical burdens upon the community in the actual process of reaching agreement.

What rule proves to be the happiest compromise depends upon many factual circumstances of the community—its size, the character and homogeneity of its members, the kinds of issues it must face. Successful democracy needs different rules for different communities, different situations, and different kinds of issues. No single rule is optimal for all.

6.3 Democratic process and decision-making rules

Good decision-making rules serve and support the democratic process by making it effective, but they are not the whole of that process. This may be shown by considering the relations of the rules to dimensions of democracy other than breadth. The employment of any decision-making rule is, at best, only the culmination of a participatory process that is continuing rather than intermittent, involves discussion and debate as well as commitment, and is manifested in a host of ways only one of which is the casting of votes [2.4]. The desire for specificity, and the impelling need to make some verifiable judgments, results in a widespread tendency to identify democracy with its decision-making rules. This is a mistake, reducing democracy to only one of its dimensions, breadth, simply because it is breadth that lends itself to quantitative analysis.

At the stage of the democratic process when decision-making rules are applied, the question has become, in effect: "Now that we have discussed the matter, what actions shall we take?" Proposals are made, and a vote in some form is taken. Reaching decisions demands some definite and publicly verifiable measurement of community opinion, so there must be resort to what is measurable—ballots cast, hands raised. We hope the rule will be fair, wise, justly administered. But no rule, however wise and consistent with democracy, can measure all aspects of the democratic process; its application can never reflect the depth of the participation of those voting.

In like manner, decision-making rules cannot reflect the range of participation either; the most complete information about the character of a rule tells us nothing about the variety of questions on which it is applied and respected. Appraising the democracy of a community, therefore, one must ask not only what rules are in effect, but where they are in effect, and how consistently they are used. Maximizing the democracy of the whole demands not only maximal range of participation, but within that range the use of differing rules of appropriate inclusiveness. Decision-making rules are the instruments of democracy; the entire pattern of their use is only one index of the health of any democracy, but it is a most important one.

6.4 Majority rule and its varieties

Of all decision-making rules, the rule of the majority is the most familiar and the most important. So closely is it associated with democracy that the two are often mistakenly identified. Majority rule, in fact, is only one of many consistent with democracy, and is sometimes less appropriate than others. Because of the combination of efficiency and protectiveness it provides, however, majority rule is commonly chosen as the happiest available compromise.

The concept of "majority rule" is itself ambiguous, on two levels. There is, first, uncertainty as to the meaning of "majority"—i.e., as to what proportion of a given body it refers to; and there is, second, uncertainty regarding the nature of the body within which the majority is required. I treat these two levels in turn.

(1) The "majority" normally means "more than half" of the group in question, but is sometimes loosely used as synonymous with "plurality," the largest single part of the group, whether or not more than half. Obviously majority rule and plurality rule are importantly different, since they can lead to very different outcomes. Plurality rule permits (but does not entail) decision-making by a distinct minority of the whole. Clearly, rule by majority (sometimes specified as "the simple majority") is more inclusive than plurality rule; it therefore provides more protection for the interests of the members, but is less efficient.

On some kinds of issues rule by the simple majority may be thought not protective enough. Rules are then devised requiring the active agreement of two-thirds, or even three-fourths, before certain kinds of action can be taken. These are often called "qualified majority" rules, each named after the fraction it requires—"two-thirds majority," "three-fourths majority," and so on. Qualified majority rules are entirely appropriate for matters of great consequence to the community. So, for example, the Constitution of the United States may be altered only when both (a) an amendment has been properly proposed by either two-thirds of both houses of Congress, or by a convention called by the legislatures of two-thirds of the states; *and* (b) an amendment so proposed has been ratified by the legislatures, or by conventions, in three-fourths of the several states. This double use of the qualified majority is highly protective; citizens may rest assured that the fundamental law of the land cannot be amended easily, or carelessly, or without the overwhelming endorsement of the people's representatives. Such protectiveness can be afforded, however, only when the need for change is very rare, and where speed and efficiency in making change is not essential, perhaps even not desirable. On matters like constitutional change, highly inclusive qualified majority rules, offering much protection and little convenience, may be a democracy's most suitable instrument.

(2) With the meaning of "majority" specified, it remains to determine the precise body within which it must be garnered. The majority of whom? There are three major alternatives. Rule by the majority may signify: *(a)* rule by the majority of those who actually vote; *(b)* rule by the majority of those who may vote; *(c)* rule by the majority of all members.

These alternatives may be viewed as points on a continuum extending from most relative inclusiveness to most absolute inclusiveness [6.2]. Another point on that continuum is the rule requiring a majority of those members qualified to vote who are actually present. This would be intermediate in absoluteness between *(a)* and *(b)* above; but its restricted applicability only to communities small enough to permit all members to meet together renders it of lesser interest. Still another possibility is rule by the majority of those members known to be affected by the outcome, assuming an issue affects some but not all. Restricting decision to those so affected is an appealing notion, but is seldom feasible because it supposes that criteria marking out the affected sub-group can be precisely specified and fairly applied. In effect, this variant of the rule seeks to circumscribe a new, smaller community within the original, larger one [2.7]. Within that smaller community the three alternatives above arise once again.

Consider, then, a hypothetical community of 100 members, all of whom will be affected by the democratic resolution of a given issue. Suppose that only 80 are permitted by law to vote (the "qualified voters"), and that only 60 cast a ballot (the "actual voters"). Seriously respecting the principle that the will of the majority should govern, of which body shall we specify that a majority should be required?

(a) Most workable (especially when the community is very large) is the rule requiring only a majority of the votes cast. In our hypothetical case that would mean a majority of the 60 actual voters, resulting in control by as few as 31 of the community's members. This is the rule most commonly employed, but it has the unhappy consequence that, if the number of actual voters should be small, the number needed for control may be very small. If, in our hypothetical community, only 25 had voted, 13 members may decide the matter for 100. (Quorum rules designed to minimize this risk can guard only against the extreme case, and are impractical in elections of large scale.) Usually we do not boggle at the consequences of this system. We know that the controlling minority is likely to be genuinely concerned, and also likely to represent, in fact, a large proportion of the non-voters. Moreover, no other rule may be feasible. Yet this interpretation of majority rule could result in outcomes in conflict with the general wishes of the community.

(b) For greater protection a majority of the qualified voters may be required. This sets a floor below which breadth of participation cannot fall—41 voters in the hypothetical case proposed. The worth of that floor depends, of course, upon the assumption that suffrage in the community is universal, or nearly so. In communities of which a significant percentage of the members are not permitted to vote, even this stronger variant of majority rule may be delusive, resulting in decisions by a small minority of the whole.

(c) In special contexts rule by the majority is interpreted in the strongest sense, as rule by more than half of the total membership of a specific community. Positive action then must have relatively wide support. To apply this rule a community must consist of a determinate number of voting members whose identities are precisely known. In the nominating conventions of political parties, for example, voting delegates are carefully identified and nominations usually require support of at least one-half the total of all delegates plus one. Such a rule may delay positive action (requiring repeated balloting) or block it entirely. It is usually feasible only where the community is relatively

small, and where the common need for some action will keep large minorities from remaining stubbornly immovable. Where suffrage is substantially universal (i.e., virtually all members are qualified voters) this and the preceding interpretation are substantially identical.

Concerning each of these interpretations we want to know the degree of efficiency and the degree of protectiveness it provides. Efficiency is an inverse function of inclusiveness (though perhaps not of inclusiveness only); since the three interpretations of majority rule are progressively more inclusive, they are progressively less efficient. Even the most efficient of the three is often clumsy; therefore the majority most commonly required in democratic communities is the majority of those who do actually vote. Anything beyond that is almost certain to retard decision-making, perhaps unduly.

Protectiveness too is largely determined by inclusiveness, hence the risk of minority control is heightened under the first, most common interpretation. However, when actual participants approach in number those qualified to participate, and those qualified approach the number of the whole, the differences in protectiveness may not be very great.

Conclusions both theoretically and practically important for democracy may be drawn. After satisfactory breadth of participation has been attained, majority rule of some variety is usually a reasonable instrument to make the popular will effective. But the rule of the majority cannot by itself guarantee satisfactory breadth. Perhaps the common identification of democracy with majority rule flows from the uncritical assumption that with such a rule breadth of participation is assured. The assumption is not always warranted; majority rule, although a valuable instrument, may prove deceptive as an index of democraticity.

What varieties of what rules a democratic community should employ must depend upon the degrees of efficiency and protectiveness it demands, the degrees of inefficiency and risk it can tolerate. Possible combinations are unlimited, ranging from highly protective and clumsy qualified majority rules, to relatively efficient but risky plurality rules. In view of its own circumstances, and the needs and wants of its own members, a democracy must choose its instruments.

6.5 Majority rule as the instrument of democracy

Majority rule, the *lex majoris partis*, is no more, or less, than one principle through which the will of the participating membership of a community is made effective. Reasonably interpreted, its use promises that, whatever the breadth of participation already achieved, a fair weighing will be given to the voices of the several participants. No procedural principle can be invoked to judge the wisdom of individual contributions, since that judgment is precisely the one that cannot be antecedently made. Nor can the depth of members' contributions be controlling, since that cannot be accurately or fairly determined. What remains to measure the popular will is, in most cases, the numerical majority, the greater part.

That majority rule is an instrument of democracy and not its substance is further evidenced by the following considerations. *First:* the fact that it is a principle appropriately subject to various interpretations [6.4] and that one of these must be deliberately selected, is indicative of its instrumental character. No particular decision-making rule is forced upon a community because it is a democracy—although some rules, it is true, will be precluded for that reason.

Second: the importance of plurality rule, and the frequency of its use, is instructive. Rule by plurality may be operative in fact, even where it has not been explicitly agreed upon. Beneath the surface of two-party conflict many points of view are likely to be contending. By receiving the support of the largest minority in the majority party (or even the largest minority within the largest minority within the majority party) one position finally wins the day. It is arguable that in this way minorities almost always, and majorities rarely, rule in a large democracy. The power of minorities is often hidden by the need for compromise within political parties, and by the technical requirement that legislative enactments receive a majority vote in the parliament.

Third: it is noteworthy that some democracies employ devices specifically designed to prevent the majority from being absolutely decisive. In the United States, such institutions as the judicial review of legislative action, the Electoral College, and the representation of each state by two senators regardless of its population, are invoked deliberately to protect minorities from exploitation by a majority. A democracy may respect and use majority rule, and at the same time rationally seek to mitigate the absolute control of the majority.

Fourth: some democratic communities do not count votes at all, when the participation of the members can be made effective through the grasp of the "sense of the meeting," its con-sensus, by its presiding officer. This power of leadership can be seriously misused, deliberately or inadvertently, but when employed sensitively and in the spirit of democracy it can result in decisions superior to those of a vote count.

The presiding officer may, subjectively but in the service of the whole, weigh the intensity of concern manifested by minorities, as well as the risk of disruption certain decisions might create. Such qualitative considerations, combined with an estimate of numbers, make possible outcomes that are deeply democratic, perhaps more responsive to the will of the community than any mechanical rule. Also, this procedure permits formulation of the group's judgment through letter or report, with a subtlety that motions and amendments following formal parliamentary procedure can rarely match. It is a delicate and risky instrument, but it, too, a democracy may choose.

All varieties of decision-making rules are attended by considerable risk; all, including the rule of the majority, have merits as well as limitations. Of all the possibilities, however, only the rule of the simple majority has this special advantage: it is the single rule that both prevents any minority, by itself, from taking positive action for the whole, and prevents any minority, by itself, from blocking the positive action of the whole. Any less inclusive role—rule of the plurality, for example—does not accomplish the former goal; any more inclusive rule—a qualified majority rule, for example—does not accomplish the latter goal. The power to block action is in some ways as important as the power to take action; any minority possessing that power can force the community to keep things as they are, a positive decision often of great consequence. The rule of the simple majority, therefore, exhibits a unique merit, and in most democratic contexts is likely to prove simplest, fairest, and most workable. This is why it has come to be viewed as the natural instrument of democracy. In just this instrumental spirit John Locke wrote of it in his *Second Treatise of Government* (1690).

> For when any number of men have, by the consent of every individual, made a community, they have thereby made that community one body, with a power to act as one body, which is only by the will and determination of the majority; for that which acts any community being only the consent of the individuals of it, and it being necessary to that which is one body to move one way, it is necessary the body should move that way whither the greater force carries it, which is the consent of the majority; or else it is impossible it should act or continue one body, one community, which the consent of every individual that united into it agreed that it should; and so everyone is bound by that consent to be concluded by the majority. And therefore we see that in assemblies impowered to act by positive laws, where no number is set by that

positive law which impowers them, the act of the majority passes for the act of the whole and, of course, determines, as having by the law of nature and reason the power of the whole.

And thus every man, by consenting with others to make one body politic under one government, puts himself under an obligation to everyone of that society to submit to the determination of the majority, and to be concluded by it. . . .

6.6 Rule by fluctuating majorities

What keeps the power of majorities from being abused in healthy democracies? The threat of a tyrannical majority is real, and has been much feared and emphasized by critics of democracy. There are democracies, however, in which majority power is used tyrannically and exploitatively rarely, if at all. How is the danger met?

Many factors may contribute to majority restraint, of course, among them constitutional prohibitions and guarantees. But if the majority is large enough, and determined enough to have its way, no external restrictions will long bind it; laws and institutions can be altered, customs can be ignored, even formal constitutions can be amended or suspended. Yet majority restraint is reasonably common (though far from universal) even where the members of the community are neither unusually altruistic nor unusually sophisticated. What keeps the natural drive for power and self-interest from wrecking a democracy?

Two elements above all encourage successful restraint. First, the habits and temperament of the individual members must be such as to permit general participation in government to continue. The attitudes and dispositions required I pass over here, to treat more fully later [Chapter 12] as among the psychological conditions for the success of democracy. Second, an institutional balance must be developed where majority rule is applied by a democracy over a considerable range of issues, and over a considerable stretch of time. The majority that rules on any given issue is not likely to be the same majority as that which rules on many other issues facing the same membership. So, while an equal (or nearly equal) percentage of the community may continue to control, as "the majority," the constituents of that percentage will be constantly varying, from issue to issue, and from time to time. What really rules, in a moderately healthy democracy, is not the majority, but majorities (and often, as noted in 6.5, only pluralities) constantly changing in membership. I call this "rule by fluctuating majorities." The rule of fluctuating majorities is operative when membership in a decisive majority is experienced by all (or almost all) of the community's members at one time or another, and when, on a range of different questions being decided during a given period, any member is likely to find himself a constituent of the ruling majority on some issues, and of a ruled minority on others.

The rule of fluctuating majorities is a key factor in the health of any large democracy. It keeps each citizen conscious of his several roles within the community: ruler, when he sides with the many; ruled, in that he is committed to obey the laws, whether he sides with the many or with the few. That he frequently finds himself one of a minority—indeed, that he is always a member of some minority—is likely to cause him, as it causes his fellow citizens also, to restrain those oppressive tendencies which the possession of power can excite. What the majority of which I am a member does to others today, a majority of which I am not a member may do to me tomorrow. Here enters into the political realm one of the noblest of ethical maxims, the Golden Rule. It enters not because of its nobility, but because of its cold practicality; and it enters in negative form, in which it is more easily understood and more readily applied. Within democracies which realize the principle of rule by fluctuating majorities, this is the Golden Rule of politics: Refrain from doing to others what you would have them refrain from doing to you.

Some have argued that the fluctuating character of rule in a democracy has the reverse effect—that rather than tending to restrain oppressive tendencies it reinforces them. John C. Calhoun, for example, in his *Disquisition on Government* (1851), wrote: "But the duration or uncertainty of the tenure by which power is held cannot, of itself, counteract the tendency inherent in government to oppression and abuse of power. On the contrary, the very uncertainty of the tenure, combined with the violent party warfare which must ever precede a change of parties under such [i.e., pure majoritarian] governments, would rather tend to increase than diminish the tendency to oppression." Similarly, Robert Michels (*Political Parties,* 1911, Part II, Chap. 1) contended that where the turnover of power is frequent, "everyone who attains to power thinks chiefly of making a profitable use of that power while it lasts," and he concludes that the genuine advantages for democracy provided by rotation in office are outweighed by "the exploitative methods of ephemeral leaders, with all their disastrous consequences."

Such arguments would be more persuasive if they were more generally supported by the facts. Dreading the tyranny of the majority,

72

these critics are convinced that the natural lust for power must make that tyranny unavoidable. Their fears cause them to view "the majority" as a monolith, hungry and irresistible. They ignore the actual condition of democratic communities and one of the most notable features of rule by majority. The search for private profit is tempered by the insecurity of elected office, and the possibility of future catastrophe. Even one who would be rapacious if he could must weigh the fact that the issues in which he has an interest are many, and that he (like all others) enjoys concurrent membership in various majority and minority groups. Intelligent self-interest must cause every citizen of a democracy to remain conscious of the uncertainty of power under majority rule and the possible consequences, to *him*,—on another issue or at another time—of his abuse of power.

This is the core of the argument in Madison's justly famous *The Federalist #10*. The brilliance of the argument of this paper lies in Madison's grasp of the way in which the continuing contest of a multiplicity of parties and interests can effectively restrain the abusive tendencies of any single party or interest. This argument he marshals in support of the proposed American union.

> Extend the sphere, and you take in a greater variety of parties and interests; you make it less probable that a majority of the whole will have a common motive to invade the rights of other citizens; or if such a common motive exists, it will be more difficult for all who feel it to discover their own strength, and to act in unison with each other. . . .

> Does it [the advantage of a healthy republic] consist in the greater security afforded by a greater variety of parties, against the event of any one party being able to outnumber and oppress the rest? In an equal degree does the increased variety of parties comprised within the Union, increase this security. Does it, in fine, consist in the greater obstacles opposed to the concert and accomplishment of the secret wishes of an unjust and interested majority? Here, again, the extent of the Union gives it the most palpable advantage.

Madison himself distrusted direct democracy, and therefore carefully avoided the term "democracy" in referring to the system he defended, which he called a "republic." But Madison's republic is nothing different from the indirect, representative democracy (of considerable size) here being discussed. Some have supposed (perhaps because of his rejection of "democracy") that in *The Federalist* Madison was proposing a new and singular theory of government—so called "Madisonian democracy." This interpretation misunderstands his enterprise, which was chiefly to provide a defense of representative self-government [14.3]. That defense consists of an acute account of the way in which one special instrument of democracy—the rule of fluctuating majorities—can serve and preserve it. Since "the *causes* of faction cannot be removed . . . relief is only to be sought in the means of controlling its *effects*." Thus, in a healthy polity, a reasonably restrained and stable balance can be achieved among a multiplicity and variety of factions. The continuing and widespread use of majority rule can greatly mitigate its own dangers.

6.7 On the misuse of majority power

Decisive majorities do not always fluctuate. Where they do not, or do not fluctuate with sufficient frequency (all questions in this sphere being questions of degree) the rule of the majority may undermine the practice of general participation, and thereby subvert the very democracy whose instrument it is. Hence there is real danger, for a democracy, in the development of a *fixed majority* in the community. A fixed or permanent majority is released from the healthy check of fluctuation; it can maintain absolute control in the areas of its interest; those who oppose it have no leverage to use against it; its use of power may become abusive, even repressive. At its worst a fixed majority can utterly destroy the delicate equilibrium of many contending interests upon which the practice of democracy so fundamentally depends [4.6].

This danger, ironically, tends to be greater where the differences of interest within the community tend to be most marked, and the need for tolerance and restraint most acute. The relatively homogeneous community need not so greatly fear the abuse of power by some of its members. Needing less in the way of protection for the individual in the decision-making rule, it can afford to provide that protection more readily, since even more inclusive rules for decision are not likely to stymie needed activities. In very heterogeneous communities, on the other hand (or at least those having sharply distinguished, stable, and intensely committed sub-groups), individual citizens have much to fear from the power of opponents, and therefore need inclusive, protective, decision-making rules. But in just these communities the operation of such protective rules is likely to prove a cause of serious inefficiency, and even to block needed community action entirely. In these more divided communities, therefore, democracy must be more fragile, its instrument of fluctuating majorities being less effective.

These observations help to explain the great difficulties in developing healthy democracy in those lands where ethnic and economic subcommunities are sharply marked and virtually fixed. This is only one of the very grave problems of underdeveloped communities that seek to develop democratic government. In such contexts democracy may be made safer for its own members, and hence more viable, if the range of issues subjected to community action be restricted to those upon which there is some measure of community consensus. But the degree of such consensus varies enormously among national communities. So, for example, what can be done effectively by collective action in a small, relatively homogeneous nation—say, Holland—may be more wisely left in private hands in a large, relatively heterogeneous nation—say, India—if the operation of the democracy is not to result in the fragmentation of the entire community. Unfortunately, the severe community problems—economic and social—of thickly populated and industrially underdeveloped lands may make essential community control over matters which (given the nature of those communities) do not lend themselves to democratic resolution. The consequent tension may be so severe as to render democracy unworkable in some communities of this kind.

Even where majorities do fluctuate, it can happen that the will of a particular majority, on particular procedural questions, may unwisely restrict the participation of some significant portion of the community on other substantive issues. It is thus entirely possible that decisions reached democratically may cripple the continuation of that very democratic procedure. Such situations are painful for the democrat, but will arise; I shall discuss them at length in treating the protective conditions of successful democracy [13.4]. Here it is sufficient to note that the power of the majority when used—even with the best of intentions—to restrict the breadth, or depth, or range of popular participation, may prove to be the instrument with which a democracy does itself to death.

There can be no absolute guarantees against such misuse of power. The rule of fluctuating majorities, and a widespread sensitivity to the requirements of democracy, can build restraint in the use of power but cannot insure it. James Thurber put it well: "There is no safety in numbers—or in anything else, for that matter."

Chapter 7

Democracy and representation

7.1 Representation as the instrument of democracy

The distinction between *direct* and *indirect* democracy is both common and reasonable. We may participate in the governing process ourselves, or we may participate in the selection of others who will govern for us. The members of a democratic community, in choosing some among themselves to represent all, do not give up ultimate control of community policy. They do give to those so elected the power to act, in certain ways and for a specified period, in the place of their constituents. These representatives then perform what I have earlier called the "administrative" functions of government [1.2]. Collectively they may properly be called a chamber of deputies, or a representative assembly, or simply the parliament.

The principle of representation, concisely formulated, is this: the administration of government may be conducted by relatively few persons, responsible to the constituent members of the community who elect them, and deriving all their authority from their constituents. All elected office holders, regardless of the branch of government in which they serve, and with them the conduct of virtually all government business, rely ultimately on this principle. It is crucial, therefore, that the citizens of any large democracy understand the proper relations between themselves and their representatives.

When the mass of citizens are believed incapable of governing themselves, a representative system will be deemed not merely a necessity but a positive good, allowing administration to remain in the hands of those thought to be more judicious and more enlightened. Having that consequence was believed, by its authors, to be one great merit of the proposed Constitution of the United States. Madison wrote: "The effect [of the delegation of the government] is . . . to refine and enlarge the public views, by passing them through the medium of a chosen body of citizens, whose wisdom may best discern the true interest of their country, and whose patriotism and love of justice will be least likely to sacrifice it to temporary or partial considerations. Under such a regulation, it may well happen that the public voice, pronounced by the representatives of the people, will be more consonant to the public good than if pronounced by the people themselves, convened for the purpose" (*The Federalist #10*, 1787).

Whether viewed as a positive advantage or a necessary evil, representation is (like majority rule), an instrument of democracy; it is not identical with democracy. As majoritarianism is a way of making the participation of the membership of a community decisive, representation is a way of channeling that participation so as to enable individual voices to be heard fairly, while increasing the likelihood that difficult decisions will be made wisely. Both instruments are extremely valuable, yet there are circumstances in which either or both may properly be rejected. In some very small democracies no system of representation may be needed or wanted, in large ones representation becomes a practical necessity. Democracy is government through general participation; representation helps make that participation effective. To suppose the identity of the two is to confuse the essence of democracy with one of the instruments through which it is realized.

The proper functioning of any instrument depends both on its quality and the wisdom with which it is used. A large democracy, therefore, needs first a system of representation that is just, designed to reflect the will of the people fully and accurately. Inferior representative machinery may stymie and frustrate even an intelligent and concerned citizenry. The most excellent representative schemes can be abused, however; if the citizenry is corrupt, uninterested, or uninformed, no machinery by itself will provide wise governors. In the last analysis, representatives will represent, as well as lead, their constituents.

A democrat should recognize the necessary consequences of any representative system, and its limitations. In it, each citizen's voice will be diminished, sometimes drowned, by the voices of the many others whom his representative also represents, and by the representatives of other constituencies within the community. But representation itself is not to blame for a reduction in the influence of each citizen; that reduction is a direct result of increasing community size. In a democracy of 500 one must expect to play a smaller role in decision-making than in a democracy of 50. With or without a representative system that will be so. When the community is one of fifty thousand or fifty million, the dimunition in the relative importance of each is proportionate. Beyond a certain size a democracy is compelled by practical considerations to use representative machinery if the individual is to be heard at all. We ought not blame the machinery for the consequence of the size that made it essential.

There are two great spheres in which a representative system must function, and be appraised. The first of these is the choosing of the representatives themselves, the elections. The second comprises all other occasions, between elections, for the people to be heard. If the system for selection is not intelligent and fair, the democracy may be undone; but after selection, too, the system must promote responsiveness by the deputies to their constituents. I discuss the first of these spheres in Sections 7.2–7.8; the second in Sections 7.9–7.11.

Many of the issues relating to representative systems are highly technical, and are properly in the province of the political scientist. Still we can, in short compass, lay out a philosophical framework within which concrete systems may be understood and judged. We must identify the central aspects of all representative systems, and indicate the kinds of advantages and disadvantages offered by the several basic alternatives. And we must grapple with certain fundamental questions arising in every representative system.

7.2 Democratic elections in general

Electoral systems are extremely complicated. Ignorance and misunderstanding of them is common, and may be exploited by those whose real intent is to frustrate democracy while professing it. It is unfortunate but true that just here, in this technical arena, the forces for and against democracy often fight their battles.

I begin by distinguishing the basic elements of every representative system. They are: *(1)* the degrees of representation; *(2)* the decision-making rule for selecting representatives; *(3)* the decision-making rule(s) used within the representative body; *(4)* the bases of representation; *(5)* the levels of representation. Each of these elements has a key role; in practice, however, it is their combined effect in one system that determines the effectiveness and justice of that system.*

---

*For a more detailed, quasi-mathematical account of some of these elements and their interrelations, see J. M. Buchanan and J. Tullock's brilliant study, *The Calculus of Consent* (1962), University of Michigan Press, Ann Arbor, to which the following discussion is much indebted.

7.3 Degrees of representation

The degree of representation is the degree to which the system approximates direct democracy; the upper limit upon the degree of representation is a system in which everyone speaks for himself. A high degree of representation is realized where the number of persons who must be heard through each representative is small, that is, where the ratio of representatives to total membership is high. As the number of constituents represented by each deputy goes down, the degree of representation goes up. The degree of representation can therefore be expressed as a percentage figure: the percentage of the total membership that will represent the whole. In large democracies it will be an extremely small percentage. So, in general, the degree of representation in a community will *in*crease as the number of representatives increases (supposing the total population constant); that degree will *de*crease as the total population increases (supposing the size of the representative body constant).

Ideally, a democracy will strive for the highest degree of representation feasible. We depart from direct democracy chiefly because size has made it impractical. Representation seeks to overcome the impracticalities of direct general participation, while keeping participation general. The lower the degree of representation (i.e., the more constituents per representative), the greater the distance between the individual citizen and the final decision-making process. I can participate more effectively in the making of laws and policies if I am one of ten electing a representative than if I am one of ten thousand. Participation may continue, but is reduced in effectiveness by the sheer force of numbers.

At the same time, the number of representatives in the governing body must not become so great as to frustrate the purposes of the representative system. Whatever the decision-making rule within that body, its efficiency in resolving the issues before it will drop as the number in the body increases. It must not be allowed to grow indefinitely. The highest possible degree of representation means, in practice, the highest degree of representation consistent with effective function in representative bodies.

The ratios that will best realize this ideal depend upon the kinds of issues dealt with by the representatives, and upon the total size of the community. Some kinds of issues can be debated in an assembly of

hundreds; some can be intelligently resolved only in very small deliberative bodies. Legislatures are often quite large; executive committees
of large organizations are likely to be very small.

The total size of the community affects the ratio fundamentally
because there is virtually an absolute limit on the size of an effective
representative assembly. The United States House of Representatives,
with 435 members, surely nears that limit. As national democracies
grow larger, therefore, they must suffer lower and lower degrees of representation. There is no escaping it. The larger the community, the
smaller is the percentage of it who can sit as deputies, and the greater
the distance between citizen and decisions. In general, democracy is
adversely affected by great size.

7.4 Decision-making rules and representative bodies

Factors *(2)* and *(3)* listed above [7.2] are largely explained by the account of decision-making rules in the preceding chapter. There must be
a rule according to which representatives are chosen (factor 2), possibly different rules for different bodies. The rule of the simple majority
of actual voters is most common for this selection, and works reasonably well where a two-party system is solidly ensconced. Where there
are three or more major candidates for an office to be filled, the requirement of a simple majority may necessitate a second, run-off election.
The inefficiency of any run-off system can be avoided only by restricting
the number of candidates to two (in which case the inefficiencies may
be moved to the primary elections in which the candidates are chosen),
or by changing from majority to plurality rule, which would make it
possible for the successful candidate to be opposed by a majority of
the voters. This choice of decision-making rule for elections is most
important since it is in the electing of representatives that citizen participation in government is most concrete. Ideally the rule for selecting
representatives will be as inclusive, as protective, as it can be without
imposing undue inefficiencies on the conduct of elections.

There must be rules, also, for the making of decisions within a
representative body already elected (Factor 3). It will be normal, as
we have seen [6.4] for differing rules (simple majority of actual voters,
qualified majorities of various sizes, etc.) to be applied to issues of
different kinds. In this context, too, we seek to combine efficiency with
safety.

The protectiveness of the decision-making rules within the representative body is commonly increased through the use of a bicameral legislature. The two houses will normally exhibit different degrees of representation [7.3] and different bases of representation [7.5]; therefore the requirement that legislation must be approved by both houses is an effective (but sometimes inefficient) way of protecting minority interests against oppressive or careless action, without imposing a decision-making rule that would require an impossibly high percentage of support for any positive action. As the degrees of representation and the bases for representation in the two houses are more nearly alike, the protectiveness of the bicameral system is reduced. Whether the safety it affords fully compensates for the inefficiencies it imposes is a question that can be answered only with full knowledge of the specific circumstances.

Between the two kinds of context just distinguished (decision in the selection of representatives, and decision within the representative body) there is an interesting complementarity. Decision-making rules may be more protective and less efficient, or less protective and more efficient [7.2]. Now greater protectiveness on the one level (say, in the selection of representatives) may reasonably encourage the use of more efficient, if less protective rules at the other level (say, within the representative body). This could work the other way as well. Very protective rules within the assembly may tend to justify more efficient if less protective rules in selecting representatives. In the end it is the combined effect of the entire system that must be appraised.

7.5 Bases of representation

Assuming the degree of representation known, and the rules both for the selection of representatives and for decisions within the representative body fixed, a key question remains: What kind of constituency is each representative to have? On what principle(s) are the several constituencies to be formed? These principles determine the bases of representation. Selecting them is the most difficult and the most important task in developing a good representative system.

There are many possible bases, all of which can be ordered on one very general continuum. At one extreme the constituency of each representative may be entirely homogeneous, comprising only persons with interests importantly similar; at the other, it may be entirely heterogeneous, comprising persons with diverse, random interests. Each of the two extremes is much superior in some respects, much inferior in others. Intermediate points on this continuum offer compromises in which advantages of one kind are traded off for advantages of other kinds. No solution is perfectly ideal; each democracy must devise the instruments best suited to its circumstances.

Illustrations will be helpful. Suppose the representative body were to consist of deputies each elected by a fixed number of members of some trade or profession. Constituencies would then be very homogeneous, and representation would be functional, in that each constituency would be delineated by the productive role or function of its members. The interests the deputy would defend would be those of lawyers, or plumbers, or teachers, and so on. Systems of roughly this kind have long been advocated by guild socialists and others. Suppose (at the other extreme) each member of the community had been assigned an identification number on a random basis, and that the representative body were to consist of deputies each elected by a fixed number of persons whose identification numbers lay within arbitrarily chosen ranges. Constituencies would then be very heterogeneous, and representation would be non-functional, because neither the special interests nor the productive role of a citizen would have any bearing upon the constituency of which he was a member. The interests the deputy would then defend would be those he believed to be the interests of the coalition, within his randomly selected constituency, responsible for his election and likely to support his reelection. He might find it difficult to know what these interests were, but would try to learn them indirectly by judging the apparent effectiveness of the several elements of his election platform. Such heterogeneity is quite nearly approached in practice, but never fully realized, in the senatorial constituencies of large and populous American states.

The full realization of neither extreme is feasible. But what are the respective advantages and disadvantages of systems near the two ends of the continuum? Functional representation has the enormous advantage of providing clear lines of responsibility for the deputy. On the one side, he knows precisely who elected him, and what interests he is therefore obliged to represent; on the other, his constituency, being homogeneous, can judge more readily and accurately how well he does his job of representing their common concerns. In such systems the rule for the selection of a representative (so long as it offers some small degree of protectiveness) is not of great moment, since the failure to represent the group's interests will be quickly noted whatever the rule, and punished by rejection at the first opportunity. The nonrepresentation of minorities within the constituency is not a serious danger, since the deputy is pretty certain to respond to the main functional concerns universally shared by his constituents. In general, such a system, to be fair, need only insure that each functional group is genuinely free to choose its own representative, and that the chamber of deputies include representatives of each of the community's major functional groups in proportionate number. So far, excellent. But within the representative body so composed the importance of protection being built into the rule for decision-making is much magnified. When the several competing interests have been institutionally divided and set in opposition, the losing interests (or losing coalition of interests) may lose everything, their concerns being defended only incidentally, if at all, by those in the majority coalition. Furthermore, as a result of the sharp demarcation of interests, the activities of each representative are likely to focus so sharply upon the concerns of his specialized constituency that his vision of community affairs as a whole may be somewhat myopic, with the result that, each looking out only for his own, the larger concerns of the community may be seriously threatened.

Non-functional representation, on the other hand, is very much more likely to result in a concern, by the individual deputy, for the needs of the community as a whole. His constituency being a random sample of the whole, he is likely to believe, correctly, that the interests of a majority of his constituents and those of a majority of the community are substantially identical, and that in defending the latter he defends the former, and so best enhances the chances of his own reelection. Provincialism is thereby much reduced. Moreover, the random nature of the several constituencies much reduces the probability that any significant minority will be entirely without representation in the ruling majority, since any effective coalition is likely to include some defenders of every major interest. The danger of minorities being oppressed by the majority is thereby reduced. So far, excellent. But the lines of responsibility between representatives and constituents in such a system will be most unclear. It will be hard for the deputy to know which of his randomly chosen constituents voted for him, or to know why they voted for him; and it will be therefore difficult for him to learn how to be of particular service to his supporting constituency. In the confusion it is possible, even likely, that some groups will get inadequate attention and defense. Where constituencies are heterogeneous the rule for the selection of representatives from the constituency becomes (in contrast to the other extreme) of high importance. That very heterogeneity calls for the greater emphasis upon protection of minorities that may lie wholly within that constituency, and must therefore be represented through it, or not at all. But the effectiveness and wisdom of any rule, even one highly protective (and therefore inefficient), will be very difficult to judge, as it will be practically impossible to say how well each deputy is doing the job of representing those who elected him.

Every large democracy is likely to devise some compromise between these two extremes, a compromise which seeks to maximize their respective advantages, while keeping their disadvantages to a minimum. James Madison and his colleagues thought the Constitution of the United States provided such a compromise. Supposing, reasonably, that an increasing number of constituents entailed increasing heterogeneity, he wrote: "It must be confessed that in this, as in most other cases, there is a mean, on both sides of which inconveniences will be found to lie. By enlarging too much the number of electors, you render the representatives too little acquainted with all their local circumstances and lesser interests; as by reducing it too much, you render him unduly attached to these, and too little fit to comprehend and pursue great and national objects. The federal Constitution forms a happy combination in this respect . . ." (*The Federalist #10*, 1787). Representation in the United States has much changed from Madison's day, but the effort to find the appropriate mean goes on. To this problem there is no final solution, because the needs and circumstances of large communities are forever changing.

7.6 Geographical and proportional representation

In establishing the bases for representation in a democracy two solutions predominate. Both are compromises; both have serious flaws; both work moderately well. On one system, the geographical, a fixed number of districts (wards, townships, states) are each permitted a fixed number of elected representatives. On the other system, the proportional, various devices are employed to insure that each elected deputy has a known and relatively homogeneous constituency supporting him specifically as the representative of their common concern. Under the latter system, if the supporters of Parties x, y and z comprise 60, 25, and 15 percent of the total population respectively, the mixture of representatives in the parliament will approximate that same proportion, each deputy sitting as a representative of voters all of whom share his views on some key issue.

Democracy and representation

Proportional representation is clearly intended to increase homogeneity, functionality in the representative system. Under it the members of each constituency will not be completely alike, of course, since voters united on some issues will be at odds on others, but it must lead to far more homogeneity than constituencies geographically determined. Geographical representation is not wholly non-functional, because many interests tend to cluster in certain places. Industrial interests (those of farming or mining, for example) or ethnic interests, often concentrate in specific areas. But a geographical district may encompass great heterogeneity, and is likely to encompass at least a good deal of it. Although neither of the two systems is pure, therefore, their relative merits are essentially the merits of the functional and non-functional ends of the continuum described above. There are, of course, many variants of each, and they can even be in some degree combined.

Geographical representation is subject to a particular flaw that is both very common and very serious in a democracy. In essence, that flaw is the distortion of the geographical districts in a way that subverts genuine and balanced representation. The "rotten boroughs" of England before 1832 (electoral districts with populations near zero), and the "gerrymandering" sometimes still practiced in America (shaping the district to concentrate the votes of a favored minority), are instances of deliberate distortion. More serious, if less blatant, injustices frequently result from accidental distortion caused by the growth and movement of populations. Where the total number of representatives in a legislative body is fixed, and the number from each geographical district is fixed, significant changes in the relative population of the several districts may result in severe under-representation of citizens in more densely populated districts, and over-representation of voters in sparsely populated areas. In effect, the degrees of representation [7.3] in the several districts then show great disparities; a rural district having half the population of a metropolitan one, but the same number of representatives in a common assembly, unfairly enjoys a degree of representation twice as high.

The population changes that create these disparities take place gradually, but their cumulative impact is enormous. With great cities grossly under-represented, it is inevitable that their needs will be inadequately met by the representative body as a whole. The metropolitan districts will contribute more than their share to the communal treasury, receive less than their share in tax expenditures. In just this fashion have American cities been abused.

85

Remedy for the distortion of representative districts is very difficult to achieve. Changing the number of representatives in the assembly, or the relative number from the several districts, is generally not feasible. The remaining alternative is the redrawing of the electoral districts on the map of the community, the painful process of legislative reapportionment. Even when the need for it is widely appreciated, reapportionment is difficult to effect. Any system of representation, once in operation, becomes habitual and ensconced. Moreover, the task of reapportioning falls naturally to the representatives themselves, and they are not likely to want to alter the system in which they have been elected to leadership and have strong vested interests. If the representatives cannot be persuaded or driven by their own constituents to reapportion, external pressure from the judiciary may be the only recourse. In the United States, the landmark Supreme Court case of *Baker v. Carr* (1962) opened the path to judicial remedy for inequitable apportionment in the several states, and brought to the surface a host of injustices in our representative systems of which few had realized the full extent. The slogan "one man, one vote," has been shorthand for the expression of the democratic ideal of equal degrees of representation for all—for every vote an equal voice.

Proportional representation has the merit of encouraging the responsiveness of the deputy to his constituency; it also tends to give minority parties large enough to elect one or two representatives under that system a voice they would probably be denied under a geographical system. But its flaws are serious too. Some versions of it oblige the use of signed "voting papers" on which the voter lists his preferences among the candidates; the need to keep these on file makes impossible a wholly secret ballot. Some versions result in the representation of so many minor parties in the parliament that definitive action requires coalitions difficult to maintain. Governmental efficiency is thus reduced. In some cases, the functional division of interests that proportional representation encourages can result in severe damage to minorities wholly unrepresented in the ruling coalition; then the decision-making rules applied within the parliament become most delicate matters. And systems of proportional representation are invariably complicated to operate. But, whether for good or ill, all versions of proportional representation may have results quite different from those that would have emerged had representatives been chosen from geographical districts by majority rule.

Every representative system—geographical, proportional, or other

—is an instrument whose purpose is to make effective the participation of citizens in communities too large to permit each a direct voice in substantive affairs. No such system will be perfect; but the continuing effort to improve old forms and devise new ones so as to make representation more just and more effective is an enterprise no democracy can wisely abandon.

7.7 Levels of representation

Any system of representation moves the sphere of actual decision-making one level away from the members represented. That process of removal is sometimes repeated, creating a second level of representation, and even a third. In each case the representatives at a given level become the represented at the next higher level, and the original body of electors come to be represented by a hierarchy of deputies, on several levels. The number of levels of representation in any given system is the number of steps above the membership at large at which substantive decisions are made. Members of a parliament elected through universal suffrage, for example, are representatives on the first level; ministers elected by the members of that parliament are representatives on a second level; administrative officers appointed by those ministers are representatives on a third level. The greater the number of levels, the less direct is the participation of the people, the less pure the democracy.

Such levels of representation are now taken for granted in most large democracies. Sometimes the indirection is a deliberate effort to insulate decisions from masses thought not competent or trustworthy enough to choose their own leaders—as with the original design of the Electoral College that was to choose the President of the United States. Open distrust of the people is less common now, but it is still widely believed that top executives, or administrators requiring technical skills, will be more wisely chosen by the elected representatives of the people than by the people themselves. The first level representatives, it is argued, will have a clearer understanding of the administrative tasks to be performed, and the talents those tasks require, than citizens at large. Such devices, in any event, although they may not defeat democracy, do tend to mute it. In some cases the argument for a second level of representation is based not on the incompetence of the masses, but on an alleged need to shelter officeholders of some kinds—judges, for example, or members of regulatory agencies—from the political pressures that would inevitably be applied to them if their selection took place on the first level of representation. There is often good sense in this argument.

Increased levels of representation do not remove ultimate authority from the hands of the members of the democratic community, but they do tend to reduce the power of the members to make their authority concretely effective. Wise or foolish, such levels are refinements of the tool of representation itself. Representation is an instrument to enable the members of a community to do for themselves indirectly what they cannot do, or do as well, directly; second and third levels of representation are modifications of that instrument to make possible the accomplishment for the community of what first level representatives cannot accomplish, or accomplish as well.

7.8 Representation between elections

When democracy operates through representatives, its depth will depend partly upon the quality of the participation of citizens in the election of representatives, and partly upon the effectiveness of the influence of constituents upon their representatives after election. This influence, between elections, is backed up ultimately by the promise of support or the threat of opposition at the next election. But whatever the sanction, that representative system is a better instrument of democracy which provides more and better channels through which public participation may be continuously operative.

Lenin said that, in Western democracies, the people have only the right to decide, at elections, who is to misrepresent them in parliament. Were he right, those democracies would indeed be fraudulent; if the consequence of the representative system is the frustration of the people's will, democracy has been subverted, not served by it. Some so-called democracies are fraudulent in this way; the mere existence of a chamber of deputies is not proof that democracy has been realized. One must know that the deputies represent their constituents truly and steadily; the representative system is only a tool that may function well or badly.

Recall, initiative, and referendum, are institutions devised to help insure better and more constant representation between elections. Recall permits the removal of a public official, by the vote of his constituency, when such a vote is demanded by a specified number of electors. This threat of removal even before the next regular election tends to maintain pressure on representatives to act as faithful deputies, to be sensitive to the intense desires of their constituents, and thus to make indirect participation by those constituents more continuously effective. Initiative and referendum have the same tendency, but operate quite differently. Instead of threatening the tenure of representatives, they threaten to take certain questions out of the hands of the representatives, and return them to the direct control of the citizens. Initiative provides that a statute or amendment having a specified degree of support must come to popular vote. Referendum permits measures already before some legislative body to be submitted to the vote of the electorate for approval or rejection. These devices aim to sensitize the representative machinery by giving the voters the power to punish or to bypass their representatives without awaiting the next general election [2.6]. The mere presence of these powers, not to mention specific threats of their use, can inhibit a representative who might seek to abuse his position, and can help to keep representatives alert to the strongly felt needs of their constituents.

Such institutions may increase the depth of a democracy, but they do not always improve the democracy; their net effects upon it may prove to be adverse. The very considerations of community size and complexity of issues necessitating representation in the first place may render damaging instruments designed to suspend representative government on specific issues and reinstitute direct democracy. At critical moments in the life of a community recall, too, may do harm. Although honestly intended to increase the effectiveness of participation, these devices may have precisely the reverse effect, by interfering with the proper fulfillment of the tasks of legislative or executive bodies. They may be employed in such a way as to subordinate long-range policy to short-run desires, while the participation of the people is made truly effective by the representative system as a whole, and over the long run.

Tension invariably arises between the need to keep the will of the membership continuously effective, and the need to encourage reasonable stability of policy and leadership. That stability it will normally be desirable to insure by protecting the authority and tenure of elected representatives. Yet on some occasions in some communities it may be appropriate to return from representative to direct democracy in order to insure the sovereignty of the people. What set of representative institutions best resolves this tension in a given community can be determined only by it, in view of its own circumstances.

7.9 The dilemma of the representative

The problem of maintaining equilibrium between the need for stability and the need for continuing citizen control between elections, has thus far been viewed from the perspective of the citizens. Consider the problem now from the perspective of the representative, one who serves his constituency with integrity in a system functioning with reasonable success. When he finds himself in honest and serious disagreement with the majority of his electors he may face an agonizing dilemma.

In such circumstances, is it the obligation of the representative to act as he knows his constituents wish him to act (say, support Policy P), or as he genuinely believes to be in their best interests (say, support Policy Q)? On most issues this conflict does not arise; but when the constituents' wishes and his judgment do conflict, what is the representative's overriding duty?

At first glance it would appear that, his position being that of deputy, he ought to vote for P if he really knows that P is what a majority of his constituents want. He has been selected, after all, to represent them, to participate in decision-making for them. To defy them would seem to betray their trust in him. His job (he may reason) is not to pass judgment on the people's wishes, but to implement those wishes. On the other hand, it is easy enough to see that certain questions arising in the parliament may be of so complex a nature that the mass of citizens do not have the time or opportunity to acquire the information necessary for intelligent decision, or the ability to organize or apply such information. In such cases the honest representative may feel that, in acting contrary to the people's will, voting against P, he is only doing what they would themselves do had they the information and understanding that he has. And he has been chosen, the argument continues, precisely for this task—to gather and apply relevant information with a thoroughness not possible for each single citizen he represents. Therefore (he may reason) it is his duty to follow the course that he honestly believes to be in the best interests of his constituents, even if they do not presently agree with him. Edmund Burke said to the electors of Bristol in 1775: "Your representative owes you not his industry only, but his judgment; and he betrays instead of serving you if he sacrifices it to your opinion."

The same general tension between continuity of citizen participation and stability of leadership described in the preceding section is here manifested in the smaller and clearer context of this deputy's dilemma. If the representative thinks his proper conduct in this situation is that of acting as he knows his constituents really wish him to, he exhibits prime concern for the continuing effectiveness of general participation in government. If he thinks it proper for him to act as he believes the best interests of his constituents require, in spite of their disagreement, he exhibits concern for the successful completion of certain tasks with which the representative body of which he is a member has been charged. There is no simple answer available to him, and the question will not down.

This tension will prove less worrisome, however, if the important distinction between questions of policy and questions of implementation is kept in mind. Our inclination to swing now to one and now to the other horn of the dilemma is partly caused by the difference in our attitudes toward these different kinds of issues. When the question is one of general policy formation, it is appropriate that its resolution be undertaken by general participation. When the question is one of policy implementation its wise resolution is likely to require technical competence and information far greater than that of the ordinary citizen, and is then appropriately the task of representatives selected for just that purpose.

Every particular question, of course, will encompass some elements of policy formation and some of implementation. There can be no simple rule which permits the definitive classification of every issue the representative confronts. Furthermore, what is an issue of policy implementation in one context may be an issue of policy formation in another, smaller context. For example, the decision to work vigorously for greater traffic safety is one of policy formation in the community that makes it. The decision to move toward this goal by enforcing traffic laws more strictly is one that may be made in the effort to implement this policy. Within the community of law enforcement officers (very likely not to be organized democratically) the decision to enforce the laws more strictly is a policy decision whose implementation requires far more detailed principles of operation. And so on. Which decisions are to be considered in which category depends largely upon the context in which it is being made. As a matter of practical fact, the representative is likely to have a keen appreciation of the community context within which he functions as deputy; without it he could hardly succeed at his job. Given an understanding of that context, the difference between policy formation and implementation, though never sharp, is clear enough on most matters. In the case of a member of a national parliament, should his constituents have indicated their strong support for the conservation of natural resources, or more social welfare legislation, or the reverse of these, it surely is the representative's duty to work for these general objectives. In the smaller context of city government, a councilman is likely to be conscious of his constituents' express desire for public housing, or an improved system of public transit, and he is then under the obligation to work for these ends. If the member of parliament or the councilman cannot support known community objectives in good conscience he is at liberty to resign his representative office—he is likely to lose it at the next election in any event. On the other hand, technical questions concerning the rules governing the use of state-owned resources, or the fares to be charged on a public transit system, are not reasonably put before the general populace. It is to resolve just such questions, as best to implement the general aims of nation or city, that representatives have been chosen.

The problem here is that of determining the proper range of direct participation within a democracy that is itself largely indirect. Which questions, or kinds of questions, are properly left to the judgment of the representatives, and which are properly decided by the popular will even when a representative system is functioning smoothly? The problem has no general resolution. But the dilemma facing the representative is not so burdensome as at first it might appear. In the first place, on most questions (in communities where representatives are fairly and frequently chosen) their will and the will of their constituents are likely to be identical or nearly so. This is more likely to be the case, of course, where the constituency is relatively homogeneous—and this approximation of identity is an important consideration weighing in favor of a more functional system of representation [7.5]. In the second place, where representative and constituents are not known to be in agreement, they will very often not be known to be in disagreement either, for the will of the constituents will not normally have been clearly and unambiguously expressed. In such common circumstances the dilemma does not arise; the conscientious deputy ought to act as he supposes they who elected him would act in the light of such knowledge as he possesses. Finally, in those rare cases in which the representative finds himself in conflict with the known will of the majority of his constituents, he must determine whether the question is chiefly one of policy, upon which the popular will ought to be decisive, or one of technique, upon which his election and professional qualifications entitle him to act in opposition to popular will, on the ground that, were his constituents in a position to know or understand the situation as thoroughly as he, they would judge the merits of the question as he does. He makes this decision knowing that he will have to answer to his constituents no later than the time of the next election.

Who, in practice, is to decide whether a given issue is chiefly one of policy or of technique? Is he, the representative alone, to make that decision? Yes; there is no one who can do it for him. But will he not always be inclined to treat questions of policy as technical questions upon which his special competence entitles him to overrule the popular opinion? No doubt there will be that inclination. The integrity of representatives, however, can never be guaranteed by written rules or prescribed codes of conduct. In being elected by the members of a community to administer the governing process in their stead, each representative occupies a position of the highest and most delicate trust. If the members of a democratic community are not capable of selecting, at least in the great run of cases, representatives whose integrity and conscientious attention to their responsibilities as trustees are sufficient to qualify them even to determine the limits of their own jurisdiction, that community will not long remain a democracy.

7.10 The conflict of local and larger interests

There is another kind of dilemma faced by the democratic representative. Suppose he sits in the parliament which serves as the highest legislative body for a large nation, N. Suppose he is a member of that parliament by virtue of his election from some smaller community, C, that is one constituent element of the nation, C being significant in its own right, but small in relation to N, of which it is a part. How is this representative to behave when faced with the necessity (to oversimplify) of supporting or opposing a policy, P, which is very much in the interests of his constituents in C, but not in the interests of the nation as a whole?

The problem is common enough; it arises in all (but not only) cases of what is called "pork-barrel" legislation. That term tends to prejudge the issue, however, causing us to suppose at the outset that the interests of C are being wrongly furthered at the expense of the interests of N. Of course representatives may act wrongly (either deliberately or by mistake) in supporting narrow interests when support ought to have been given to the overriding interests of the larger community.

When there is general agreement that support has been wrongly given no theoretical difficulty arises.

Really problematical for democratic theory, however, is the kind of case in which the relative weight of the apparently conflicting interests is not clear, and the representative is understandably perplexed about what he ought to do. If he honestly believes that P is much in the interest of his constituents in C, he is likely (as a matter of fact) to persuade himself that P is genuinely in the interest of N also. Whether right or wrong in this, if he comes to believe it he faces no dilemma. Suppose, however, that, although he sees the benefit that P will yield to his constituents, he also sees and fully comprehends why P is disadvantageous to the nation, N. Then he is faced with the task of deciding which set of interests he ought to defend in the battle over P.

One is tempted to reply immediately that the supposed conflict of interests is illusory. What is genuinely disadvantageous to the nation, N (the argument might proceed) is equally disadvantageous to all of its elements, including C. So there is no real issue. This is simply to say that any interest of N always overrides any interest of C, and that is the end of the matter.

This argument is superficial; it does not face up to the realities of democratic process in large nations. If we know that policy P is in fact disadvantageous to N, it follows that it is, that far, also disadvantageous to its element, C. But what is disadvantageous to C in some respects may be highly advantageous to C in other respects, and this precisely is the case in some puzzling situations. For example: the retention of a national military installation in one community, C, may be a matter of intense concern to the citizens of C because of the important role of that installation in C's economy; while it may be generally agreed that that installation is somewhat obsolete, and serves the defense needs of N inefficiently. From the viewpoint of N as a whole it would appear wise to close the installation permanently, thereby saving money, or reserving those funds for more effective expenditure elsewhere. From the viewpoint of the residents of C, who may recognize and admit some wastefulness, closing the installation will have immediately painful results of far greater intensity, in the form of unemployment, depressed business activity, and so on. Now it is easy to say that the interests of N are of greater concern than the interests of C, and all may agree to that principle stated generally. Does it follow that every interest of N (say, small savings in defense expenditure) overrides every interest of C? That is not at all obvious; and it is in such circumstances that the representative from c must decide to support or oppose the closing of the installation. "After all," the residents of c may say, "our representative in parliament is *ours*; he was elected by us to represent us in affairs of national scope. Here is a national issue that affects us intensely; we have every right to expect him to defend our interests above all."

The conflict between the interests of c and n is largely illusory, but not for the reasons earlier suggested. The conflict is illusory not because the interests of n must always dominate but because the final determination of the interests of the nation, n, also requires that the damage done to each of its constituent elements be carefully weighed, considering not only financial advantage to the whole, but the intensity of injury to the parts as well. It is quite plausible to suppose that, after weighing the likely injury to c, the national government will refrain from enacting p on the ground that severe economic dislocation outweighs the increase in efficiency that closing the base makes possible. Or similarly, it is plausible (although not as likely) for the residents of c, after recognizing gross inefficiency in the continued operation of an obsolete base, to accede to its elimination on the ground that the savings it effects outweighs the temporary local hardships that may ensue. Either of these decisions, under appropriate factual circumstances, might be rational. Such supposed conflicts of interest are dissolved by showing that a given course of action is in the best long range interest of both communities. The apparent conflict, then, stems chiefly from the fact that the real interests of one or the other (n or c) had not been carefully enough weighed—that is, that it had not been recognized how integrally the interests of one are in fact part of the interests of the other.

Were the interests at stake of precisely the same kind (as might be the case, say, in the determination of proportionate tax burdens) it is natural to suppose that the interests of the larger community will always override the interest of one of its constituent communities. If it is in the interest of n that all of its members' incomes be taxed at a given rate, and in the interest of c that its members alone among the citizens of n be taxed at half that rate, we have no hesitancy in saying that the interests of the larger community in such a case are controlling. That seems only a single instance of the general principle of distributive justice, that equals be treated equally. This decision is easy because the conflicting interests of n and of c are (by hypothesis) of exactly the same kind. In fact this is rarely the case; dilemmas of this kind normally arise just because the interests of the two communities, larger and smaller, are (with respect to some specific issue) of different kinds entirely, and if not incommensurable, are nearly so.

So we are forced back to the situation in which the representative must decide, in the light of conflicting considerations of different kinds, what he ought to defend or oppose as the conscientious deputy of his constituents. One can't say flatly that the interests of the larger community always override those of the smaller. The problem faced by the representative is just that of deciding, in particular cases, which set of interests deserve his support. The fact that such conflicts of local and national interests are usually only apparent may ease his burden but cannot eliminate it. He still may have the job of weighing national apples against local watermelons, in different qualities and quantities; in some cases every judgment he might make will be subject to attack.

Is it unrealistic to expect the representative of the smaller community, C, to weigh the concerns of the entire nation, N, in deciding what is in the interest of his constituents? Not always. If the policy in question is one that seriously affects the nation—say, subjects it to grave danger—even very considerable advantage for C will not outweigh that consideration, from the viewpoint of the resident of C as well as from other viewpoints. A grave danger to N is as grave a danger to C as it is to all the rest. Sensitivity to the concerns of the larger community will be heightened where the individual constituency is more heterogeneous, more like the membership of the whole; this is a consideration weighing in favor of a more non-functional system of representation [7.5].

If, on the other hand, the consequences of a given policy for the nation are not entirely clear, but its benefits to C are obvious and marked, the representation of C in the national parliament may appropriately support that policy with vigor. What is finally determined to be in the interest of the larger whole will emerge from the pushes and pulls of the several subordinate interests involved. It is the more likely to be determined wisely if those interests are fairly represented. If there are other constituent communities that do not derive benefits from the policy in question, but must help pay for it, they will then be heard from; if that policy creates dangers for the nation that should be weighed, the representatives of other communities will then be quick to point them out. The evaluation and resolution of these conflicting (or apparently conflicting) interests is precisely the purpose of the deliberative process which is the major business of a representative assembly.

Democracy and representation

The task of weighing and choosing between the interests of the smaller and the larger community presses inevitably upon the representative in a democratic system. Making that choice is part of his job, and he will feel the tension most acutely because the pressures for both narrower and wider interests are likely to be organized and articulate (as well as internal) and because these pressures are likely to focus sharply upon him. But the dilemma he faces is essentially no different from the dilemma faced by every member of every democracy, representative or not. The citizens must know and feel themselves to be members of the larger as well as of the more parochial community and must appreciate their stake, as private individuals, in the preservation and advance of both [12.9]. Without such multiple community consciousness and concern, the single-minded pursuit of subordinate interests, whether expressed directly or through representatives, will eventually cause the democracy to disintegrate.

Part Four

THE CONDITIONS OF DEMOCRACY

Chapter 8

Democracy and its conditions

8.1 Relations of democracy to its conditions

Democracy sometimes fails, or develops incompletely, even where its presuppositions have been realized and its instruments provided. The degree of its success depends, additionally, upon various kinds of conditions that its practice requires. The conditions of democracy are many, each subject to different degrees of fulfillment. Most are difficult to realize in the concrete, and difficult to maintain once realized. All are important for the success of democracy, but the degree and nature of their importance varies. A major task for any theory of democracy is the identification and elucidation of these conditions.

This enterprise can take either of two forms. As a quest for the techniques and institutions that have proved successful in democratic government, it is the appropriate inquiry of the political scientist. The forms, procedures, machinery of government are of the first importance, their variations and consequences of enormous interest in the practice of politics. That practice also supposes, however, the fulfillment of conditions of a more general, theoretical kind. The inquiry to follow seeks not the particulars of organization or procedure, but the kinds of circumstances required for the successful operation of a democracy. The improvement of particular institutions demands an understanding of the larger purposes those institutions are created to implement; without that understanding even the best of institutions are without direction, and the democracy that employs them not likely to be well served. This theoretical inquiry into the conditions of democracy, therefore, is of the highest practical importance.

The logical relations between democracy itself and its several conditions are difficult to formulate precisely. The conditions of democracy are not its logically necessary presuppositions, in the sense in which community and rationality are [Part Two]. Unlike those, one or more of these conditions may be done without for a time, and in many existing democracies one or more of these are realized only partially. It is rarely if ever true, in fact, that in any given community any one of the conditions of democracy is entirely absent, or perfectly fulfilled.

Whether, taken as a set, these may be considered the sufficient conditions of democracy, is moot. If, in some hypothetical community, all these conditions were realized to perfection, perhaps democracy would inevitably arise. In real communities it remains conceivable, although unlikely, that each condition could be realized in substantial measure although a non-democratic government is retained. The relations involved here are not logically strict.

While neither logically necessary nor logically sufficient, these are nevertheless the practically necessary conditions of democracy. Most of them will have to be present in generous measure in any community in which democracy meets with sustained success. Transposing this we may say that if, in a given community, a significant number of these conditions are not adequately met, democracy in that community will not long continue. What constitutes a "significant" number, and what degrees of fulfillment are "adequate," are matters not decidable in general. Some of these conditions are more crucial than others; which will prove most essential for a particular democracy will depend on the special character and special problems of that community.

8.2 Relations of the conditions of democracy to one another

There is no necessary harmony among the several conditions of democracy. Some are mutually supportive; it can also happen that the maximization of one condition counters, or in some manner tends to restrict another. So, for example, the drive for economic growth, entailing large accumulations of investment capital, may conflict with the drive for an equitable distribution of the national product; economic growth and economic justice do not always go hand in hand. Or again, the need to protect a democracy against internal subversion, and the concurrent need to maintain in a democracy the widest freedom of speech and press, may create tensions not easily resolved. Such disharmonies help to explain why democracy so generally exhibits an air of incompleteness and imperfection.

On the other hand there is no necessary incompatibility among the conditions of democracy. In contributing to a single social fabric they are likely to fit well together. So, for example, the constitutional protections needed by democracy and the individual habits and attitudes it requires are likely to be mutually reinforcing, and both may be enhanced by the intellectual and economic circumstances independently required. In general, the conditions of democracy tend to prove consonant one with another, although they do not invariably do so.

8.3 Democracy and its conditions distinguished

The ties between democracy and certain of its conditions are so close and so obvious that there is a natural but mistaken tendency to amalgamate these conditions with democracy itself.

Common misconceptions of some so-called "democratic freedoms" serve as good examples of this confusion. The freedom of speech is a crucial condition of the success of democracy, but strictly it is not a "democratic freedom" if that expression implies that such freedom is somehow a part of democracy, or associated only with it. Nor are most of the rights we prize properly considered "democratic rights" if by this is meant either that a democracy cannot curtail them or that a non-democratic government cannot protect them. Reference to the freedom of speech as a "democratic freedom" or to certain rights as "democratic rights" is very common, and springs from the correct belief that these rights or freedoms are somehow very closely and very importantly related to democracy. They are indeed, being practical necessities of its operation. But what is *required for* democracy is not thereby *part of* democracy, and should not be identified with it.

Underlying this confusion is the common supposition, reinforced by careless thinking and loose talk, that democracy must somehow embody all other political virtues. So rich and positive is the emotive content of the name of democracy in these times that everything desired in the social sphere is called by it. Freedoms cherished become "democratic freedoms"; rights are indiscriminately called "democratic rights"; and virtually all that is held by some to be properly ideal, from Christianity to the poll tax, is dubbed by its supporters "democratic."

My complaint here is directed not against mere habits of speech, but against the philosophical misunderstandings those poor habits engender and reflect. When the term "democracy" has absorbed everything even remotely associated with self-government, the vital distinctions between democracy as a form of government, and the conditions of the successful employment of that form, are obscured. The result is confusion, not because we cannot put our finger on what is democratic, but because virtually everything we put our finger on turns out then to be "democratic."

This is a lamentable state of affairs. It is very important and very useful to distinguish the many virtues of the political world. Democracy is one thing; freedom another; order is a third; peace, equality, security, are also valuable and distinguishable. All of these may be ideals of ours, but nothing is gained by forcing them all into one. Political ideals are vague and confusedly related under the best of circumstances; amalgamated they become foggier still, and even more difficult to pursue. Discourse about political theory then becomes, as it frequently has been and is, an intellectual mush.

Once distinguished, the several conditions of democracy may well prove highly desirable in their own right [14.6–14.8]. Nothing I shall say about material well-being, for example, or the toleration of dissent, or like matters, should be taken as denying the intrinsic worth they may possess, or their instrumental value in some different context. One or more of the conditions to be discussed may be necessary for individual self-realization quite apart from their connections with democracy; or they may in some other way make important contributions to the good life. My present concern with these institutions, dispositions, and states of affairs, however, is with their role as conditions of a successful democracy. If properly called "democratic," they are so only because of their relation to the practice of democracy; only that relation is the object of my inquiry in what ensues.

8.4 The kinds of conditions of democracy

The conditions of democracy fall into several great groups or classes. Although these groupings are for the most part natural, any such classification must inevitably impose some measure of arbitrary ordering upon its materials. The several classes are not without cross-relations, to which I shall point from time to time, nor do the separate treatments of them and their sub-categories imply sharp lines of division. I distinguish five major kinds into which the conditions of democracy can be sorted.

(1) The Material *Conditions of Democracy*. These include such matters as geographical environment and the brute machinery of participation. They also include the material circumstances of the citizens and the economic arrangements of the community as a whole. Although they appear easy to specify and agree upon, it is with regard to these material conditions that some of the most bitter ideological disagreements arise. Ironically, these are least appreciated as conditions of democracy where they are best realized. To them I devote Chapter 9.

(2) The Constitutional *Conditions of Democracy.* These concern the principles, embodied in the organism or constitution of a community, which protect the rights of the citizens to act as they must be able to act if they are to participate fully and genuinely in the governing process. The right to speak freely, to criticize leadership, to assemble freely, to publish without censorship—these are leading examples of the constitutional conditions of democracy. Of all the conditions of democracy these present the most difficult theoretical problems. Although honored in name, they are seldom fully met. To them I devote Chapter 10.

(3) The Intellectual *Conditions of Democracy.* These concern the capacities of the citizens to perform the tasks that democracy imposes, and the provision of the information and training essential for the proper employment of those capacities. More than any others the intellectual conditions of democracy are unstable, the levels of attainment required increasing with the advancing state of human knowledge and powers of control. They too receive universal lip-service, but pose enormous practical problems still. To them I devote Chapter 11.

(4) The Psychological *Conditions of Democracy.* These consist of a complex of dispositions and attitudes that must be manifested by the individual members of the community if democracy is to function. Fallibilism, a willingness to compromise, a capacity for self-restraint when holding power, are only some examples of the personal traits democracy requires in generous measure. About conditions in this category we know the least, and over them we appear to have the least control. They are difficult to cultivate, difficult to maintain; yet their effect upon democracy is profound. To them I devote Chapter 12.

(5) The Protective *Conditions of Democracy.* These concern the capacities of the democratic community to defend itself against external onslaught, and against internal deterioration. Defenses needed against attackers of different kinds sometimes conflict with one another; vigorous discipline to protect against attack from without may erode other conditions of democracy within. Agonizing practical difficulties are sometimes created, therefore, by these protective conditions. Unlike the others, however, they tend to be almost exclusively the concern of national democracies (or democracies otherwise sovereign); and of all the conditions these are the most extrinsically related to democracy itself. To them I devote Chapter 13.

THE CONDITIONS OF DEMOCRACY

These five—material, constitutional, intellectual, psychological, protective—are the classes of conditions that must be met if democracy is to emerge, and to maintain itself. Some of the important things to be noted about these conditions are rather obscure; some are obvious. No harm is done by recapitulating clearly what is commonly but vaguely understood; and there is much advantage to be derived from a thorough review of all of democracy's conditions, putting into order a mass of argument and evidence rarely thought through. Specifying the conditions of democracy consists largely of laying out the common sense of the matter; but organizing the content of that common sense is essential if it is to be effectively brought to bear on practical problems.

Chapter 9

The material conditions of democracy

9.1 The kinds of material conditions

The reasonably successful operation of a democratic government requires, first of all, certain material conditions that are very far from universal. The need for some of these conditions is obvious; concerning others there rages continuing dispute. In identifying the material conditions of democracy, I group them under three headings. Conditions under the first two present no serious theoretical problems, although their practical attainment meets with the gravest obstacles. Under the third heading lie conditions subject to sharply conflicting interpretations which I shall examine and weigh.

The three categories are: (*1*) *environmental* conditions of democracy; (*2*) *mechanical* conditions of democracy; (*3*) *economic* conditions of democracy. To each of the first two I devote one brief section; the remainder of this chapter will be devoted to the third.

9.2 The environmental conditions of democracy

Democracy—especially in the political sphere—requires physical circumstances that render the general participation of the membership feasible. On the one hand the natural environment—climate, topography, and the like—must not too greatly interfere with this participation; on the other hand the human control of the physical environment—systems of transportation, communication, and the like—must be developed to take advantage of favorable natural surroundings, or to overcome natural hindrances to that participation.

Geographic features, like mountain ranges and large bodies of water, have historically and understandably formed the natural boundaries of communities. Where technology has been primitive, but some community has extended beyond such barriers, that community has rarely been able to sustain a democracy. In this century, with high speed transportation and electronic communication, we can bind the most diverse of geographic regions. But, for the great majority of the earth's population, sheerly environmental factors remain severe obstacles to the development of community participation over large areas.

THE CONDITIONS OF DEMOCRACY

The absence of roads and harbors, the presence of mountains and deserts, the crude state of communications, all still do interfere with democracy. Even smaller communities, themselves unified, find democracy more difficult when environmental factors hinder the development of other conditions themselves essential for democracy.

Much is in our power. With the imaginative application of growing technology, we can hope to overcome the purely environmental obstacles to general participation. For the present and near future, however, the relatively hostile environments in some portions of the planet continue to present serious problems for the growth of democracy in those regions. Physical circumstances must temper political hopes and expectations.

9.3 The mechanical conditions of democracy

Democracy requires concrete machinery through which participation is made effective. Here it is not the representative system and the like, but machinery in the brute sense to which I refer—ballot boxes, filing cabinets, legislative chambers and offices. Such mechanical needs may be negligible in small democracies; where communities are very large the physical machinery of participation becomes exceedingly complicated and very expensive. A democratic community must be able and willing to bear that expense.

Once provided, this machinery requires continuing care and attention. Buildings must be kept in repair; clerical forces must be constantly bringing records up to date; elections must be organized, conducted, inspected. Endless details must be attended to, all demanding the expenditure of time, effort, and cash. Without the will to use them in proper spirit no buildings or ballot boxes can by themselves make democracy successful. But neither is that will to maintain a democracy enough by itself. As the machinery without the spirit is fruitless, so the will without the machinery is ineffective.

Inadequate development of its mechanical conditions is a sign that something is seriously amiss in a democracy, and the results will quickly show. Whether for the lack of vigorous effort, or the lack of money, the mechanical conditions of democracy are very often incompletely realized, and this incompleteness is sure to reduce both the breadth and depth of participation. Moreover, this incompleteness is likely to invite the abuse of such machinery as has been provided, which then serves to support the appearance but not the reality of democracy.

9.4 The economic conditions of democracy

Economics is the study of the production, distribution, and consumption of wealth in all its forms. "Economy" is a term derived from the Greek word for the management of the household; the economic system of any community is the system of its household operations. Obviously, the organization of that national household will largely determine how fully the material needs of its members will be met. The fulfillment of these material needs, and the economic system that insures it, so far as these are required for the operation of a democracy, I call its economic conditions.

Many philosophers argue—some Marxists, some capitalists, some neither—that democracy (especially national democracies) cannot succeed without some particular set of economic arrangements, though they differ sharply over the nature of the set required. It is important to assess the truth of these claims, for three reasons: first, to improve our general understanding of democracy; second, to expose the fraudulent claims of communities in which genuinely requisite conditions are not satisfied; third, to guide economic reform if democracy is desired and its economic conditions not yet realized.

Three common claims regarding these conditions I propose to distinguish and evaluate. They are: *(1)* That some level of economic well-being is a condition of democracy; *(2)* that "economic democracy" is the condition of any genuine democracy; *(3)* that economic equality is a condition of democracy. Of these I shall argue that the first is true, the second false, the third neither flatly true nor false.

9.5 Economic well-being as a condition of democracy

No community can long expect to be self-governing unless the members of that community enjoy a minimum level of material well-being. This first claim distinguished above now meets with universal agreement, but its importance for contemporary national democracies is not fully enough appreciated.

In being a participatory system, democracy depends fundamentally upon the capacity of the citizens to play an active public role. In large measure that capacity is physical; a healthy democracy requires healthy citizens. Where the members of a community suffer from chronic malnutrition and frequent illness, participation in common affairs that is both broad and deep is difficult to maintain. Where the lot of the masses is often that of acute hunger, or where disease runs rampant, the expectation of any genuine democracy among such masses is naive. Economic circumstances which cause the physical well-being of the citizens to deteriorate, and which tend to compel their attention to be given largely or exclusively to the problem of survival for self and family, will not support a vigorous democracy.

The minimal standards democracy requires cannot be exactly specified; they will vary with time, and place, and the character of the community. But the basic claim is true: democracy requires that its citizens enjoy a reasonable level of economic well-being.

Economic well-being is a condition always relatively well or relatively poorly satisfied. This relativity arises on two levels. First, on the level of individual circumstance, the requirement of economic well-being may be satisfied more or less fully from the viewpoint of the citizens considered separately. Second, on the level of community circumstance, the proportion of the whole meeting the required standards may greatly vary, the condition being more or less fully met by the citizenry taken as a unit. Democracy may be feasible, if imperfect, where a small fraction of the community are impoverished; as that fraction grows, democracy in that community is less likely to succeed. Where prosperity is enjoyed by only a few, the masses living in degradation and poverty, democracy cannot be realized, and the use of its name is only a rhetorical trick. But, of course, even where prosperity is virtually universal, democracy may be imperfect, or wholly unrealized, for non-economic reasons.

Impoverishment may have different effects upon the different dimensions of democracy. Material discontents may cause a growing number to cast ballots (if they are allowed to do so) thereby improving the breadth of democracy, while its depth continues to suffer. Persons driven by insecurity to improve their condition at whatever cost are unlikely to have the time and patience deep democracy requires. Severely impoverished masses are simply unable to inform themselves adequately on public affairs, to discuss public issues effectively, to organize efficiently, and keep contact with their deputies. In general, extreme poverty defeats democracy, rendering participation uninformed and superficial, even if widespread. It is the affluent who can afford to be public-spirited citizens.

What is readily enjoyed is often little appreciated. So it is with material well-being among many of those in Europe and North America who have enjoyed prosperity long and fully. They have frequently striven to ameliorate material conditions in poorer parts of the globe, if not for altruistic then for selfish reasons, because prosperity elsewhere tends to support prosperity at home. Nevertheless, the wealthy have generally failed to understand the dependence of their own democracy upon material well-being. Westerners, Americans especially, have too readily assumed that economic well-being requires only industry and the use of political forms open to everyone, ignoring the fact that the successful employment of these political forms itself requires a measure of community prosperity much of the world has never enjoyed. We are then puzzled and frustrated when, in underdeveloped lands, democracy stumbles or falls. I paraphrase a colleague's verse (Kenneth Boulding, in the *Principles of Economic Policy*, 1958):

> Poor countries can't afford to be
> Democratic, just and free.
> So there are many virtues which
> Are practiced only by the rich.

9.6 Is "economic democracy" the condition of any genuine democracy?

Marxists, being materialists, have been highly sensitive to the importance of the economic conditions of democracy. It is a very general principle of theirs that all political and social arrangements are determined by the economic base, or substructure. From this they infer that democracy, too, must have an economic foundation. This insight in one direction, however, is counterbalanced by blindness in others. The neglect of economic considerations in political analysis is a mistake often made in the West; to argue, as Marxists often do, that economic considerations are the only ones that really matter is a mistake at the other extreme, equally serious. It results in the neglect of a host of other considerations, of a non-material kind, also essential to democracy. "Economic democracy" the Marxist concludes, is the condition of any genuine democracy. I argue that this is false.

What is "economic democracy"? It is not, for the Marxist, a system of government, but a special state of economic affairs. "Economic democracy" he believes, exists only where the means of production and distribution rest in the hands of the entire community. It is the public ownership of the economic "substructure" that he seeks, and he holds that only after the economic system has been thus revolutionized can any "real" equality or "real" freedom be achieved in the political sphere. This belief in the overwhelming causal efficacy of economic change is an assumption, often dogmatically defended if defended at all. In fact, no single set of institutions, economic or of any other kind, will lead inevitably to a community of free and equal persons.

Putting this enormous oversimplification aside, any argument framed in terms of "economic democracy" is needlessly confusing and deceptive. With all the variations there have been in theories about the nature of democracy, there has been virtually universal agreement, from the classical Greeks onward, that it is some form of government. Earlier I argued that the essence of this form lies in the participatory mode of making community decisions. In the Marxist argument the favorable emotive connotation of the word "democracy" is capitalized upon to further particular economic objectives. The public ownership of the means of production and distribution one may hold to be the necessary or sufficient condition of other social virtues, or worthy in its own right. But one who argues so, even if correct, is not justified in calling public ownership "democracy." Public ownership may or may not lead to, or permit, democratic decision making, but *it* is not democracy; to call it that is to extend a flexible term beyond reason. Humpty Dumpty says (in Lewis Carroll's *Through the Looking Glass*), "When I make a word do that much work, I pay it extra!"

To this criticism the Marxist is likely to reply: "I insist that public ownership of the productive forces is correctly called 'economic democracy.' It is only through public ownership of these forces that the mass of the people can participate in making the economic decisions that affect them all. So you see, I accept your analysis of democracy as participatory decision-making. That, in the fundamental economic sphere, is just what I am after. In short, (he continues) I argue as follows: public participation in community affairs requires public participation in economic decision-making; public participation in economic decision-making requires the public ownership of all productive forces; the public ownership of all productive forces *is* economic democracy; therefore, real democracy requires economic democracy—economic democracy is its necessary condition."

This Marxist reply again confuses democracy with what is claimed to be the conditions of its success. In failing to distinguish the democratic process of decision-making on the one hand, from the institutional arrangements that he believes will foster that process, on the other, he badly muddies the intellectual waters. Now the claim that public ownership is the condition of the public participation is precisely the point at issue, and cannot be decided by reiteration. The one may promote the other; that remains to be determined in fact. But that public ownership is a necessary condition of public participation in decision-making is a very much stronger claim, and it is false.

Democracy, especially in large communities, does not require direct participation by every citizen in all or even in most decisions of public concern. Where matters to be judged are complex or technical, the community may elect to have the run of decisions made by persons better equipped to make them than themselves. This is part of the justification for representative systems in large democracies, and recalls an earlier distinction drawn between the sovereign and the effective range of a democracy [2.6]. Public participation in economic decision-making is certain to be indirect, therefore, even where public ownership is a fact. The crucial issue, then, is whether indirect public participation is possible in economic affairs (i.e., whether economic policy lies within the sovereign range of the democracy) under economic systems not publicly owned.

Clearly the answer to this question is yes. The system chosen by a community for the administration of affairs in a given sphere need take no one special form. Production and distribution may be managed by elected representatives, or the appointees of elected representatives, but surely that is not the only alternative open to a community. Nor does such a system necessarily insure the greatest effectiveness of public participation in forming economic policy. If there is widespread belief that complete public ownership would result in an economy less responsive to consumer needs, less efficient, and less productive than one administered by private enterprisers, it is certainly reasonable for the members of that community to choose, and choose freely, a system of economic organization that relies wholly or in part upon private economic activity and the operation of market forces. It is reasonable for them to select any system of economic organization, embodying any combination of private, cooperative, and public enterprises that they have rational grounds for believing will serve them best in the many ways they seek to be served.

In sum, "economic democracy" is not a necessary condition of any genuine democracy. Democracy within the sphere of economics itself does not require any particular economic system, entailing either public or private ownership. It is not the special scheme of economic arrangements that constitutes economic democracy, but the ability of the community to choose its own scheme.

To see that democracy in any sphere of community activities does not require any single form of ownership, or participation, one has only to reflect upon the varieties of participation in some non-economic spheres of community concern. Consider: democracy in the arts does not require that all decisions concerning artistic production and support be made by elected representatives. It does require that the people be free to participate (directly or indirectly) in deciding what systems of artistic enterprise will be allowed or encouraged. Traditionally, we have chosen to leave artistic activity almost wholly in private hands, and there are good reasons for that choice. Similarly, democracy in education does not demand that all educational decisions be made by the majority or their deputies. It does demand that the system of education which the community will provide for itself be chosen freely by the members of that community. Historically, we have chosen to develop a system mixing, in various ways, the private, parochial, and public institutions of formal education. So it is likewise with economic affairs. In the United States we have chosen, for many reasons, to rely chiefly upon privately owned enterprises, publicly regulated. Such a system has produced materially satisfactory results for the greater part of our population. During the twentieth century we have experimented more and more with patterns of public ownership, in some cases finding them quite successful. Very possibly we shall continue to move in that direction, but democracy does not make a necessity of such movement. Whatever our future course may be, it is to be hoped that it will be determined not by its accord with any dogma, of the right or left, but experimentally, after careful reflection upon the probable consequences of the several possible patterns of economic organization.

The original claim that "economic democracy" is the condition of any genuine democracy may be given the yet stronger interpretation that public ownership of the means of production and distribution is the sufficient condition of genuinely democratic process; that is, that from such public ownership democracy in other spheres will inevitably ensue. This claim for sufficiency flows from two premises accepted by practically no one save Marxists: (1) that political institutions are nothing but the reflection, in idea, of the economic "substructure," and, (2) that democracy in the political sphere is the correlate only of public ownership in the economic sphere. The second of these has already been rejected. The first—a strong form of economic determinism—has been subjected to repeated refutation not necessary to review here. The falsity of this economic determinism, and of the claim for sufficiency, is evident on two grounds. *First:* the argument exhibiting other necessary conditions of democracy [Chapters 10–13] shows that economic circumstances cannot be by themselves sufficient. *Second:* the fact that there are national governments in which the ownership and management of the economy do lie in public hands, while the process of decision-making remains very far from democratic, provides concrete evidence that public ownership gives no guarantee of democracy.

A *third* interpretation of the original claim—that "economic democracy" is both the necessary and sufficient condition of democracy —calls for no further comment. Although sometimes asserted by orthodox Marxists, it is doubly false, suffering all the disabilities of its two component elements.

9.7 Democracy and economic systems

"Economic democracy" is an awkward expression at best. Used to refer to a specific set of economic arrangements—public ownership and the like—it is, deliberately or accidentally, deceptive. Used to refer only to the operation of democratic process within the economic sphere it is at least misleading. In the latter case the difficulty stems from putting the term "economic" in adjectival position. Use of the expression "economic democracy" certainly seems to imply that there is at least one other, possibly several other, kinds of democracy. Then we might also speak of "educational democracy," "religious democracy," and so forth. Nothing is seriously wrong with this so long as we, not the words, remain the masters. Political discourse will be much clearer, however, if such adjectives are not used to modify democracy.* More accurately we should speak of democracy in the educational system, or in the school or classroom, or we should speak of a democratic religious community, and so on. None of these is a condition of democracy; they are all applications of it.

Because the expression "economic democracy" seems to refer to

---

*Another expression causing confusions of the same sort (in other contexts) is "participatory democracy." In this case the use of "participatory" as a modifier suggests, incorrectly, that one among several kinds of democracy has been identified. In fact, all genuine democracy is participatory; that adjective serves only to remind one of the true character of democratic government. In doing that, however, it does serve a useful function.

democracy of a certain kind, its use encourages the unfortunate theoretical mistake examined earlier. If "economic democracy" is one sort of thing, it is easy to suppose that "political democracy" is another; then arises a natural temptation to compare or contrast them. Now "political democracy" (if that expression makes any sense at all) is democracy in the body politic, which is to say, in the civic community as a whole. Properly then, democracy in the economic sphere is one part, although a very important part, of political democracy. If, however, "economic democracy" and "political democracy" are contrasted as kinds of democracy (as the adjectival, modifying expressions suggest they may be) the former is identified with particular economic institutions (public ownership of the means of production, etc.), while the latter is identified with particular political institutions (elections, parties, etc.). Both identifications are mistaken. They not only invite invidious comparisons of the two, but cause widespread misunderstanding of what it is, in either set of institutions, that is genuinely democratic.

Most of those who talk about "economic democracy" and its superiority to "political democracy" are chiefly interested not in democracy at all, but in universal economic well-being, and the public ownership they believe will promote it. How these economic objectives are achieved is for them secondary. As a tactical matter they are more likely to succeed in reaching their goal of public ownership by attaching to it the name of democracy, now having universal appeal. The identification of a particular economic system with democracy brings a threefold loss: *First:* fundamental agreement between those, Marxist and non-Marxist, who genuinely seek to improve general economic well-being, is obscured in disputes over who is or is not a supporter of "economic democracy." *Second:* significant progress in determining what forms of economic ownership or control will in fact further mutually shared objectives is hindered by dogmatic quarrels over whose economic patterns are "truly democratic." *Third:* on all sides substantive ends are unhappily confounded with procedural ideals. If a given state of economic affairs (say, public ownership) is democracy for them, a wholly different state of economic affairs, it is concluded, (say, "capitalism" or "free enterprise") must be democracy for us. All attention riveted on the particular arrangements defended or attacked, what is genuinely democratic in each is lost on its critics, while the failures of each to protect participation in depth and breadth is lost on its supporters.

"Economic democracy" is neither a kind of democracy, nor a condition of democracy itself. If ever properly employed, the expression "economic democracy" means democracy in the sphere of economics; it is present when the members of a community have the power to choose the economic objectives they shall pursue, and choose as well the economic means to the attainment of these objectives. If democracy is absent in the economic sphere, entirely or in part, the range of democracy is restricted. When democracy is eliminated in certain spheres, it may be more easily restricted or eliminated in other spheres, because the habits of democratic process know no artificial boundary of subject matter. But the claim that "economic democracy" is the necessary or sufficient condition of "real democracy" is a confused and confusing mistake.

In the continuing controversy over the material conditions of democracy, the virtues of the two sides (call them "Marxist" and "anti-Marxist") have been curiously complementary. Marxists base their argument upon the underlying thesis that all political systems, including democracy, have purely economic foundations. The anti-Marxists argue that democracy is much more than the reflection of economic structure, and requires, for its realization, many complex conditions of a non-material sort. The anti-Marxists are right in this: they justifiably condemn governments that suppress political freedom, restrict opposition, stage fake elections, and call themselves democratic because the means of production and distribution are publicly owned. Anti-Marxists insist that where there are nominations and elections but no real choice on the ballot and only one party's voice may be heard, the forms of democracy may be present, but the substance is not. In a word, one of the virtues of the anti-Marxist argument is its emphasis upon the non-material conditions for democracy. Marxists erroneously belittle these conditions. Their contention that socialist nations are necessarily governed democratically, or that non-socialist nations are necessarily governed undemocratically, is false, flowing from a faulty understanding of democracy and its conditions, or one at best incomplete.

On the other hand, intense concern with economic matters has brought Marxists to see, correctly, that economic conditions essential for democracy are not being met in large parts of the globe under Western influence. The Marxists may be mistaken about what the needed conditions are, but their philosophical position has made them sensitive to the absence of material requirements that anti-Marxists have often failed to appreciate. So Marxists have insisted that many governments with several political parties, freedom of speech, and other of what they call the "trappings" of democracy, are really fraudulent; they exhibit the forms of democracy but do not possess its substance. This criticism is often correct. The open contest of political opponents, and the conduct of apparently free elections are the usual mark of democracy, but by themselves are not enough to ensure it if the material conditions of participation are not met. So it has been the virtue of the Marxist side to see the necessity of material conditions (although seeing them with a special theoretical bias), and the fault of the anti-Marxist, often enjoying prosperity, to overlook the necessity of those conditions.

Each side condemns the other as fraudulent. Each says of the other: "Your system presents the forms of democracy, but not its substance." Insofar as necessary conditions (but different ones) are being neglected by each side, there is justice in the complaints of both.

9.8 Economic equality as a condition of democracy

Relations between democracy and economic equality are intricate. On the one hand absolute economic equality is certainly not a necessary condition for the operation of democracy, as long experience shows. Neither is economic equality a sufficient condition of democracy, since the most perfect equality at an economic level low enough would effectively cancel the possibility of a healthy democracy. Economic equality may be desirable for other reasons, or in its own right, but a condition (either necessary or sufficient) of democracy it is not.

On the other hand, when economic inequalities are gross, the circumstances are not propitious for democracy. This is not because economic inequality, as such, blocks participation, but because great inequalities tend to distort the participation of many. Enormous wealth held by few, or relative poverty suffered by many, provides the opportunities for the participation of some to be manipulated, even controlled, by the participation of others. The economic conditions of democracy, in short, involve not only the absolute circumstances of the citizens, but their relative circumstances as well. Economic equality is not strictly a condition of democracy, but for maximal success democracy does require the elimination of gross economic inequalities.

Even gross inequalities are not an absolute bar to democratic process. If reasonable affluence is enjoyed by the great majority of the citizens, the powers of the individually wealthy to influence the participation of others are markedly reduced. Some reasonably healthy democracies enjoying general prosperity have tolerated and do tolerate great economic disparities among their citizens. Moreover, while great wealth can lead to improper manipulation of others, it need not, and may even be put to the service of democracy.

The elimination of all economic inequalities may not be in the interest of a democracy, for two kinds of reasons. *First:* where economic development is needed, large capital investments are required. Such investments, at least from the private sector of the economy, are virtually ruled out if incomes and accumulated wealth are fully equalized. This equalization, even if just, may, by retarding growth, do more to hinder than to promote the material conditions essential for democracy.

Second: economic equality may not prove conducive to other conditions of democracy of a psychological or intellectual kind. Variety of skills and activities seems to correlate with variety of economic circumstances; whether the great diversity of attitudes and interests needed by a democracy can be maintained in a community of economic equals is a question still moot. It is possible that although reduction of gross economic inequalities is required for the improvement of democracy, the elimination of all economic inequalities is not even its appropriate ideal.

Economic well-being is one thing, economic equality is another; both are tied to democracy, but in different ways. They are often confused because the effort to improve general well-being, especially in the early stages of economic development, normally entails the reduction of gross inequalities. So it is inferred that the fullest realization of the material conditions would bring the elimination of all inequalities. This inference is unwarranted. Improving the lot of the poor is an objective intertwined with, but distinct from, that of increasing economic equality.

Complete economic equality, whether or not attainable in practice, may be a defensible ideal quite apart from its relation to democracy, given certain principles of distributive justice. After democracy has been realized in some community, its material and other conditions reasonably satisfied, the citizens of that community may choose to adopt policies aiming at the achievement of complete, or almost complete, economic equality. Democratic communities may even have some natural tendency to move in that direction. Whether a particular democracy should choose complete economic equality as its aim remains an open question, however, to be decided for each community by its own members.

Chapter 10

The constitutional conditions of democracy

10.1 Introductory note on constitutional conditions

The constitution of a community—political, fraternal or of any other kind—is, in John Calhoun's happy phrases, its "interior structure," its "organism." It is the way the community is constituted. The constitution may be embodied in a specific document—the Constitution of the United States of America, for example—or it may be unwritten, as in the English tradition. Written constitutions sometimes do not give an accurate account of the internal structure of the community they purport to govern; what is promised in the document may not be realized in the life of the community, and all that is realized there may not be written down. What deserves the name "constitutional" in any community are those elements of principle truly central to its life.

Certain principles must be incorporated in the constitution of any community in which democracy is to be practiced. These are the principles that guarantee that citizens will be permitted to do, and protected in their efforts to do, the kinds of things that participation in community government requires. These guarantees are the constitutional conditions of democracy.

Like democracy itself these conditions will be realized in degrees, more or less perfectly in different communities. Like democracy they need not always take the same form; in different contexts different institutions may give them effect. And like democracy these conditions may be vigorously sought as ideals in their own right. These similarities, plus the fact that the constitutional conditions often take concrete form in institutions themselves very closely associated with democratic governments, result in the frequent confusion of the constitutional conditions of democracy with democracy itself. And, again like democracy, their names frequently become hollow shells into which very different contents may be stuffed.

10.2 Freedom and rights

The constitution of a democracy must guarantee that every citizen will be free to engage in certain kinds of activities, and that these freedoms will be protected. Before turning specifically to the freedoms democracy requires, some general remarks about freedom are in order.

Democracy and freedom are distinct ideals. What democracy is I have already tried to make clear [Chapter 1]; what freedom is I cannot here explicate in the same detail. It will suffice for the present purpose, however, to say only this: an individual's freedom depends upon a combination of his *external circumstances*, and his *capacities to act* within those circumstances. Both sides of this complex are essential. The courses of action open to him in the world must be various; the more they are limited the less he is free. In addition, he must be capable of exploiting the opportunities that arise in his external circumstances; the more limited his capacities the less he is free. If he is restrained by external forces—laws, or customs, or geography, or chains—even highly developed capacities will not free him. But if the entire world were open before him, and he lacks the capacity or training essential for certain activities, the mere fact that avenues have not been closed does not enable him to pursue them. Traditionally, the absence of external restraint has been called "negative freedom," (freedom *from**) while the power or capacity to do or enjoy (freedom *to*) has been called "positive freedom."

Properly understood these are not two kinds of freedom, but the two essential aspects of every genuine freedom. Where men are truly free there is real concern for both. Yet it is possible, for specific purposes, to attend chiefly to one or the other aspect of certain freedoms, and I shall do this in discussing the constitutional conditions of democracy. It is the external aspects of certain freedoms, "negative" freedoms, that are of chief concern here; I shall attend to the constitutional guarantees against any governmental or other interference with certain kinds of activity. The internal, "positive" side of these freedoms is equally essential; these capacities of the agent I discuss in Chapters

---

*Freedom's what's inside the fence
Of Morals, Money, Law, and Sense,
And we are free if this is wide
(Or nothing's on the other side).

We come to Politics (and Sin)
When your fine freedoms fence Me in,
And so through Law we come to be
Curtailing Freedom—to be free.

Kenneth Boulding, *Principles of Economic Policy* (1958), p. 110.

11 and 12 in treating the intellectual and psychological conditions of democracy.

The freedoms essential for the operation of democracy are often identified as rights. In calling them this we emphasize their necessity, their essential place in democratic government. It isn't merely that we like to be free to do certain things, but that we must be free to do them. That "must" is part of what we convey in saying that "such-and-such is my democratic right." The same necessity is recognized by the community as a whole, sometimes by writing that guarantee of freedom into a "Bill of Rights," but always by exhibiting its willingness to bring the force of law to the defense of any citizen's acts within the sphere of that right. Whether codified or not, certain kinds of activity—the freedom to do certain kinds of things—are the democratic citizen's rights.

10.3 Democracy and freedom

Certain freedoms are related to democracy as they are to no other form of government, for the nature of democracy is such that its citizens must have the right—the constitutionally guaranteed freedom—to participate in community decision-making, and to do all that such participation entails. Some other freedoms, however valuable intrinsically, have no direct bearing upon the process of participation, and are therefore not essential to democracy. Freedom of religious practice is one example, freedom to engage in private economic enterprise is another. Such freedoms may be protected *by* democracies, but they are not conditions *of* democracy.

Autocracy—government in which all authority resides in one man —is the antithesis of democracy, and I take it here as the archetype of non-democratic forms. But autocratic government may provide wide ranges of freedom to its citizens. Some benevolent autocracies have, in fact, protected freedoms wider, in some spheres, than those found in many democracies. However, while autocracy may protect freedom, it need not. There is nothing at all inconsistent with autocracy in the restriction or elimination of any freedom whatever. Such freedoms as it does provide are provided at the pleasure of the autocrat, to be restricted or withdrawn at his pleasure. Autocrats have generally found it advisable to offer (or seem to offer) such freedoms to their subjects as they safely could; but they have found, too, that citizens' freedoms in certain spheres are not conducive to the safety of absolute rulers, or to the stability of their regimes.

The freedom to engage in some special activities the autocrat can never allow. These freedoms, incompatible with autocracy, are precisely the freedoms most essential to democracy—the freedoms involved in really governing the community, in directing its policy and making its decisions. The autocrat may listen to the requests or complaints of his subjects (if they are permitted to express them) but ultimately he acts on his own authority. Democratic governments, by contrast, can act on no other authority than that of the citizens, and therefore not only may, but must protect their freedom to express and make effective their individual and collective concerns. What democracy requires and must protect, autocracy must forbid.

In the ensuing sections I shall show why certain freedoms are essential for the practice of democracy. Beyond that I aim to show why certain arguments often presented in defense of these freedoms are not strong enough for the purposes of a democracy. Part of my object is to provide a supplementary and stronger defense of these freedoms, a defense I think will prove compelling for those who accept the ideal of democratic government. The freedoms we prize, of course, are of many different kinds, and they bear quite different relations to democracy; for those freedoms not essential to democracy I shall present no argument at all. Clearly freedom may be defended as intrinsically worthwhile, or instrumentally valuable in other connections; one would have to be hypnotized by democracy to maintain that only through it could any freedom be justified. Furthermore, even some of those freedoms essential for democracy are defensible on other, independent grounds, and those grounds might apply even were one to reject democracy as an ideal. I specifically disclaim the effort to provide the only or the whole defense of freedom in general; I shall be concerned with the analysis and defense of certain freedoms because of their close and special connections with democratic government.

10.4 Political freedoms

The freedoms essential for the operation of democracy are too many to treat separately. Two major categories can be distinguished, however, into which these freedoms fall. These are: *(1)* political freedoms, and *(2)* freedoms of speech. The former I shall discuss very briefly in this section; to the latter I shall devote the remainder of this chapter.

By political freedom I mean simply the freedom to do those many kinds of things entailed by self-government. These include, fundamentally, the freedom to use the instruments through which a citizen's voice can be heard and become effective in the government.

Above all, the citizen of a democracy must be free to vote. Each member of the community must count for one, and his right to be so counted must be protected. This requires, of course, the development of just systems of representation [Chapter 7], the restrained use of majority power [Chapter 6], and a variety of technical instruments through which individuals can influence their government. Such instruments and systems must be administered fairly, in the spirit of the democracy they are intended to serve.

Given the machinery of participation, with all of its complexity, the right of the individual citizen to use it freely must be safeguarded. Safeguarding this right entails scrupulous attention to a mass of detail, the careful protection of a host of particular and concrete freedoms. The citizen must be free to participate in the nomination of candidates for office, free to run for office himself, free to cast his ballot without fear of retribution, and so on. Taken together, these freedoms are absolutely essential if democracy is to work.

Because they are so essential, these freedoms must be guaranteed by the constitution of any genuinely democratic community. They need no further defense. So central is their function that in common speech we often comingle these freedoms with democracy itself, failing to distinguish the concept of government by participation from the basic freedoms to do the things that such government requires. These political freedoms are not identical with democracy, but without them no democracy can succeed.

10.5 Freedoms of speech

The constitutional conditions of democracy are of two kinds, political freedoms [10.4] and the freedoms of speech. Freedoms of speech can be further divided into sub-categories, of which the two most important for democracy are *(1)* the freedom to propose, and *(2)* the freedom to oppose.

(1) Democracy requires that its citizens be free to propose alternative courses of action, literally to place them before the community for its consideration. Without the freedom to propose the citizen might retain the opportunity to express his preference among the alternatives presented to him, but opportunity for his most constructive participation

will have been denied. Any limitation of the freedom to propose is a restriction not only upon him who would make the proposal, but upon every member of his community who is thereby kept from considering that proposal. By such limitation the depth of the participation of all is reduced.

Unlimited freedom of proposal may sometimes result in too large a number of alternatives from which everyone must choose. When citizens are forced to select from among long lists of candidates most of whom they cannot reasonably be expected to know much about, or from among many alternative programs whose variations are of high refinement, the ends of general participation may not be well served. The remedy for such excess lies not in restricting that freedom, however, but in devising orderly procedures for its use, and in having these procedures administered by intelligent and conscientious representatives. In any case, the danger to democracy arising from overly numerous or subtle alternatives is never so great as the danger arising from the arbitrary restriction of alternatives. The main lines of action open to the community will rarely be obscured simply by a superabundance of proposals or candidates.

Even if only some candidates or some alternative policies or parties are refused a hearing, the democracy will be seriously injured because whatever degree of participation then remains cannot in consequence be fully effective. As a result even of partial constraint or coercion, it can never be certain that an election (or other participatory process) expresses the true will of the community membership. Any restriction whatever upon the alternatives that may be proposed by the members to the community cripples democracy, directly by reducing the depth of participation, and indirectly by rendering suspect the genuineness of whatever participation does continue.

(2) Democracy requires that its citizens be free to oppose such candidates or policies or parties as have been presented for community consideration. The freedom to oppose is literally the freedom to place one's self against, or publicly to place argument against, any program or nominee.

There can be no sharp line between the freedom to propose and the freedom to oppose; to propose one alternative is, at least indirectly, to oppose others, or at least to invite such opposition. But indirect opposition is not enough in a democracy. Alternatives must not only be given comparative weighing, but should also be subjected to attacks of the most negative character. Proposals put before the community must be able to stand the test of community inspection; before final adoption they must win the support of the majority in spite of the open and organized opposition to any vigorous critics. Not to permit this opposition, or to place any restriction upon it, either by silencing individuals or proscribing ideas, is to block a major form of participation, and thereby to subvert democracy.

The right to oppose, like the right to propose, must be protected not only out of concern for the critic, but because it is essential to the well-being of all the members of the community who must in some way pass judgment upon the issue with which that critic is concerned. Whoever is not permitted to hear the arguments in opposition cannot be fully informed, cannot decide upon the issue as wisely as otherwise he might. Where any opposition whatever is silenced, the depth of the participation of the entire community is impaired.

Unlike the freedom to propose alternatives, however, the freedom to oppose them (or to oppose parties or candidates) can hardly be carried to excess. Unlimited proposals may confuse; unlimited opposition serves only to subject what has been proposed to closer scrutiny, and to expose such deficiencies as it may harbor. Continuous vigorous criticism can help to avoid hasty action, and it is likely to encourage the development of new proposals not subject to the same criticism. The advantage lies not wholly with the critic. If the channels of communications are kept fully open, criticism may be met with refuting evidence and argument; vigorous opposition calls forth vigorous defense. The candidate (or party or program) meriting community approval will be he (or that) best enduring the trials of this battlefield.

These two—the freedom to propose and to oppose—together constitute the freedom of speech democracy requires. Here "speech" is not restricted to vocal activity, but includes all forms of utterance, oral and written, and the communication of ideas through any of the various media normally used for that purpose—radio, television, books, newspapers, magazines, pamphlets, handbills, and the like. Freedom of speech thus encompasses the freedom of publication (a "free press") which is the freedom to make public facts and ideas of public concern, without fear of punishment.

Everyone agrees that freedom of speech is of fundamental importance in a democracy. Some, however, support that freedom superficially, or halfheartedly, and are quite ready to see it restricted, or even denied to those whose views they believe dangerous. Usually (but not always) efforts to limit the freedom of speech are undertaken in the honest belief that doing so will protect the democracy. This belief is tenable only when the true relation between democracy and the freedom of speech is not fully understood.

Democracy is government through the participation of the governed. Participation in decision-making calls for joint intellectual activity, and therefore relies upon the continuing expression and communication of facts, ideas, and arguments. The freedom to present and discuss these publicly, therefore, is a condition of democratic process. Insofar as that condition is restricted or impaired, the democracy that requires it is restricted or impaired. It is not merely that freedom of speech is nice, or desirable, or wise to protect. It may not seem so nice on occasion, and some may even question its ultimate desirability or wisdom. It is nevertheless a necessity and must be built into the structure or organism of any community that hopes to remain truly self-governing. The freedom of speech is a constitutional condition of democracy.

Many grant the truth of this without fully realizing its implications for the practice of democracy. Agonized discussions then ensue concerning the limits which might be, or ought to be, placed upon the the freedom of speech. Should there be such limits at all? If so, what form should they take? Should speech be constitutionally protected even when its exercise threatens stability and order? What shall we do when the freedom of speech is used by those who seek eventually to destroy the freedom of speech? Must we protect the freedom even of those who aim to subvert that very freedom?

These are the questions with which the remainder of this chapter will be directly concerned. No principles that will resolve every particular problem in this sphere should be expected. "As in other sciences," Aristotle writes (in Book Two of the *Politics*), "so in politics, it is impossible that all things should be precisely set down in writing; for enactments must be universal, but actions are concerned with particulars." Nevertheless, correct answers to the question above can be got, and a wide understanding of these answers is vital to the success of any democracy, especially any national democracy of great size and internal diversity. To develop these answers I shall examine three different defenses that may be offered for the freedom of speech. My aim is to show that the successful operation of democracy requires that no restrictions be placed upon the freedom of speech, and that because that is true two of these defenses (the two most commonly relied upon) are inadequate for the theory and practice of democracy.

10.6 *Absolutist defense of free speech*

The freedom of speech may be defended on absolutist grounds, typically as an inalienable human right. To contend that a right is inalienable is to insist that it cannot be taken from a human being, alienated from him, under any circumstances, even if he were willing to give it up. "We hold these truths to be self-evident," the authors of the Declaration of Independence confidently wrote, "that all men are created equal, that they are endowed by their Creator with certain inalienable rights. . . ." On this view there is no room for argument or doubt; the absolutist will insist that whoever claims not to recognize these truths as "self-evident" is deceived, or deceiving, or intellectually or morally blind.

Such defenses of free speech are common; they tend to result in a conception of the relation between this freedom and democracy rather different from that I have proposed. The absolutist defends the freedom of speech unconditionally, and therefore with no regard for the governmental forms it may or may not serve. He may agree that free speech and democracy go hand in hand, but he is likely to believe this is true because he thinks democratic government offers the best protection for this and other inalienable rights, and not the other way about. His concern for these rights is primary, for the democratic process secondary; his chief aim is the preservation of God-given rights, and one of his fundamental principles is that "to secure these rights governments are instituted among men. . . ."

On just such grounds the founders of the American republic believed, in 1776, that they were fully justified in overruling the allegiance of the former colonies to the English Crown. It was not so much the Crown's denial of democracy—of which there was then little enough on either side of the Atlantic—but its refusal to protect the inalienable rights of men that caused them to insist that it was their right, even their duty, "to throw off such Government, and to provide new guards for their future security." That was a stirring and effective defense of the American Revolution.

As a defense of the freedoms essential to democracy, however, "self-evidence" is quite unsatisfactory. It suffers from weaknesses that have been exposed and explained on innumerable occasions, by philosophers and jurisprudents. These weaknesses have, ultimately, the same core: when conflicts arise over the nature or extent of self-evident rights, or between such rights, there is no rational recourse through which resolution of these conflicts may be achieved. Consider:

(1) When the self-evident truths recognized by one person or group conflict with the self-evident truths recognized by another person or group, what is to be done? Assuredly, at least one of the conflicting parties is mistaken. But how decide which? Obviously the issues cannot be decided by counting noses, or by measuring intensities of belief. No inquiry of a scientific kind can resolve the matter, for none could be relevant to the establishment of truths which, by the hypothesis of both parties to the conflict, are open to immediate and certain determination by each person. What remains? If self-evidence is claimed as the ultimate ground of rights and freedoms, self-evidence is the only court to which we may reasonably appeal when conflicts among them arise. But then whose self-evidence will rule? Every attempt to make some higher appeal to self-evidence, or immediate perception, may encounter the same conflict of judgment that arose on the original substantive issue. To one whose absolute freedom to speak is self-evidently inalienable, it will be equally self-evident that his self-evidence is absolutely reliable, and that what his opponent calls self-evidence is only mistaken opinion. The opponent, finding by self-evidence that freedom must be otherwise construed, reasons in precisely the same way. Between them there can be no resolution short of surrender. If one of the conflicting parties will not surrender, they must change the subject of their discourse, or resort to force. This force may take the form of legal action at one extreme, or at the other, the appeal to arms.

(2) Self-evidence may also conflict with other kinds of evidence, publicly verifiable, called scientific. Again the conflicting parties are likely to deny each other's intellectual credentials. When such conflicts do arise it is highly probable that scientific authority will be generally accepted, which shows that we trust claims based on self-evidence, if at all, only so far as we are ignorant of any better grounds for conviction on the matter at hand.

(3) What is self-evident to a given person at one time may directly conflict with what is self-evident to the same person at a different time.

How is one to decide which of his own views is truly self-evident? He is likely to rely on his most recent opinion; but there is no reason to suppose a later judgment of this kind is invariably superior to an earlier one, nor is it clear why the passage of time should have any effect upon judgments which, when rendered, claim absolute certainty. Indeed, when we realize how frequently philosophers, theologians, and the mass of men have maintained as "self-evident truths" propositions later found to be very dubious, or plainly false, and corrected by later judgments, we can hardly deny the possibility that truths now believed "self-evident" are equally uncertain, being subject to the same sort of correction. With that realization, self-evidence, immediate intuition, and the like, lose their force in defending rights or freedoms absolutely and unconditionally.

(4) Even for a given person at a given time, self-evident rights of one kind may conflict with self-evident rights of another kind. My right to speak freely may conflict with my neighbor's right to privacy. Or self-evident duties may conflict with one another. My duty to tell the truth may conflict with my duty to keep a promise of secrecy. Or self-evident rights may conflict with self-evident duties. My right to live my life as I please may conflict with my duty to realize as best I can my intellectual or moral capacities. The puzzles and paradoxes of the epistemology of self-evidence are endless.

When self-evidence is replaced or supplemented by some alleged faculty all men are held to possess—"moral sense," or "ethical intuition," or "rational insight," or "the natural light"—essentially the same difficulties arise. No really secure defense of rights or freedoms can be grounded upon unverifiable kinds of knowledge, or special powers that are alleged to lead necessarily, when correctly applied, to a unique and certain result. The universal possession and recognition of such special knowledge or power has been repeatedly denied by a great many astute and reflective thinkers—philosophers and plain men of every age—all of whom are not likely to have been morally blind. The universal and infallible application of such intuitive powers in the defense of human rights is too much even to hope for. Common experience speaks loudly and conclusively against the reliability of arguments so grounded—especially when those arguments are employed in defense of persons who would speak critically of those in authority. Allegedly infallible intuitions or insights may never be absolutely disproved (their very peculiarity enabling those who claim them to dodge such proof), but neither can their reliability or even their existence be clearly established, except to the satisfaction of those who do not need to be persuaded.

These faculties, or kinds of knowledge—intuitions or self-evident truths—are nevertheless appealing. They seem easy, straightforward; they fit nicely with the simplicity and absoluteness of the moral injunctions we learn as children. By their standard things are good or bad, right or wrong, and there appears no need to hedge or hesitate. Unfortunately, such simple standards, simple judgments, and the infallible faculties needed to stand behind them do not work in the real world of mature human beings.

Absolute defenses of the freedom of speech (or other freedoms) are particularly attractive to those with a theological orientation. Viewing the world as properly governed by a set of divine commands, they are inclined to resort to supernatural authority as the certification of the absolute standards proclaimed. But the very same unsolvable problems discussed in connection with self-evidence arise again in the effort to determine the correct and unequivocal interpretation of divine commands. Political problems are then exacerbated, however, because contending parties have not only their own wisdom at stake, but (many believe) the truth of their religious beliefs as well. The resort to theology explains nothing in the sphere of practical politics; it helps not one whit in resolving concrete political issues. Rigidity is only reinforced when beliefs about God are taken as the ground for the defense of rights or freedoms.

When, relying upon some such theological base, rights so derived are held to be "natural," confusion is compounded. In this way, Abraham Kaplan has argued,

> ... religion is naturalized, and the supernatural projected onto the face of nature as a principle of cosmic order. . . .
>
> The whole apparatus of natural law adds nothing to the moral content of our politics, but only changes its form of expression. Beginning with whatever code of political rights and duties our needs and knowledge, traditions and experience have produced, we covertly construct from it a system of natural law, present this as objective in origin and universal in application, then triumphantly derive from it the rights and duties with which we started. . . . Rights to be defended as *our* ideals and secured through *our* efforts can then be seen as antecedently guaranteed, absolute and fixed in the nature of things. Such a conviction may indeed produce a show of courage: with a stacked deck a man will

stake everything. But when we are challenged by competing absolutes, the courage called for must have deeper roots, or it will vanish. . . .

Natural law is not the ground of political morality but its projective expression. (*American Ethics and Public Policy,* 1958, pp. 14–17)

There is an additional practical reason why the effort to ground political principles in religious beliefs is unfortunate, and can be dangerous to a democracy. Religious communities are voluntary; if we disagree with the doctrine of a church we may leave it freely, and join another, or join none at all. The sovereign political community is not voluntary in the same way or to the same degree. To insist upon any theological defense of rights necessarily universal within the political community, therefore, is to oblige a theological uniformity that is likely to prove intolerable. Even the threat of that imposed doctrine may disrupt the community democracy presupposes.

I conclude that civil freedoms—among them the freedom of speech —are not safely grounded if their ultimate defense is so vulnerable a shield as the varieties of absolutism, theological or metaphysical. And although very commonly professed, such views are not commonly acted upon. Of those who profess to defend the freedom of speech as an absolutely inalienable right, it can usually be said that, in practice, their good sense gets the better of them.

10.7 Utilitarian defense of free speech

The utilitarian argument in defense of free speech holds, essentially, that the protection of speech is justified not by natural law, or self-evidence of any kind, but by its own practical consequences. The argument is effective as far as it goes, but it does not go far enough to defend the full freedom of speech needed for the practice of democracy.

In classical form, as presented by John Stuart Mill in *On Liberty,* the utilitarian argument has three divisions. The first and fundamental division of the argument holds that the suppression of opinion does not serve truth, because the very determination of what is true depends utterly upon the free play of contesting opinions. To silence any opinion, therefore, however false or noxious we may think it, is to assume we cannot be mistaken in that matter. Such infallibility, all history attests, is possessed by no man, no party.

The critic replies: "I claim no more infallibility in silencing a false and pernicious opinion than is claimed by those who pursue all other serious acts of government. Recognizing the possibility of error we must act with care, but when convinced that the dangers of the circumstances demand it, we must also protect the public interest as best we can. That protection may entail suppression."

The utilitarian rejoins: "The case of suppression of opinions is importantly different from all other acts. In most matters our acts are based upon judgments whose truth we think to have been tested and established. In the case of suppressing an opinion we deny the opportunity to test and establish the truth both of that opinion and our own." Mill writes: "Complete liberty of contradicting and disapproving our opinion, is the very condition which justifies us in assuming its truth for the purposes of action; and on no other terms can a being with human faculties have any rational assurance of being right."*

The whole strength of human judgment rests upon the corrigibility of its errors, that it can be set right when it is wrong; therefore, reliance can be placed upon any judgment for the purpose of guiding action only when the instruments for the correction of judgments are available and in use. Mill concludes:

> The beliefs which we have most warrant for, have no safeguard to rest on, but a standing invitation to the whole world to prove them unfounded. If the challenge is not accepted or is accepted and the attempt fails, we are far enough from certainty still; but we have done the best that the existing state of human reason admits of; we have neglected nothing that could give the truth a chance of reaching us; if the lists are kept open, we may hope that if there be a better truth, it will be found when the human mind is capable of receiving it; and in the meantime we may rely on having attained such approach to truth, as is possible in our own day. This is the amount of certainty attainable by a fallible being, and this the sole way of attaining it.

The unhappy effects of suppression upon our capacities to reach truth in difficult matters are manifested concretely in a host of ways. *First*: where suppression in any form is practiced, those who would defend minority views if they could are obliged, for the sake of their own safety, to disguise their true opinions, or at least to refrain from a full and open statement of their judgments. Honest convictions are swallowed; arguments are presented not because they are truly persuasive but because they harmonize with established authority; citizens are con-

*This and other citations from Mill in this section are from the second chapter of *On Liberty*, 1859.

strained to become, in Mill's penetrating phrase, "time-servers for truth." A sort of intellectual pacification is achieved—but at the price of "the sacrifice of the entire moral courage of the human mind."

Second: heretical opinions that are false, and could not stand the test of full and fair exposure, do not die as they ought, but continue to smolder, as attractive mysteries.

Third: great harm is done, not only to those who defy control and express their heresies, but to the whole society through the loss of those potentially bold and original thinkers whose mental development is cramped, and reason cowed, by the fear of heresy. If worthwhile intellectual advances are ever to be made, men must be free to follow their intellects wherever they lead, without threat of punishment or reprisal, legal or other. "Truth gains more," Mill contends, "even by the errors of one who, with due study and preparation, thinks for himself, than by the true opinions of those who only hold them because they do not suffer themselves to think."

Fourth: most painful of all is the price paid in the destruction of an intellectual atmosphere in which an intelligent and inquiring citizenry can develop. Not only great thinkers, but average human beings lose, by suppression and the threat of it, the circumstances under which they can best realize their own capacities. "Where there is a tacit convention that principles are not to be disputed; where the discussion of the greatest questions which can occupy humanity is considered to be closed," Mill concludes, "we cannot hope to find that generally high scale of mental activity which has made some periods of history so remarkable."

The second division of the utilitarian argument holds that, supposing some minority opinions were known infallibly to be false, suppressing them, or silencing their supporters, would be evils still. Even in such hypothetical (and in fact unattainable) circumstances, the restriction of criticism undermines our grasp of the truth. However true one's opinion may be, Mill argues, "if it is not fully, frequently and fearlessly discussed, it will be held as a dead dogma, not a living truth." Really knowing the truth entails knowing the grounds of one's beliefs; knowing these grounds requires that opposing claims and arguments be fully heard and honestly met. "He who knows only his own side of the case knows little of that."

Not only are the grounds for conviction lost through suppression, but sometimes the very content of one's own truths as well. Without criticism, once-living beliefs become empty phrases learned by rote.

Convictions turn gradually to doctrines, and then to dogmatic creeds, passively received, encrusting and petrifying the mind.

To avoid this petrification, to revivify and strengthen our grasp of the meaning and force of our own most important truths, we must hear them contested, and must answer the arguments of those who defend opposing views not merely as an academic exercise, but in earnest. In the interest of the convictions we most deeply cherish we must protect the freedoms of our critics—not merely as their right, but as an instrument in our service. If critics do not arise spontaneously, we must, for our own sake, create them. Mill comments: "That, therefore, which when absent, it is so indispensable, but so difficult, to create, how worse than absurd it is to forego, when spontaneously offering itself! If there are any persons who contest a received opinion, or who will do so if law or opinion will let them, let us thank them for it, open our minds and listen to them, and rejoice that there is someone to do for us what we otherwise ought, if we have any regard for either the certainty of the vitality of our convictions, to do with much greater labor for ourselves."

The third division of the argument holds simply that, in fact, the whole of the truth is likely to lie neither on the side of received opinion nor on the side of its critics. To supply that portion of the truth that the minority (but not the majority) view incorporates, the outspoken nonconformist is essential, and must be protected, even though he blends his truth with serious error. Indeed, those elements of the truth needing to be specially prized and cultivated are not the ones commonly recognized and accepted, but those which are, for the time, neglected or misunderstood. If, therefore, majority and minority opinions are in conflict on serious issues, it is the minority views that, in the interests of all, deserve not merely toleration, but even encouragement. The majority views will take care of themselves. Thus may we hope to arrive at a better grasp of the whole truth—through "the rough process of a struggle between contestants fighting under hostile banners."

This utilitarian defense of free speech has not here been cast in specifically political terms, but its political impact has, in fact, been considerable. Most famous, in American constitutional history, is its appearance in Justice Oliver Wendell Holmes's dissent in the case of *Abrams v. U.S.* (1919): "When men have realized that time has upset many fighting faiths, they may come to believe even more than they believe the very foundations of their own conduct that the ultimate good desired is better reached by free trade in ideas—that the best test of truth is the power of the thought to get itself accepted in the competition of the market, and that truth is the only ground upon which their wishes safely can be carried out" (250 U.S. 616).

Splendid as this argument is in many contexts, it does not, unfortunately, go far enough. In some circumstances this utilitarian defense cannot protect the freedom of speech as broadly and strongly as the full success of democracy requires that it be defended.

Nothing in this utilitarian agreement commits one to democracy. If democratic government is consistent with the liberty of thought and opinion, so much the better for it. Mill himself was far from being a wholehearted democrat; he distrusted the masses in some ways, and wished to enlarge the influence of an intellectual elite. Like many utilitarians, he prized other political values more highly than democracy, and was prepared to sacrifice the latter on occasion. The pure utilitarian is bound to agree that his argument in defense of free speech gives no special place to democracy. His condemnation of the suppression of opinion is based upon his conviction that such suppression leads to serious evils, whatever the governmental form.

Therefore, the pure utilitarian is compelled also to admit that, in some special circumstances, unrestricted freedom of speech *may* lead to even greater evils, to such irreparable danger or disorder that, on utilitarian grounds alone, we are justified in limiting that freedom. It may be hoped that such circumstances will prove rare, but they are surely conceivable. In short, the pure utilitarian argument cannot defend complete freedom of speech when, all things considered, the danger that freedom appears to present is greater than the dangers known to be entailed by its restriction.

Unhappily, in concrete political contexts, where the defenses of freedom have been primarily utilitarian, these very special circumstances have been claimed to arise with remarkable frequency. Every national crisis, every war, every international threat, brings that claim. By itself, the utilitarian arguments cannot stave off the demands of those who argue honestly and persuasively that permitting all speech without restriction is a course too dangerous to follow. The kind and degree of the threats to security that may justify suppression have been much disputed, of course, in legislatures and courts. Countless formulations of the allowable risks have been proposed and debated from the time of the Alien and Sedition Laws of 1798 to the present. The upshot is a principle first formulated by Justice Holmes himself, in 1919, and still commonly applied in American law—the doctrine of "clear and present danger."

In the case of *Schenk v. U.S.* (249 U.S. 47) the United States Supreme Court held that since Congress is constitutionally authorized to declare war and raise armies, it may constitutionally punish (specifically, under the Espionage Act of 1917) those who interfere with that function by keeping men out of service. So far, no question of free speech arises. But the Court further held that *persuading* men not to register for the draft, or not to enlist, is punishable interference, and also that *efforts so to persuade* are punishable, even if unsuccessful. Speech is but one way of acting, on this view, and when its bad tendency is immediate and severe, it may be silenced, on utilitarian grounds, in the interest of national security or the prosecution of the war. Justice Holmes wrote for the court: "The character of every act depends upon the circumstances in which it is done. . . . The question in every case is whether the words used are used in such circumstances and are of such a nature as to create a clear and present danger that they will bring about the substantive evils that Congress has a right to prevent."

This "clear and present danger" doctrine is the natural outcome of a purely utilitarian approach; I argue that it is bad law, not consistent with the full realization of democracy. In the first place it is probably an incorrect interpretation of the basic intentions of the authors of the United States Constitution. In the second place, whatever their intentions may have been, it is an interpretation that vitiates the constitutional protection of unrestricted freedom of speech that the practice of democracy requires.

The clearest proof of the real intentions of the authors of the American Constitution are the words they used. Few men have possessed a talent of exact and elegant expression equal to that of James Madison and Thomas Jefferson. Their language in the First Amendment was perfectly lucid and straightforward; it is difficult to suppose that they did not grasp the full force of the plain words they deliberately chose. The First Amendment to the Constitution of the United States reads as follows: "Congress shall make no law respecting an establishment of religion, or prohibiting the free exercise thereof; or abridging the freedom of speech, or of the press; or the right of the people peaceably to assemble, and to petition the Government for a redress of grievances."

The clarity and undeniable meaning of this language has been repeatedly emphasized by one of the greatest of the Justices of the Supreme Court, Hugo Black:

I believe the words do mean what they say. I have no reason to challenge the intelligence, integrity, or honesty of the men who wrote the First Amendment. . . . I learned a long time ago that there are affirmative and negative words. The beginning of the First Amendment is that "Congress shall make no law." I understand that it is rather old-fashioned and shows a slight naivete to say that 'no law' means no law. . . . But what it *says* is "Congress shall make no law respecting an establishment of religion," and so on. (*N.Y.U. Law Review,* June 1962)

The historical and practical purposes of a Bill of Rights, the very use of a written constitution, indigenous to America, the language the Framers used, the kind of three-department government they took pains to set up *all point to the creation of a government which was denied all power to do some things under any and all circumstances, and all power to do other things except precisely in the manner prescribed.* (*N.Y.U. Law Review,* April 1960; italics mine)

We do not need to rely, however, upon the analysis of any contemporary scholar. James Madison, himself the sponsor of those proposals that eventually became the Bill of Rights, and the most influential member of the Constitutional Convention, spoke clearly to the question. One of his proposals was transformed into the present First Amendment, and read as follows: "The people shall not be deprived or abridged of their right to speak, to write, or to publish their sentiments; and the freedom of the press, as one of the great bulwarks of liberty, shall be inviolable." Madison himself, in defense of this proposal, said in Congress that, under it, "the right of freedom of speech is secured; the liberty of the press *is expressly declared to be beyond the reach of this government"* (italics mine).

Indeed, if the authors of the American Constitution had intended to establish the principle that 'Congress shall make no law abridging the freedom of speech except when such freedom creates clear and present dangers of certain kinds' they surely could have said so. They intended to be explicit and unambiguous, yet did not formulate the Amendment in that way. Had any exceptions been thought by them permissible they would have indicated the general nature of such exceptions, at least. If the authors had believed—as Justice Holmes and others have seemed to believe—that the applicability of the Bill of Rights is restricted by the authorized functions of Congress, so that in performing these functions the prohibitions of the Bill of Rights do not apply, they would certainly have said that. They might then have written: *"Except in the exercise of its duly authorized powers,* Congress shall make no law abridging the freedom of speech. . . ." Clearly such qualifications would have robbed the First Amendment, and the rest of the Bill of Rights, of all their bite. To permit the Congress to do certain things only when it feels the need to do them is to forbid virtually nothing. That is what the "clear and present danger" doctrine says: "Do not restrict the freedom of speech in any way—unless you think you really must." Just in that way are constitutional guarantees emasculated. The "clear and present danger" doctrine, and similar principles, permit Congress to do, in times of crisis, what the First Amendment clearly says Congress may not do.

Thus far I have shown only that the "clear and present danger" doctrine is not consistent with our own, written Constitution. I must next show that such principles are inconsistent with the constitutional conditions of any genuine democracy. To that end, I present a third defense of free speech, more powerful in some respects than either the absolutist or utilitarian defenses just reviewed.

10.8 A conditional defense of free speech

May the freedom to speak or publish be in any way rightly limited or qualified in a democracy? I argue that it may not, and that the doctrine of "clear and present danger," and all similar doctrines, are therefore untrue not only to the intentions of the authors of the American Constitution, but also untrue to the spirit of the democracy they founded. In any democracy, the freedom to speak and publish must be in no way restricted.

An absolutist defense of free speech, although in many ways attractive, is basically unsatisfactory [10.6]. The utilitarian defense of free speech although profound and effective, proves insufficient, by itself, to protect against unfortunate abridgements of that freedom [10.7]. By insisting that no restrictions be placed on speech or publication, do I not simply return from the utilitarian to the absolutist position? Assuredly not. How then can complete freedom of speech be defended? I answer: *conditionally.*

Absolutist defenses of free speech are unconditional. They rely upon "natural" or "inalienable" rights; they suppose some infallible faculty through which such rights are known, or claim that they are "self-evident" to all. Such epistemological foundations are too weak to stand the strain that the exercise of truly free speech will put upon them. Conflicts among supposedly infallible faculties and supposedly self-evident rights render such an approach hopeless.

The complete freedom of speech can, nevertheless, be successfully defended; but this defense will be conditional upon the acceptance of the democratic ideal. *If we wish to maintain a democracy*, speech must be entirely free. The liberty to criticize, to express dissenting opinions—however unpopular, noxious, or perverse they may be—must remain, in a democracy, absolute. Its absoluteness stems not from direct intuition or any other special faculty or evidence, but from the operating requirements of government by participation. The free and open discussion of all sides of all issues of community concern is a condition of full and effective participation. The complete freedom of speech, therefore, is not merely a benefit to democracy but a necessity for it. What limits the freedom of speech in any way, that far limits the democracy in the community. Really successful and long lasting democracy requires that the guarantee of this freedom be built into the constitution; any effort by parties in power—however patriotic or well-meaning—to stifle criticism or opposition undermines the constitution of that democracy.

This position may be called "conditional absolutism." The preservation of democracy demands that the freedom to speak and publish be absolute. It is not, however, the absolute a priori right of every human being to speak without restraint; it is the a posteriori but absolute requirement of a democratically governed community that its citizens be entirely free to speak and criticize. Freedom of speech is not the inalienable right of every man; it is the *constitutional* right of every citizen of a democracy.

Those who feel no commitment to democracy, and no obligation to defend it, will of course find this defense of free speech ineffective. "If," as Justice Holmes wrote on one occasion, "you have no doubt of your premises or your power and want a certain result with all your heart, you naturally express your wishes in law and sweep away all opposition." When the result is so much more important than the process by which it is obtained, let the process be damned. Then, as Holmes said, persecution for the expression of opinions is "perfectly logical" (*Abrams v. United States,* 250 U.S. 616, 1919). For one who holds the democratic process of higher worth than any particular result, however, the necessary conditions of that process must be religiously honored and safeguarded. Therein lies the source of the sanctity and priority given to certain "First Amendment" freedoms. Being essential for the proper operation of the entire system, we hold them inviolable. This inviolability is based not on their supernatural origin or certification, but upon our resolve to give them always first place. We could alter this resolution if we wished. But whenever we have ignored these principles or underestimated their essential role, our democracy has suffered. Two centuries of deeply satisfying self-rule reaffirms the wisdom of our decision to revere the principles that are the condition of our national self-government. That reverence we manifest by writing these principles into our Constitution, saying plainly of the freedom of speech, press, assembly and petition, that even the Congress is not permitted to abridge them. In one form or another the constitution of every democracy must incorporate these fundamental guarantees.

This conditional defense of the freedom of speech in a democracy permits no exceptions. It applies to all opinions and all persons, however mistaken or perverse, and however much displeasure the majority is thereby caused. Being without exception, the argument applies not only to persons and views thought loathsome, but also to those thought dangerous.

The doctrine of "clear and present danger" is applied by well-meaning democrats who believe that it is sometimes necessary, for the safety of the nation, to restrict free speech. While that freedom must indeed be always revered, they argue, there are times when some opinions, or the speech of some persons, must not be permitted in order that the nation be preserved. Only a consideration of that magnitude, they might insist, could justify such a limitation of constitutional guarantees; but that consideration—national preservation—will sometimes justify suppression. The danger must be clear, and it must be present; when it is both, the opinions or persons who create that danger may be silenced.

I put aside now the clear incompatibility of this doctrine with the plain words of the First Amendment. I put aside also the fact that the doctrine is easily and commonly misapplied, sometimes used to suppress dangers both unclear and future. More importantly, that doctrine is fundamentally incompatible with the spirit and operating principles of the democracy it was devised to protect. Four counter-arguments, taken together, are compelling.

First: intelligent participation by citizens in their government requires that they be allowed to hear all that can be said for, or against, or about every proposal of joint concern; they must therefore be permitted to hear arguments or ideas thought by some to be dangerous. If they are not allowed even to hear such talk they cannot decide wisely concerning it—and the democracy depends entirely upon the wisdom of its citizens and no one else. By interfering with the development of that wisdom, "the clear and present danger" doctrine cripples democracy.

Second: the "clear and present danger" doctrine manifests a fundamental distrust of the people, a lack of confidence in their capacity to judge for themselves. Democracy requires the very reverse of this—a confidence in the citizens that justifies placing ultimate community authority in their hands. Any doctrine resting upon the premise that, in times of crisis, the members of the community cannot be trusted, is profoundly incompatible with democracy.

If some opinions are too dangerous to allow to be heard, or some persons too dangerous to allow to speak freely, who is to make this decision for the community? Any such doctrine implicitly supposes that some may safely hear the nasty person or idea, but that the rest must be kept from contamination by it. It supposes, in short, just what democracy denies—that because the mass of people are incompetent to govern themselves they need a set of enlightened governors who will protect them from "dangerous ideas."* The "clear and present danger" doctrine flies in the face of democracy.

Concerning the censorship of books and printing as a way of protecting citizens from "dangerous" opinions, John Milton wrote (*Areopagitica*, 1644): "Nor is it to the common people less than a reproach; for if we be so jealous over them as that we dare not trust them with an English pamphlet, what do we but censure them for a giddy, vicious, and ungrounded people, in such a sick and weak estate of faith and discretion as to be able to take nothing down but through the pipe of a licenser? That this is care or love of them we cannot pretend. . . . Lords and Commons of England, consider what nation it is whereof ye are, and whereof ye are the governors: a nation not slow and dull, but of a quick, ingenious, and piercing spirit, acute to invent, subtle and sinewy to discourse, not beneath the reach of any point the highest that human capacity can soar to." It is true that

---

*The U.S. Government, in its brief in support of the prosecution of Lloyd Barenblatt (1959) for refusing (on First Amendment grounds) to answer questions about alleged Communist affiliation, speaks of the "communication of unlawful ideas"!

142

the advocates of the "clear and present danger" doctrine do not usually propose a general censorship of the kind Milton was attacking. All principles, however, having the effect of censorship injure democracy in precisely the same way. They patronize the people by forbidding them to hear the 'dangerous' ideas upon which they must ultimately pass judgment.

Third: if the nation is "preserved" by silencing or censoring, what is saved may not be worth the saving. In abridging freedom we may destroy the very system we set out to preserve. The suppression of free speech necessarily denies—so far as it is employed—the democracy it purports to protect. And the injury it does is not a danger merely; it is not a threatened but an actual deterioration of democracy.

Fourth: any principles restricting the freedom of speech rest on the absurd premise that the security of the nation depends upon its power to punish people for the expression of ideas. They suppose that, were certain people or views not suppressed, the entire society is jeopardized. This premise is plainly ridiculous. The welfare and safety of the nation never hang upon the silencing of any person or party. If ever the nation did prove that insecure, we should be gravely concerned about the wisdom and justice of its policies, and all the more anxious to hear everything that might be said about them.

In a famous dissent, Justice Hugo Black wrote: "I . . . deny that ideas can be proscribed under our Constitution. I agree that despotic governments cannot exist without stifling the voice of opposition to their oppressive practices. The First Amendment means to me, however, that the only constitutional way our Government can preserve itself is to leave its people the fullest possible freedom to praise, criticize, or discuss, as they see fit, all governmental policies and to suggest, if they desire, that even its most fundamental postulates are bad and should be changed. 'Therein lies the security of the Republic, the very foundation of constitutional government' " (*Barenblatt v. United States*, 360 U. S. 109, 1959).

10.9 Incitement and advocacy

The constitutional guarantee of free speech does not protect persons who, by means of speech, deliberately and directly incite criminal acts. This is no restriction on what may be said; it is a restriction, as reasonable as countless others, on what may be done. It is essential, therefore, that incitement and advocacy be carefully understood, for under the guise of punishing criminal incitement, the freedom to oppose the government or to criticize it severely is too easily abridged.

Incitement may be accomplished by a great variety of means, but it is incitement through speech, verbal incitement, with which I shall here be concerned. Verbal incitement, however, has two distinct senses, one generic, the other specific, which are importantly different. In the former sense incitement is provocation—stimulation of interest and concern that certain things be done. In this generic sense incitement falls clearly within the purview of the constitutional protection of free speech, for it is precisely the stimulation of interest and concern that the citizens of a democracy must be free to receive and to impart, and that is essential to their full participation in their own government. It is in this general sense that Justice Holmes used the term when he wrote, in his dissent in *Gitlow v. New York*: "Every idea is an incitement. It offers itself for belief, and, if believed, it is acted on unless some other belief outweighs it, or some failure of energy stifles the movement at its birth" (268 U.S. 652, 1925). This generic sense of incitement as any provocative idea is an overly extended and extraordinary use of the term. Because it does enter into these discussions, however, this usage is a source of considerable confusion.

In the specific sense, incitement is instigation, the deliberate and direct arousal of another to do a particular act. In this sense I incite you to commit a crime when I urge and advise you to perform a particular criminal act, and you do it. This specific sense of urging or advising is the normal and more commonly accepted sense of incitement, and it is the sense in which I shall use that term.

One essential distinction between the two senses of incitement is this: no speech or writing (or any other conduct) can be considered specific incitement unless the act urged is actually performed. Until it is performed the speech that urges it can only be treated as general provocation, which may or may not be in good taste, depending upon its object and its manner, but—in a democracy—can never be unlawful.

Advocacy is one subclass of generic incitement; it is provocation in the form of support or recommendation of a course of action, the pleading of a cause. Other kinds of generic incitement which do not take the form of advocacy create no problems in this context, and may be ignored here. The contrast of key importance is that between advocacy (one form of generic incitement) and incitement (i.e., specific incitement).

The crucial difference between the two is that advocacy does not entail the performance of the act advocated, while specific incitement does logically entail the commission of the act incited. Whether advocacy has taken place depends wholly upon the speaker and what is said; advocacy has no logical tie with the consequences of the utterance. I may advocate a life of poverty and chastity, even if no one pays any attention to me. More exactly put, advocacy takes the form of what are sometimes called illocutionary acts, acts performed in saying (or writing) something; specific incitement takes the form of perlocutionary acts, acts which accomplish certain results through saying (or writing) something. Advocacy being essentially an act of speech, it can never be criminal merely because of what is advocated. The commission of crime presupposes responsibility for the consequences of the act; but the advocate is never, by his advocacy alone, responsible for the doing of what he advocates. All advocacy must be protected where the constitution guarantees free speech. In a democracy one must be free to advocate anything, anything at all.

Specific incitement is another matter. Being directly linked to the act resulting, it can involve responsibility for that act and its consequences. Of course specific incitement may result in action that is lawful as well as action that is unlawful. This point is so obvious as to require special notice. One may be specifically incited to vote Republican, breed his bitch, or change his job; or he may be specifically incited to assassinate the Queen, or set fire to the presidential palace. Incitement can't be unlawful unless the act incited be unlawful; lawful incitement is very common and not problematic.

The grounds upon which some specific incitements may be held unlawful must be carefully discerned. There is nothing in the constitutional protection of free speech that keeps the state from enacting and enforcing laws which forbid certain kinds of overt acts as criminal. Neither does anyone deny that overt attempts to perform criminal acts, even when not successful, are also punishable as crime. So, too, utterances deliberately and directly causally linked to the performance of a specific crime become part of that crime. Holmes was right in saying that no competent person ever supposed that to make criminal the counseling of a murder within the jurisdiction of Congress would be an unconstitutional interference with free speech (*Frohwerk v. United States,* 249 U.S. 208, 1919).

Specific incitement, therefore, poses no special exception to the constitutional protection of free speech. When it can be proved that any person, through his speaking or writing, deliberately caused certain specific illegal acts to be done, that speaking or writing may be treated as part of the unlawful act. He may then be subject to penalty—not because of the content of his views, or his making of them public, but because of what he did, outside the realm of speech. Abraham Lincoln asked: "Must I shoot a simple soldier boy who deserts, while I must not touch a hair of a wily agitator who induces him to desert?" The answer is clear; whether or not desertion be a capital offense it is surely a crime, and therefore any government may rightly and constitutionally punish him whose words deliberately and directly helped to plan and prepare it.

Similarly, when Justice Holmes understandably insisted that "The most stringent protection of free speech would not protect a man in falsely shouting fire in a theatre, and causing a panic," he rightly calls our attention to the fact that one can, through speech or writing, do things that are criminal; these, however, are acts that are criminal however they are done, their criminality does not depend upon the instrument through which they are done. Deliberately causing a panic in a theatre is a criminal act, and when speech is used to achieve that result, such speech becomes part of the crime. No sensible person would defend such conduct. Note that it is shouting fire falsely that Holmes uses as his example; were the shout an honest warning of a real fire it would probably be considered an unwise, but perfectly natural way to call attention to a serious danger. Furthermore (supposing it a false warning) even if no panic results, it is against the law to rise and shout in a theatre for no good reason; what may then be punished is not the public expression of an opinion, but the act of shouting inappropriately and thereby causing public disturbance and inconvenience.

The right to speak freely, to advocate unpopular causes openly, is not the right to speak anywhere, at any time, in any way. Of course I may not shout freely or falsely at a theatre or concert; neither may I deliver reasoned speeches at my pleasure in restaurants or butcher shops; nor may I freely enter another's living room to express my criticism of the present administration's foreign policies. These acts are not culpable because of the content of my views, but because of what, through speech, I am doing unlawfully.

The same principle applies to the laws of libel and slander. These are not exceptions to the constitutional protection of free speech. Libel or slander may be punishable as crime, or be actionable in a civil suit, because what is written or said is a malicious attack upon another, or causes him demonstrable injury. As we may not injure people by deliberately beating them, causing harm to their person, so we may not injure people by deliberately defaming them, causing harm to their reputations. It is not the expression of views that is at issue, but what has been done by means of that expression. In the same way the author of a fraudulent letter, or the sponsor of a false advertisement, may be held for criminal trial.

Libel and slander present particularly touchy problems. In the first place it is often very difficult to establish injury as a result of verbal attack, or to establish the degree of such injury. In the second place, malicious injury may be caused by deliberate publication of what is perfectly true, but private. For this reason it is a long-established principle of the common law that the mere fact that a deliberately injurious public utterance is true is no defense against an action for libel. The truth of the injurious material is often relevant in libel suits, however, because if true, and published with honorable motives or justifiable objectives, its publication is likely to be protected. This underscores my thesis that speech is actionable at law only when wrongful injury is proved, and it is this injury that is punished (or for which remedy is given) and not the speech content itself which is restricted. In the third place, it is often very hard to determine whether the motives for the publication were good, or whether its objectives were justifiable. Often the plaintiffs in libel cases are public officials, or figures frequently and willingly before the public eye for other reasons, and must reasonably be presumed to have anticipated criticism and personal attack upon entering public life. Argument over their fitness for leadership must frequently verge upon such attacks, and those who seek controversial appointment must be understood to have invited them. When the issues involved are of genuinely public concern, and the persons involved active in community affairs, even the most damaging remarks will very probably be excused as part of the robust and uninhibited debate essential for the operation of democracy.

Deciding particular cases in this sphere is often difficult, but the general principle is clear. One may say and write what he pleases in a democracy, but he may not do whatever he pleases; when speech behavior constitutes or contributes deliberately and directly to an illegal act, it too may be illegal.

So important, however, is the open discussion of public issues in a democracy, that it constitutionally protects all utterances until they can be proved to have been part of an illegal act. For that proof they must be shown to have resulted in overt disobedience to law. The belief that some utterances may do so, or are likely to do so, or that similar utterances have incited crime in the past, is never enough. The presumption, in a democracy, lies always on the side of freedom in speech and publication. Writing and speaking may, on occasion, be part of a crime, but only after guilt for the other, non-verbal part of that crime has been established. Justice Black says: "I believe with Jefferson that it is time enough for government to step in to regulate people when they *do* something, not when they *say* something, and I do not believe myself that there is *any* halfway ground if you enforce the protections of the First Amendment" (*N.Y.U. Law Review*, June, 1962).

But isn't saying something doing something? Of course it is, in one sense; but that kind of doing—speaking and writing and publishing—is precisely what the constitution of a democracy protects, without restriction as to content. It does not protect what would in any case be a crime, or the integral parts of that crime.

It is true, as Sidney Hook (in *The Paradoxes of Freedom*, 1962, Chapter 1) and others have argued, that the distinction between advocacy and what I have called specific incitement is a "functional" one. That is, to decide whether written or spoken words are the direct cause of an illegal act does require an examination of the way these words actually function in the circumstances. What might be reasonable advocacy in one context could prove to be criminal incitement in another. This functionality, however, reinforces the need to establish a direct and immediate causal connection between specific speech acts and specific criminal acts, before the former can be held criminal. That the distinction is functional by no means justifies Hook's conclusion that words "trigger action" in the same way in both cases (incitement and advocacy), only having in the case of advocacy a "slightly delayed function" (ibid., p. 36). Such reasoning is catastrophic; from it follows the conclusion (for example) that no real distinction can be drawn between the intellectual discussion of revolutionary ideas, and the command to attack in a revolutionary situation.

On such a view any hint of a causal connection between the expression of certain ideas and the performance of related criminal acts might result in the punishment of that expression as criminal. This position not only fails to appreciate the requirements of democratic process, but ignores as well the realities of the legal situation. The determination of specific criminal incitement requires much more than that the ideas expressed had some vague role in a developing historical situation. If that were the criterion for guilt, there would be few among us not subject to punishment for the incitement of unlawful conduct.

That position fails also to recognize the enormous difference between words that have triggered past action, and words that may trigger action some time in the future. Hook writes that, "When they [ideas of any kind] count in specific historical situations in such fashion as to incite, *threaten*, or create violence, they have no constitutional protection" (ibid., p. 37; italics mine). Suddenly, under the guise of eschewing violence, he reaches the conclusion that speech which merely threatens violence, perhaps only obliquely, should not be protected. Opinions only believed to be dangerous may then be silenced. But it simply does not follow from the fact that an utterance may become specific incitement in some circumstances, that any utterance may rightly be silenced if it is believed (by whom?) that there is genuine danger that it will incite. We cannot know in advance what will in fact incite to violence, and we may not guess, or assume that we know, for purposes of suppression.

The power of the state does not need to be extended in this way. If it is within the physical power of the authorities to silence persons who utter or publish inflammatory remarks under tense circumstances, it is equally in their power to abort any attempt to perform the violent acts they may induce, or the violent response they may meet. There is nothing about democratic process that keeps public law enforcement agencies from maintaining good order, punishing unlawful injuries to property or person, whether by the speaker or his audience. If it is violent opposition to the speaker that is feared, it is the job of police officers to prevent hostile threats against lawful speakers from being carried out, and to prevent persons attempting to disrupt a lawful assembly from doing so. Justice Black again: "The police of course have power to prevent breaches of the peace. But if, in the name of preserving order, they ever can interfere with a lawful public speaker, they must first make all reasonable efforts to protect him" (*Feiner v. New York*, 340 U.S. 315, 1951). A democracy cannot allow its constitutional protection of the right to speak and demonstrate to be abridged by the least tolerant element within it. When a public meeting or demonstration erupts into riot it must be brought to order; but free speech must not be curtailed because of the fear that the exercise of this right may result in riotous disturbances by lawless opponents.

On the other hand, if the specific act induced by the speaker himself is illegal, and if an overt attempt is made to perform it, then, *and not before*, the verbal incitement becomes culpable. We cannot determine in advance, for example, how a crowd will react to a revolutionary orator; they may shout him down, or laugh him off, or simply ignore him. He may be a rabble-rouser, but they may be no rabble.

Alexander Meiklejohn, in testimony before the Senate Sub-Committee on Constitutional Rights in 1955, put the matter eloquently. Advocacy, he pointed out,

> even up to the limit of arguing and planning for the violent overthrow of the existing form of government, is one of those opinion-forming, judgment-making expressions which free men need to utter and to hear as citizens responsible for the governing of the nation. If men are not free to ask and to answer the question, "Shall the present form of our government be maintained or changed?"; if, when that question is asked, the two sides of the issue are not equally open for consideration, for advocacy, and for adoption, then it is impossible to speak of our government as established by the free choice of a self-governing people. It is not enough to say that the people of the United States were free one hundred seventy years ago. The First Amendment requires, simply and without equivocation, that they be free now.

The same right to advocate whatever one pleases, in whatever manner one pleases, extending to all opinions and all parties however extreme, applies with equal force to advocacy in writing. It is virtually impossible to establish direct causal links between what is read and what is done, and without such links to overt crime, no written material can be rightly held culpable. A democratic citizenry must be free to read and to publish for others to read, without restraint. Meiklejohn again:

> The principle of the Constitution (that Congress shall make no law abridging the freedom of speech) tells us that we may attack the Constitution in public discussion as freely as we may defend it. It gives us freedom to believe in and to advocate socialism or communism, just as some of our fellow citizens are advocating capitalism. . . . It tells us that such books as Hitler's *Mein Kampf*, or Lenin's *The State and Revolution*, or the *Communist Manifesto* of Engels and Marx, may be freely printed, freely sold, freely distributed, freely read, freely discussed, freely believed, freely disbelieved, throughout the United States. And the purpose of that provision is not to protect the need of Hitler or Lenin or Engels or Marx "to express his opinions on matters vital to him if life is to be worth living." We are not defending the financial

interests of a publisher, or a distributor, or even of a writer. We are saying that the citizens of the United States will be fit to govern themselves under their own institutions only if they have faced squarely and fearlessly everything that can be said in favor of those institutions, everything that can be said against them.

The unabridged freedom of public discussion is the rock on which our government stands. (*Political Freedom,* 1960, p. 76)

The effort to abridge the complete freedom of speech, "only when clear and present danger threatens" or "only in times of serious crisis" misconceives the fundamental character of democratic government. It is in times of crisis that the constitutional protection of the right to speak and publish freely is of particular importance. Under just such circumstances, if violence and illegal specific incitement to violence is to be avoided, there must be public discussion of the issues, easy access to the channels of public communication, open debate, and the possibility of lawful and orderly change. The more tense the situation, the more jealously must constitutional rights be safeguarded and kept inviolate. Without them violence, disorder, even rebellion, are more, not less likely; the suppression of views which threaten to rock the boat will do nothing but hasten its capsize.

Is there not a risk that such unrestricted freedom of speech will result in numbers of people being fooled, misled, or persuaded to act unlawfully or unwisely? Of course there is. That is a risk that democracy, being government of the people by themselves, always runs, and always must run. A democratic community proclaims openly that its citizens are competent to govern themselves, and that they are, collectively, prepared to run the risks of doing so. There is no democracy without some danger of error in public policy. If false claims and fallacious arguments threaten to mislead the citizens of a democracy "the remedy to be applied," as Justice Brandeis wrote in *Whitney v. California* (1927), "is more speech, not enforced silence." *If we are committed to democracy* we will trust with Thomas Jefferson that "the good sense of the people will always be found to be the best army. They may be led astray for a moment, but will soon correct themselves. The people are the only censors of their governors; and even their errors will tend to keep them to the true principles of the institution." Similarly, Alexander Meiklejohn argues that the insistence upon complete freedom of speech is not merely a visionary ideal, but an intelligently developed principle based upon long and bitter experience. From this experience we reach the sober conviction that in a society pledged to self-government, it is never true that, in the long run, the security of the nation is endangered by the freedom of the people. Whatever may be the immediate gains and losses, the dangers to our safety arising from political suppression are always greater than the dangers to that safety arising from political freedom. Suppression is always foolish. Freedom is always wise. That is the faith, the experimental faith, by which we Americans have undertaken to live. . . .

Whenever, in our Western civilization, "inquisitors" have sought to justify their acts of suppression, they have given plausibility to their claims only by appealing to the necessity of guarding the public safety. It is that appeal which the First Amendment intended, and intends, to outlaw. Speaking to the legislature, it says, "When times of danger come upon the nation, you will be strongly tempted, and urged by popular pressure, to resort to practices of suppression such as those allowed by societies unlike our own in which men do not govern themselves. You are hereby forbidden to do so. This nation of ours intends to be free. 'Congress shall make no law . . . abridging the freedom of speech!' " (*Political Freedom,* 1960, p. 112)

I conclude that the only circumstances under which writing or speaking may be held unlawful in a democracy are those in which the utterance in question has been proved to be an immediate cause and integral part of an act otherwise illegal. It must be shown beyond reasonable doubt to have been the deliberate and specific incitement of a non-verbal crime already committed. Until all that can be shown, speech in a democracy cannot be suppressed or punished without subverting the constitution.

10.10 Free speech and the anti-democratic minority

Those who would restrict the freedom of speech frequently resort to the following argument: "What you say about the need for freedom in a democracy is all very well, and should apply to those who accept and support the Constitution [of the United States, or some other democracy]. It does not apply, however, to those who advocate subversion and sabotage, and who seek the violent overthrow of our democratic government. Whether technically citizens or not, they must be silenced, for we cannot allow them to claim the privileges and protection of the Constitution while making every effort to destroy it. To do this is to commit national suicide. Surely neither justice nor good sense requires that we safeguard the freedom of those who, had they the power, would put an end to that freedom for others. Freedoms so abused should be withdrawn, for the sake of democracy."

This argument is as bad as it is common; it misconceives the place of free speech in a democratic society. The objection supposes that the guarantees of a democratic constitution are essentially trades, deals between those who have power and those who do not. "We will protect your right to speak and publish," the implicit covenant might read, "providing you behave yourself, promising always to support and defend us. Should you fail to live up to your part of the bargain, our obligations to protect you cease." This is precisely what the protection of free speech in a democracy is not. The First Amendment to the Constitution of the United States is not a bargain; its guarantees are not given in trade for support of the Constitution, for citizenship, for loyalty to the country, or for anything else whatever. The Constitution protects the free and open expression of all criticisms and all proposals not merely as a privilege to him who writes or speaks, but as a fulfillment of a condition that democracy requires. It is not the loyal citizen alone who is free to speak; all are free to speak—citizen and alien, supporter and critic, loyal and disloyal alike. They must be free to speak because the rest must be free to hear. That is why the political objectives of the speaker, however scurrilous or subversive, are not relevant to the protection the Constitution promises him. If he seeks to put an end to democracy, and to replace it with some form of despotic state, his proposals—in a truly open society—are not likely to meet warm support. If one thinks that that is his hidden but not explicit aim, the surest defense is public argument and exposure. We may be mistaken about him; if we are not, suppression only leaves his true goals in doubt, preventing the people from rejecting them intelligently. In any event, if a democratic government is to be maintained, it is the principles of democracy that must guide the conduct of its citizens and not the principles of its enemies.

Justice Jackson wrote, in *W. Va. State Board of Education v. Barnette* (319 U.S. 624, 1943): "The freedom to differ is not limited to things that do not matter much. That would be a mere shadow of freedom. The test of its substance is the right to differ as to things that touch the heart of the existing order."

This does not mean that we cannot or may not distinguish between heresy and crime. Proof, going beyond any speeches or writing, that criminal acts have been actually attempted or begun, changes the issue from one of free speech to one of guilt or innocence. Serious crimes are not to be lightly or carelessly alleged. When there is good evidence of the commission of such crimes, or of overt attempts to commit them, criminal prosecution should be begun. Short of that evidence, criticism of the government or its leaders or policies, talk about the cruelty and injustice of the existing system, and even the advocacy of lawlessness and revolution must, in a democracy, be protected. The guarantees of free speech apply to moderates and extremists with equal force.

Finally, if we recognize and fully protect the right of an avowedly anti-democratic minority to speak their piece openly, how serious is the danger we then face? That there is some risk of the people freely electing leaders who will put an end to their freedom must be admitted. How grave is this risk? Those who would suppress subversive opinion assume that allowing the public advocacy of revolution is suicide, flatly inconsistent with the preservation of democratic society. This claim is simply false. In long run and short, nothing can better strengthen democracy than the opportunity to hear and evaluate the argument of those who would deprive us of it. What have we to fear? Is it that the citizens of a democracy know too little or too much? Have we so little confidence in the depth of democratic convictions among ourselves as to suppose that only hearing the advocacy of revolutionary views will incite our fellow citizens (never ourselves!) to violence or sabotage? Where democratic principles are so weak as to be safeguarded only by the suppression of serious discontent, there is little hope for the democracy in any case. We may seek to save the democracy by pulling from library shelves all books which advocate, under any circumstances, violence or disobedience to law. We may begin with Marx, Lenin, Hitler, and Mao Tse-Tung, finishing up with the suppression of the works of John Locke and Thomas Jefferson, among the most successful and most explicit of revolutionaries. If it is ridiculous to silence the great revolutionaries, how much more foolish it is to attempt to silence the insignificant ones. The whole enterprise of suppression in a democracy is useless, inconsistent, and absurd.

The principle, that a democracy must be able to defend itself, is sound. But it does not follow from this principle that public advocates of violence or revolution so greatly endanger the society as to require their being silenced. When democratic principles have had a reasonable opportunity to prove their workability they develop a strength that does not need the support of suppressive devices. Too many democrats labor under what James Thurber wisely called "a false sense of insecurity." In a healthy democracy those who advocate the violent overthrow of constitutional government are likely either to be laughed at or treated as beneath contempt. Jefferson said in his First Inaugural Address: "If there be any among us who would wish to dissolve this Union or to change its republican form, let them stand undisturbed as monuments of the safety with which error of opinion may be tolerated where reason is left free to combat it." Nor need we worry that some time in the future we may have cause to fear the success of radicals or revolutionaries. Should the day arrive when injustice is so prevalent in our own society that the advocates of violence or revolution find a large sympathetic audience, on that day we, too, will have every good reason to want to hear them.

The true relation between the utilitarian [10.7] and the conditional [10.8] defenses of free speech may at last be seen. The latter employs the former, but goes beyond it. The arguments of John Stuart Mill show how necessary is unrestricted thought and discussion for the discovery of truth, the correction of error, and the appreciation and defense of truths already possessed. The successful practice of democratic government requires that such intellectual advancement be fully within the power of the members of the community. The utilitarian arguments defending free speech, therefore, *are* the arguments of the democrat. But, he insists, in the context of a working democracy, the utility of free speech cannot be outweighed by danger. He is obliged to defend free speech universally, arguing as follows: if a community intends to govern itself democratically, its members must apply to all of the affairs of that community the conviction that underlies Mill's argument—that truth and human well-being are always best pursued through unrestricted inquiry and debate. Free speech is thus defended as absolute, but the defense itself is conditional; it is conditioned by a prior commitment to democracy, grounded upon the fact that completely free speech is the condition—the constitutional condition—of successful democracy.

Chapter 11

The intellectual conditions of democracy

11.1 Introductory note on intellectual conditions

The intellectual conditions of democracy are those which make possible the application of the citizens' rational capacities to their common problems. Rationality—the native ability to devise and to apply rules or plans of action—is one of the presuppositions of democracy [Chapter 5], and is the foundation of its intellectual conditions. These conditions consist largely of the growth and refinement of that rationality, and of the provision of the materials needed for its social employment. Their realization is essential for the successful direction of the public business through the participation, direct or indirect, of the public.

The intellectual conditions are closely related to other elements of democratic theory, but especially to the constitutional conditions—political freedoms and freedoms of speech—which both support and require the growth of intellect. Indeed, one may view the development of the citizens' intellectual abilities as part of those freedoms, their positive, internal aspect [10.2].

Three major categories of intellectual conditions may be distinguished, each of which I shall discuss in turn: (1) the *provision of information* upon which the citizens of the community may act intelligently, (2) the *education of the citizens* to make possible the intelligent use of information provided, and (3) the *development of the arts of conferral* to make possible the cooperative application of intelligence to community problems.

11.2 The provision of information

If the members of any community are to govern themselves successfully they must have easy access to a reasonably accurate and reasonably complete account of the facts needed for intelligent decisions upon the issues facing them. When inconsistent versions of the facts appear all must be made available to the public. The inadvertent bias of some reporters can be balanced by the efforts of other reporters who may be biased differently; deliberately distorted or colored reports of important factual situations can only be recognized through the scrutiny of other reports.

Facts and figures, although essential, are not by themselves enough. Quantitative detail must be interpreted; facts must be integrated so as to present to the public eye an intelligible picture of past, present, and predicted states of affairs. Honestly differing interpretations of some situations are inevitable; their proper arbiter is an informed public, amply supplied with competing analyses and opinions, each with the evidential support it can muster.

The copious provision of such materials is an intellectual condition of successful democracy. If the members of a community jointly decide important issues—or choose representatives who will do so—without the information intelligent decisions require, or on the basis of deceptive or one-sided accounts, they invite catastrophe. The principle is as true of a self-governing community as it is of a self-governing man. A man must hold himself responsible for the acquisition of the information needed to conduct his own affairs successfully. A community, if it hopes to make democracy succeed, must hold itself responsible for the provision and publication of all the information required for government by general participation. I speak here not simply of the freedom to publish facts and opinions. That freedom is, indeed, a constitutional condition of democracy. Beyond the freedom to publish there must be actual publication; without the fact of publication the freedom to provide it is a practically hollow shell.

When, as in all large democracies, day-to-day administrative decisions are made not by the mass of citizens but by their elected representatives, it is the deputies who must be most completely and accurately informed. Still it is essential that the citizens have the information they need to choose their representatives wisely. A democracy, whether direct or indirect, cannot expect to be governed well if its governing citizenry is kept in ignorance.

To inform a man is to *in-form* him. The word "inform" also means, by virtue of its origin, "to be the formative principle of" and hence, "to animate." This information received gives shape to the issues, helps to form opinions and principles, invites appropriate action. A public fully and correctly informed is a public fully and correctly formed, animated. Where the information provided is distorted or incomplete, so also will be the character of the public policy relying upon that information. The flow of essential information and ready public access to it, are vital conditions for a thriving democracy.

157

A vigorous press must therefore be encouraged and protected in a democracy. The "press" here includes not only newspapers and other periodicals but also radio and television, and other public and private agencies of transmittal. Their vigor is manifested not merely by their freedom to publish, but their quickness to report and eagerness to expose the facts and opinions relevant to public issues. The cultivation of such a free and healthy press is an on-going task of utmost importance and great delicacy in every political democracy.

On the one hand, the independence of newspapers and broadcasters must be maintained and defended. The people need to hear all criticism of their own administration and must see to it that their leaders do not molest a press that attacks the policies and even the personal conduct of those leaders. The news must come to the people honestly and fully. They must never be restricted to hearing only what those in authority want them to hear, or to hearing things only in the way or at the time those authorities find suitable. Such honesty and fullness require a press having courage and strength. These qualities develop only over a period of years, slowly becoming part of the tradition and pride of individual institutions. The great newspapers, periodicals, and broadcasting stations that do exemplify these virtues are few and must be treasured by a democracy, safeguarded against the near-sighted and dangerous effort to control news in order to make a given policy or administration appear wiser or juster than it really is. The news must never be managed.

On the other hand, a democracy must guard against situations in which the private management of the press, entirely unhampered, becomes irresponsible. The absence of regulation may result in a press technically "free," while the provision of full and honest information on public issues remains a condition sorely unfulfilled. The problems met in publishing newspapers provide the best illustration of this side of the problem. Newspapers are not the kind of thing that can be founded, or properly operated by anyone at his pleasure. Collecting and editing the news, organizing and printing it quickly and clearly, distributing the resulting paper widely and speedily—all are expensive and complicated tasks. The result is that most municipal communities can adequately support only one private newspaper; even the largest cities normally support only a very few private papers for general distribution. These brute limitations of private newspaper publication are serious obstacles to public participation that is fully and fairly informed. The ownership and management of the major newspapers (or the only newspaper) in a community by one or two private parties with special economic or political interests can be as menacing to the democracy of that community as can the government management of those newspapers. Particularly is this true when—as in the United States—ownership of newspapers lies commonly in the hands of the very rich. Some papers under such ownership have been published with utmost integrity. But when any single party, governmental or private, controls the flow of information and editorial analysis to a community, democracy in that community is endangered. Yet the circumstances of newspaper publication encourage single-party control. Hence the delicacy of the problem.

There is no simple resolution of it. On the one side, the reporting and analysis of the news should be provided by persons neither in nor of the administration in power, while the freedom to oppose and criticize government policy must be protected by that administration. On the other side, without restricting their essential freedom, the community must oversee the independent agencies which perform this vital informative function so as to insure the fair and adequate publication of all important and conflicting views on issues of community concern. "It is a melancholy truth," Thomas Jefferson wrote, "that a suppression of the press could not more completely deprive the nation of its benefits than is done by its abandoned prostitution to falsehood."

Jefferson had a profound understanding of the central role of the press in a democracy. The way to prevent the breakdown of government by the people, he argued, "is to give them full information of their affairs through the channel of the public papers, and to contrive that those papers should penetrate the whole mass of the people. The basis of our governments being the opinion of the people, the very first object should be to keep that right; and were it left to me to decide whether we should have a government without newspapers, or newspapers without a government, I should not hesitate a moment to prefer the latter. But I should mean that every man should receive those papers and be capable of reading them" (from a letter to Edward Carrington, Paris, 1787). But by the time the country was twenty years older, Jefferson had serious doubts that the public papers were performing their vital functions satisfactorily. In 1807 he expressed (in a letter to John Nowell) intense dissatisfactions with the press of his day. To some of the public prints of our day his criticism is appropriate still. "Nothing can now be believed which is seen in a newspaper. Truth itself becomes suspicious by being put into that polluted vehicle. The real extent of this state of misinformation is known only to those who are in situations to confront facts within their knowledge with the lies of the day. I really look with commiseration over the great body of my fellow citizens who, reading newspapers, live and die in the belief that they have known something of what has been passing in the world in their time; whereas the accounts they have read in newspapers are just as true a history of any other period of the world as of the present except that the real names of the day are affixed to their fables."

In Jefferson's time a healthy press meant, essentially, healthy newspapers; today it means much more. The ubiquity of radio and television, great advances in information storage and retrieval, and all the possibilities of electric circuitry now greatly complicate the task of informing the public fully, with needed balance. Highly sophisticated communication systems, together with the proliferation of transmission and reception stations, greatly ease the task of reaching people; effectiveness in conveying information and opinion increases constantly. At the same time, the very directness and ubiquity of these media magnify the threat to democracy arising from the possibility of their manipulative use.

Where the collection of information is centralized, and its dispersal uniform, as in government news agencies, and in "united" or "associated" news-wire services, radio and television "networks," that threat becomes concrete. When a single account and a single interpretation is distributed in canned form, in the same words, for myriads of local newspapers and broadcasting stations, everyone is put under its spell. All receiving identical information, every mind is formed in the same way; the community loses the varied and competing interpretations of events that democratic process sorely needs. The task of editing the news, of collecting and sifting the sheer mass of materials that pours in every day and of deciding what deserves publication and what calls for emphasis and detail, is one demanding large staffs and monumental energies. How it will be done must in each case depend upon the perspectives and judgments of the editor; no community can expect that job to be done satisfactorily by any single person or institution. The community that fails to devote to this task the breadth of effort and concern it requires will suffer proportionate deterioration of its democracy.

Techniques of control must therefore be devised that will at once protect essential freedoms and guard against their abuse. The democratic community must steer between governmental suppression or distortion in the interest of its own security, and the suppression or distortion that may arise from the private ownership of the press. Some regulatory activity by the community as a whole is essential, above all in the sphere of radio and television broadcasting, where the number of possible channels is clearly limited. What form this regulation ought to take is a question having no universal answer; there are many different practices through which the conditions of democracy may be realized.

The health of the press can always be improved. On issues of public concern, more facts and more accurate accounts of the facts are always in demand. New interpretations of events, differing analyses of contemporary affairs are always arising and might give us new perspectives on our common problems, if we would but have the opportunity to reflect upon them. A democracy, therefore, ought never rest satisfied with the existing means of collecting and distributing information. It must continually foster every agency, old and new, that may assist in reporting and editing the news, and cultivate assiduously every channel through which the information so essential to democracy may flow.

11.3 Democracy and secrecy

Democracy thrives on publicity—public concern with public problems, by members of the general public. Hence we think of it as an essentially public thing, a *res publica*, a republic. Secrecy is the enemy of democracy. There may be occasions on which the demands of self-defense are so pressing and military secrets so crucial to that defense, that information in special categories is made available only to those who must use it. But these occasions should be very much the exception rather than the rule. Democracy is threatened when the alleged requirements of "internal security" close off from the great body of the public the facts regarding the need for, or the costs and probable consequences of far-reaching community enterprises.

What begins as secrecy in the interest of security is soon likely to result in widespread ignorance concerning issues of grave public concern. Intelligent participation is thus undermined. In this way secrecy and distrust of the people become viciously self-justifying. When the people are not informed because it is believed they cannot be trusted to act wisely with that information (or because the information is allegedly not safe to publicize) the capacity of the people to act wisely is further reduced. Then the likelihood increases that yet more information will have to be kept from them for the same reasons. Secrecy invariably tends to create the need for more secrecy. Deliberate restrictions upon the flow of information thus begin by injuring the intellectual conditions of democracy, but may eventuate in the elimination of democracy in some spheres, in the curtailment of its range. The deterioration of the conditions of democracy leads to the deterioration of democracy itself.

One sign of this danger is the discouragement of citizens' inquiries into the facts of any affairs they deem of community importance. When the reports of public agencies are difficult to come by; when public access to the meetings of governmental bodies is forbidden; when administrative decisions are made in closed sessions, and kept from the public; and when all this is done for reasons not publicly explained— the result is the perversion of citizen participation. Not only is the range of democracy then clearly restricted, but over its remaining range its depth is reduced.

The restriction of travel is one form of governmentally imposed secrecy. To limit movement within the country or to forbid or discourage the travel of citizens to certain other lands is direct interference with the citizens' opportunities to learn the facts. Such policies cripple news-reporting agencies and render impossible the honest comparison of societies and policies that a participant in democracy is likely to find extremely helpful. Travel, within and without national boundaries, is not merely a privilege to be granted or withheld by the government at its pleasure. It is a needed element in the intellectual growth of citizens. Travel *is* broadening, and citizens with breadth of experience are essential for democracy. The unrestricted travel of citizens and visitors is part of the intellectual conditions of self-government. Where such travel is feared or curtailed, there is reason to wonder if the democracy is healthy, or even if it is genuine. Of the great Athenian democracy Pericles proudly said, "The gates of our city are flung open to the world."

11.4 The education of citizens

An educated citizenry is the second major intellectual condition of democracy. It is a truism that where the powers of government lie ultimately in the hands of the governed, their education is essential to the wise direction of that government. Even copious, accurate, and impartially presented information will be of little use to rational citizens who have not learned how to absorb and apply it and who have not the skills needed to deal with their common problems. Education does not guarantee wise policy, of course, but without an educated citizenry democracy stands little chance of lasting success.

How much education does the operation of a democracy require of its members? The answer depends upon the nature and difficulty of the problems faced by that community. So long as the character of that community's problems is largely within the scope of its citizens' understanding, intelligent participation will be possible for them—supposing the other conditions of democracy met. Even in relatively primitive communities, offering a little or no formal education, democracy may be sustained if the rough and tumble of the citizens' circumstances forces an education upon them adequate to cope with their common problems. Formal schooling is far from the only measure of education; in many communities—in classical Greece for one example, and on the American frontier for another—democracy could succeed with a minimum of institutional support of education. So it is still in some small, remote communities of the present day.

Similarly, in democratic communities of a non-political kind, only that education is essential which renders the members of the community able to deal with the issues of that community. Members of a democratically organized club or special interest group must be at a level of sophistication only high enough to evaluate proposals concerning the common needs of that club or group. For the members of a chess club to conduct their affairs democratically the education required concerns chiefly such matters as the conditions of chess play, the nature and problems of chess tournaments, and the like. The problems of a democratic religious congregation will be far more varied and profound, but will not normally exceed the intellectual capacities of any normal, stable adult who adheres to the traditions of that religion. The education that is democracy's condition is always relative to the problems of a given democracy.

The educational demands of a contemporary, national democracy are high. These demands are mitigated, however, by the fact that most of the more technical issues facing the national community are directly handled not by the members at large, but by their representatives; hence the education chiefly required for the members is that needed to select representatives wisely. A citizen cannot be expected to know, and does not need to know, all that is necessary to resolve every community problem. But he must be able to judge the solutions and the consequences of the solutions proposed by others. One who is unable by himself to prepare the feast, as Aristotle points out, may yet be very competent in appraising it [14.2], but that competence needs to be developed. The cook needs a fuller education in culinary technique; he for whom the cook toils needs an educated palate. Even in representative democracies, therefore, the education of the members is a condition of success; the citizens must be intellectually prepared for the tasks that participation in their government imposes.

The word "educate" comes from the Latin term meaning "to lead forth"; education is the leading forth of a man, drawing the best out of him and developing his skills in dealing with his world. Education that is the condition of democracy is intellectual development aimed at successful cooperative coping with a common social world. The intellectual skills required by democracy are of four related but distinguishable kinds: *(1)* practical education; *(2)* basic education; *(3)* technical education; *(4)* humane education.

Practical education is preparation for dealing with the everyday problems of human intercourse. It is the development of that "common sense" so often remarked as essential for the wise conduct of human affairs. It is common, being the natural outcome of a normal upbringing, and the more or less well developed talent of most human beings. For those so sheltered from the problems of life as to be without practical education democracy would not be feasible. Such deficiency is happily rare. When the chief problems of the community can be resolved by the application of common sense alone—when they closely resemble problems of individual life writ large—education acquired through work or family life may be enough. But the problems of most political democracies are more complex and more difficult than these. Issues of war and peace, economic growth and social welfare, public health and population control, require for resolution citizens with much more than practical education.

Basic education is training in the handling of the fundamental intellectual tools of men, letters and numbers. Its simplest measure is the literacy rate, the percentage of those in the community who can read and write. Trivial this may seem to those reading this book—but basic education is sadly lacking among vast majorities in political communities around the globe. Even in relatively advanced nations there are millions of persons (in the United States over ten million at midcentury) who remain essentially illiterate. Illiterate citizens cannot read the newspaper, cannot be fully informed on the alternatives presented to them, cannot effectively criticize or make proposals of their own.

They cannot even read the ballot. When, therefore, under some auto-cratic rule, the literacy rate shows no significant improvement, we may infer that any claim that "power is being held only to prepare the ground for democracy" is almost certainly fraudulent. Where basic education is missing, democracy may be professed, but can hardly be realized.

Technical education, requiring years of study and specialization, is essential for those in the community called upon to grapple with the narrow issues for which all cannot be prepared. Such education is neither possible nor desirable for everyone. The political community need not consist of scientists and engineers, but it cannot do without them. For a political democracy to succeed, therefore, it must develop, among its citizens, those special capacities its intelligent management requires. As the technical complexity of its problems increases, so must the capacities of its technical servants, as well as the capacities of the citizenry to appraise their services in its behalf.

Humane education is least common and least well appreciated. A democratic community must choose ends as well as means, and to do this wisely its members must exhibit—if not universally at least widely —a considerable measure of humane enlightenment. Monies will be expended and technical skills employed only on those affairs that the members, directly or through their representatives, recognize as de-serving concern. Experts on technical matters are important; more im-portant is the wisdom of those who hire the experts, and those who select and influence the men who do the hiring. In a democracy the wisdom and humaneness of policy depends, ultimately, on the wisdom and humaneness of the citizens who determine it.

If this sounds commonplace, one must reflect upon the contrast between the actual expenditures of effort and money by powerful de-mocracies, and their professed goals. Rich nations, America in the forefront, continue to spend fantastic sums—great chunks of their pub-lic treasuries—on military arsenals whose overwhelming destructive capacities almost pass human comprehension, and are matched only by their outright wastefulness. Concurrently, these nations devote the tiniest fractions of their energies to the strategies and problems of inter-national peace, to genuine disarmament, to the realities of global popu-lation growth and global undernourishment. The problems of fertility, hunger, health, environmental control, employment, and international harmony are so grave as to demand rapid solution on pain of world catastrophe. This message has been broadcast repeatedly. The citizens hear but do not listen, continuing to act as though the time to find so-lutions is inexhaustible. Repeated and gross failures by some national democracies to make wise assessment of the order of priorities in com-munity life does not augur well for their future.

Above all it is widespread education in the humanities that is es-sential for political democracy. The study of history, the appreciation of great literature, the practice and criticism of the arts, the understand-ing of philosophical inquiry—these are the intellectual requirements of a people who would wisely govern themselves. Too often priority is given to scientific or technical studies out of fear that national prestige or military advantage may otherwise be lost. The greater danger is that, in failing to develop a citizenry wise in choosing ends and making judg-ments, the capacity will be lost to direct the skills already possessed. The needs for humane study, widely undertaken, cannot be overem-phasized—but it is just here that the educational systems of democra-cies are often weakest. This is our case in America, and we may very soon have cause to regret it sorely. Thomas Jefferson wrote: "If a na-tion expects to be ignorant and free in a state of civilization, it expects what never was and never will be."

11.5 The arts of conferral

If participation in government consisted solely in a multitude of private acts, each member acting independently on the basis of his best knowl-edge and to the best of his ability, information and education might be all that was needed in the intellectual sphere. Effective participation, however, although requiring independence of mind, demands also the cooperative use of fact and opinion. Depth of participation depends largely upon the interaction of men and minds; that interaction, in turn, requires special intellectual skills. Taken together, these skills are the arts of conferral.

To meet the many needs and interests—conflicting, overlapping, diverse—within a community, its several members must engage in con-tinuing interchange. Opposition between parties must be discussed and argued to be fully appreciated; the effects of proposed legislation upon competing interests must be talked over and anticipated. The larger needs of the entire community must be jointly investigated, solutions jointly appraised. Only so can the indvidual hope to participate effec-tively in government over the several sectors of a community, and over the run of years. Discussion, criticism, argument, intellectual exchange of every sort—not merely the freedom to engage in these, but their actual practice—are, taken together, a third set of intellectual conditions of successful democracy. Without these arts of conferral, it is true, some participation is possible, but only with them can democracy be mature.

Development of the skills of communication will always remain, therefore, a central aim of education for democracy. Any joint effort to deal with communal concerns depends upon communication—through papers and books and electronic media, of course—but equally, through direct interpersonal conference as well. Democracy needs members who have learned to talk clearly and to the point; who listen attentively and with comprehension; who can write lucidly and effectively. Citizens cannot be mere listening posts; they must be able to transmit their own ideas and those of others; they must be able to express their own concerns and perspectives. Successful conference requires genuine exchange, the capacity of the conferee to understand another's position and grasp the force of his arguments. These are sophisticated intellectual skills; they develop informally, but also require effort and training. They are greatly needed, but far from universal even in the best of political communities.

Cultivation of the arts of communication is an unrelenting demand the citizens of a democracy must place upon themselves. In part they fulfill it through formal institutions—public schools, libraries, museums, universities, foundations, and so on. Such institutions are concrete manifestations of a community's concern to develop and sustain the intellectual capacities of its members. But communication must extend well beyond and below formal institutions. It must pervade the community at every level—through public lectures, discussion groups and forums, street harangues and committee meetings, and above all in private conversation. We can learn from Athens here. Benefitting from tools of communication of which the Athenians could hardly dream, we have allowed the arts of conversation—not to speak of incisive argument or effective oratory—to degenerate badly. Good conversation is a verbal 'give and take'; it can occur only when the participants know how to give what is in them, and how to take and use what is offered. Conversation is the finest and probably the most effective of communicatory instruments; a democratic society is one in which the members are in frequent *con verse*, turning ideas and proposals about, one with another.

A democratic society is a talking society. It is therefore fitting that the institution most perfectly characteristic of a working democracy is called a parliament. Its name identifies its original and proper character as a place for talk, for speaking with one another. One great function of a parliament is to talk things out, to provide the place where opponents may argue, parley until some mutually satisfactory way of proceeding can be found. That is not the whole of its purpose, but if much good talk does not go on there, it is not likely to be succeeding in its tasks. A parliament is a talk-fest. Those who criticize it for being that do not understand the essential conditions of democratic process.

In this parliamentary spirit the members of a democracy must participate in their government—largely by talking, listening, reading, writing, and arguing about community affairs. In unions and business organizations, clubs and fraternal orders, street cars and street fairs, at ball games and cocktail parties, in newspapers and periodicals of every stripe, in books and handbills, and letters to editors and friends—in every reasonable way the members of a democracy must be forever exchanging ideas and opinions, forging thereby the links of their community. *Idiotes* was the Greek term for one who refrains from all such participation, who lives in a community but concerns himself with his own affairs only. He will be ignorant, dumb, truly an idiot in the pejorative sense as well. Of the democracy in Athens, Pericles said:

> Our citizens attend both to public and private duties, and do not allow absorption in their own various affairs to interfere with their knowledge of the city's. We differ from other states in regarding the man who holds aloof from public life not as 'quiet' but as useless; we decide or debate, carefully and in person, all matters of policy, holding, not that words and deeds go ill together, but that acts are foredoomed to failure when undertaken undiscussed. For we are noted for being at once most adventurous in action and most reflective beforehand. Other men are bold in ignorance, while reflection will stop their onset. But the bravest are surely those who have the clearest vision of what is before them, glory and danger alike, and yet notwithstanding go out to meet it. (Thucydides, *The Peloponnesian War*, II, 40)

Finally, the realization of the intellectual conditions of democracy is a matter never easy to assess. Figures regarding literacy rates, school and university attendance, library book circulation, and the like, are helpful indexes, but not conclusive. The quality of interpersonal communication is hardly measurable in quantitative terms; it is a complex function of native capacities, the degree of their development, and the inclination to apply them. Jacques Barzun suggests that "the temper of democratic culture is tested at every dinner table and in every living room—just as much as at school, in the pulpit, or on the platform" (*Teacher in America*, 1945, p. 239). By this test national democracies are generally poorer than we like to think, while local democracies are often better than we suppose.

The failure to realize fully enough the intellectual conditions of democracy is often the cause of catastrophic errors by democratic governments. Some believe that mistakes by democracies are the rule rather than the exception. Walter Lippmann, for example, has claimed that "prevailing public opinion has been destructively wrong at the critical junctures." He continues: "The people have imposed a veto upon the judgments of informed and responsible officials. They have compelled the governments, which usually knew what would have been wiser, or was necessary, or was more expedient, to be too late with too little, or too long with too much, too pacifist in peace and too bellicose in war, too neutralist or appeasing in negotiation or too intransigent. Mass opinion has acquired mounting power in this century. It has shown itself to be a dangerous master of decisions when the stakes are life and death" (*The Public Philosophy*, 1955, pp. 23–24).

The picture is drawn too bleakly. But in any case the evidence, if it could support such criticisms, would serve to show not that the people are invariably bad governors, but that they have made grave mistakes when ill-educated or misinformed. The remedy for this danger lies not in the abandonment of democracy, leaving the government in hands likely to be no more intelligent but far less scrupulous, but in the improvement of its intellectual conditions. Jefferson put the matter concisely and elegantly: "I know of no safe depository of the ultimate powers of the society but the people themselves, and if we think them not enlightened enough to exercise their control with a wholesome discretion, the remedy is not to take it from them, but to inform their discretions by education."

Chapter 12

The psychological conditions of democracy

12.1 Psychological traits as dispositions

Most fundamental of all are the psychological conditions of democracy —the traits of character and habits of mind that members of a community must possess if they are to make democracy work. Ultimately, the locus of these conditions is in the internal state of the individual citizens, their psyches. But as a practical matter the emphasis must fall upon the external, behavioral manifestations of character traits. These traits may properly be viewed as dispositions, tendencies to behave in certain ways. We may say of a man that he has a friendly disposition, or an angry one, meaning that he is most often disposed to act in certain fashions; we then generalize in describing his disposition. The psychological conditions of democracy are, in this sense, *dispositional*; they are the habits and attitudes which dispose the several members of a community to act in ways that self-government requires.

Other conditions of democracy depend essentially upon these. Neither educational institutions, nor informational media, nor the arts of communication are likely to be well developed or properly used if appropriate traits of character are not common among the citizenry. Constitutional conditions too—protection of the right to participate, and especially of the right to speak freely and criticize the government openly—are likely to be underdeveloped, or abused, if the geat majority of members are not temperamentally disposed to conduct themselves with the restraint such protections entail.

Although the dispositional conditions have (with some exceptions) no formal embodiment in laws, documents, or institutions, they lie behind these and support them. Ultimately, the conduct of the courts and the legislatures, the editing of newspapers, and the honoring of constitutions all rest upon the character of the citizens. The machinery of democracy is lubricated by the manners of its members. The absence of external embodiment for these conditions is simply a consequence of their being dispositions, having their locus in individuals and individual acts. That locus largely accounts for the great difficulties met in seeking to promote them, or to measure their presence in any given community.

Smooth functioning institutions of certain kinds will be indicative of certain widespread traits, but the traits themselves may be manifested in an unlimited variety of ways. The lines between these dispositional conditions of democracy and other conditions they support cannot be sharply drawn.

How widely the dispositional conditions must be exhibited by the members of a democratic community cannot be precisely specified. Quantitative analysis in this sphere is notoriously difficult, and its use is much complicated by other variable factors—the size of the community, its external circumstances, and the degree to which other conditions of democracy are fulfilled in it. We can say, surely, that not every member of a community need display these dispositional traits, nor need any portion of the community display them constantly. But democracy does require that a goodly percentage of the participating members must exhibit these dispositions a goodly percentage of the time. Especially must they do so at critical times, and with regard to controversial issues. The psychological conditions of democracy, like all others, are realized only in various degrees; their less satisfactory fulfillment will lead, by degrees, to the less satisfactory realization of democracy.

The set of dispositional traits I shall discuss could be otherwise arranged. They overlap, are not sharply distinct from one another, tend to support one another. Although not exhaustive in detail they include, if generously understood, the major dispositions democracy requires. Together they constitute what has been called "the democratic frame of mind" (Z. Barbu in *Democracy and Dictatorship*, 1956).

Virtues of character are commonly treated as substantive and referred to with nouns—e.g., honesty, justice, courage. This can mislead by encouraging the hypostatization of what are essentially modifiers. Virtues are best understood not as things, but as ways of describing persons (that they are honest, just, brave) or their acts (which were performed honestly, justly, bravely). We risk the confusion, putting these modifying concepts in substantive form, because we are often attending chiefly not to the act or person described, but to the ways in which he is or should be acting. In order to generalize about these ways, we talk as if each way were a thing; this, however, is only a manner of speaking or writing..

In what follows I shall, for clarity, sometimes refer to these psychological conditions in adjectival form (e.g., "The democrat needs to be ————," where the blank is filled by an appropriate dispositional

171

term); sometimes in adverbial form (e.g., "The democrat needs to act ——————ly); sometimes, too, I refer to these traits as nouns. But it is with reference to the character of the citizens that these traits are of chief interest here. Citizens are properly so described when these traits identify the normal patterns of their conduct, when they are disposed to act in the ways indicated. Not things to possess, but dispositions to act in certain ways constitute these psychological conditions. Whatever the mode of expression, I am concerned not merely with a catalogue of assorted virtues, but with the specific dispositions, whether virtues or not, that the successful operation of a democracy requires that its citizens manifest.

12.2 Fallibilistic citizens

The citizens of a democracy need to be fallibilistic. Not just fallible; this they surely are, and were they not democracy would not be necessary. It does not take much experience in the world to realize how prone men are to mistake even on matters of the highest import, and in opinions they hold with the deepest conviction. Human fallibility is taken for granted, not argued, here. Democracy, then, needs citizens who are conscious of their own fallibility, who realize the inescapability of human error.

Fallibilism is a dispositional trait when it is manifested in the conduct of persons with regard to their acceptance or rejection of beliefs and opinions. The democrat needs to develop a frame of mind in which no position—respecting facts, or doctrines, or moral principles—is treated in practice as absolutely beyond correction. Said Cromwell: "Is it infallibly agreeable with the Word of God, all that you say? Think it possible, on the bowels of Christ, that you may be mistaken."

Fallibilism does not entail the denial that some beliefs or principles are true, and ought to be defended; it entails only the denial of the infallibility of any claim for truth, no matter who the claimant. Neither does it entail that the democrat cannot feel certain of anything. He can, of course; there are an untold number of truths about which most men feel certain, and on which they base their everyday lives. Some of these are trivial—that the house key is under the doormat, or that the Post Office will be open at noon; others are far from trivial—that equals ought not be treated unequally, that love is better and healthier than hate, and so on. Many such opinions one may never find reason to doubt seriously. Such feelings of certainty are consistent with fallibilism, so long as one recognizes the possibility that he may be in error.

This attitude has important consequences. If all opinions are subject to error, no decision on any issue of importance ought to be made without at least giving audience to the competing positions. In a sense fallibilism is the most basic of all the dispositions of the democrat—for in rejecting the absolute wisdom of any party it encourages participation in decision-making by all concerned. If any person or group could be known to be infallible it would be only rational to place the government of all affairs in his (or their) hands. For the fallibilistic citizen argument on fundamental matters is not only permissible but very much in order. For democrats, who must expect always to be arguing about fundamental matters, that attitude is essential.

The attitudinal condition of fallibilism is integrally related to the intellectual condition of publicity [11.3]. The need for a manifold of open channels of information flows from the conviction that no single source, in government or out, can be fully trusted. A free press may not logically presuppose fallibilism, but it is not likely to prosper where that temper is absent. The converse is also true, but less obvious. Where competing reports and opinions are not there to be heard, all channels presenting but one view, the inclination to make critical appraisals will atrophy, the spirit of fallibilism will wither.

Nothing in his fallibilism commits the democrat to the childish view that all opinions are of equal worth. They surely are not. Many beliefs are mistaken, some are foolish; convinced that this is so in particular cases, a democrat must be prepared to defend his convictions. But what seems foolish to one person at one time, may seem wise to another, or at a different time. Precisely because opinions are not of equal worth the democrat must be disposed to hear them in contest, in order that truth and error may be exposed. "Our whole theory of freedom of speech and opinion for all citizens," wrote George Bernard Shaw, "rests not on the assumption that everybody is right, but on the certainty that everybody is wrong on some point on which somebody else is right, so that there is a public danger in allowing anybody to go unheard" (*Socialism for Millionaires*, 1901).

Whether "skepticism," then, is the proper attitude of the democrat depends on how we understand that attitude. If it is intended to suggest that there is no truth, and that all claims to it are equally vain, that attitude will do more to obstruct than to support democracy and is surely not what fallibilism involves. But if by skepticism one means the insistence upon a critical review of all important beliefs, it is a consequence of fallibilism, and is appropriate for the democrat. He seeks to objectify rational inquiry in the community context, and the very fact of such inquiry supposes that some knowledge is attainable, even by fallible beings. The practice of democracy, therefore, supposes that some judgments are indeed better than others, and that making that determination is a never ending task in governing. Successful performance of that task by the membership at large requires that they be fallibilistic.

12.3 Experimentally minded citizens

The citizens of a democracy need to be experimentally minded. Faced with problematic situations, with which all government is replete, citizens need to be disposed to put a variety of proposed solutions to test —the test of argument first, but also, when appropriate, the test of experimental practice. Experimentalism commits one to no specific doctrines or outcomes, of any stripe. It entails only that all serious proposals for community action be seriously entertained and that their feasibility and desirability be objectively determined, where appropriate by actual trial. Experimentalism and fallibilism go hand in hand. The latter is an awareness of the ubiquity of error; the former is the disposition to apply methods that will expose errors. Once granted that no person or party is infallible or in possession of the whole of the truth, it remains to act in such a way as to remedy to the deficiencies in our knowledge. The best antidote for error or ignorance is an experimental and systematic inquiry into the merit of the several candidates for belief or adoption.

In the sphere of the natural sciences receptiveness to new ideas, a willingness to try them, and an honest appraisal of what works and what does not, are all essential for successful advance. Experimentalism is the combination of these. It is the controlling attitude of the intelligent scientist, and a leading attitude of the intelligent statesman. In a scientific investigation the candidates before us are competing theories, or hypotheses, and their advocates; in a democratic polity the candidates before us are competing principles or policies, represented by persons or parties. As it is the nature of scientific inquiry to weigh carefully and impartially the evidence for and against each candidate, so it is the nature of a democratic process to weigh, with all the care the circumstances will permit, the merits of alternative proposals or nominees.*

An experimental frame of mind both requires education and supports it. Here again the dispositional and intellectual conditions are closely linked [11.4]. Educational institutions cannot be fully or deeply used where the inclination to treat problems experimentally is missing; and the cultivation of that experimental temper requires the objective support of schools, libraries, museums, and all the arts of communication. Experimental inquiry demands training and sophistication—training to know how others have proceeded and what they have accomplished, sophistication to extend these efforts and to grasp the consequences of what is newly learned.

Similarly, the dispositional conditions of democracy and its constitutional conditions intertwine. Central to the latter is the freedom of speech, within which I distinguished earlier the freedom to oppose and the freedom to propose. They stand to one another in the constitution of the community much as do fallibilism and experimentalism in the constitution of the citizen; the pairs are tied. It is the conviction that all are fallible that supports the freedom to oppose. That support is reciprocal, since a people can hardly be expected to cultivate a behavioral trait whose outward manifestations meet with assorted punishments. Likewise, the conviction that empirical test is essential to rational inquiry supports and is supported by the practice of presenting and defending concrete alternatives—whether they be candidates or lines of action—in community practice. This experimental spirit, foreclosing no reasonable line of practical inquiry, is widely shared in the community of scientists and is fundamental to success there. In like manner that spirit must be widely shared in any democratic community and is essential for its continuing success.

---

*Experimentalism implies a general willingness to modify beliefs or theories in the light of new evidence, when necessary. The experimental attitude involves a readiness to revise, and is therefore essentially revisionist. It is worth noting that what is, in Marxist-Leninist dogmatics, a prime heresy—"revisionism"—is for the democratic process a leading virtue. Ironically, Marx himself labored arduously to adjust his theories to the social and economic facts of the world, and to test his theories against those facts. He never tried to prove anything about the world by quoting from authorities who wrote in the previous century, nor did he hesitate to revise his own views when he found them in error. His contemporary disciples would do well to follow his example.

12.4 Critical citizens

The citizens of a democracy need to manifest a critical attitude toward their leaders. Ideally, the relations between the members of a community and their elected officers will exhibit mutual confidence and good faith. But successful democracy requires that the confidence of the citizens be tempered by a dose of critical spirit, by a reasonable measure of distrust of all authorities.

The plural form—authorities—is used advisedly here. It is not authority as such that democrats need to distrust; that will be solidly based on the participation of the membership if the democracy is genuine. The respect of citizens for the authority of law is in fact encouraged by democracy; the laws of a democracy are, in no metaphysical sense, their laws [14.5]. But it does not follow that all who play a direct role in formulating the laws, or enforcing them, possess great wisdom. Legitimate authority deserves respect and receives it in the form of general obedience to law. Particular authorities may or may not prove worthy of respect. To determine that, they and their acts are always properly subject to the critical review of those whose delegated power they use.

No degree of intelligence or good faith exempts the legislator or executive from all error. The complexity of his tasks, the number of issues upon which he must pass judgment, the exigencies of election to office, the pressures exerted upon him by conflicting interests among his constituents, and the delicacy of his trust—these and other factors make it at least as likely that the public officer will err in doing his job as that anyone else will err in his. But power has a tendency to dull the awareness of elected leaders of their own proneness to mistake. And the mistakes of the powerful, because of their power, are the more serious. To reduce the frequency of errors and to speed remedy for their injurious consequences when it is needed, the public acts and judgments of elected officers must be subjected to constant public criticism.

There is a natural tendency to suppose that "they"—the holders of office, the men of fame and public esteem—are in so much the best position to pass judgment on affairs of consequence that their decisions on such affairs are not to be questioned. The premise is reasonable, but the conclusion does not follow. The judgments of leaders should be respected, but they must also be questioned, else control over the conduct of public officials is lost, and with it the continued sovereignty of the general public.

The authorities will doubtless find this constant criticism none too pleasant. They, after all, have been chosen by the public to do the job of law-making and law-enforcement; they bear the responsibility for seeing that it is done properly. It is easy to criticize, not so easy to perform. Public officers are sure to resent accusations of negligence or error and particularly to resent the shadows that such accusations cast upon their own integrity. Nevertheless vigorous criticism must go on. It is not, at least in most cases, the integrity of the officeholder but his judgment that is being questioned, and that process of questioning is one to which he opens himself by choosing to run for office. Constant criticism ought to be the lot of every official in a democracy. It is a burden, but it must be borne as part of the price to be paid for good government. For the conscientious officeholder there is recompense enough in the knowledge that his job is being done properly and in the rewards and honors that a grateful public may eventually bestow. We need have little fear that constancy of criticism will result in a dearth of candidates for public office.

It is wise, therefore, to give deliberate support to persons whose official business is the criticism of elected leaders. The British custom of paying the leader of the minority party in view of his special responsibilities is one concrete expression of this spirit, also splendidly manifested in the very name there given to the party out of power: "Her Majesty's Loyal Opposition." Loyalty, in a democracy, does not entail agreement—least of all hypocritical agreement—with current leadership. Support of one's government not on particular issues but with respect to ultimate goals is a more worthy form of loyalty. A democracy needs a loyal opposition, and is deeply wise to honor it.

Intelligent distrust of leadership is further manifested in the disposition always to regard the power of authorities as delegated, derivative, and therefore limited by the ultimate judgment of the electors. Concretely, this is given force by limiting the tenure of elected officers, sometimes to the point of outlawing self-succession. New leaders give opportunity for experiment with new policy; but more fundamentally, short tenure assures the return of power to the membership and helps to protect it against abuse. Instruments may also be devised for punishing abuse even between elections—impeachment, or recall. Critical citizens must be prepared to give muscle to their criticism.

The spirit with which leaders are personally regarded will also exhibit the strength of this critical temper. Absolute monarchs and dictators are regarded by their subjects more with awe than with respect.

They are glorified by grandiloquent titles (Royal Highness, Redeemer, Maximal Leader); addressed indirectly by reference to their alleged magnificence (Your Majesty, Your Excellency); dressed in ornate robes and uniforms; adorned with crowns, scepters, and medals; housed in palaces and seated on thrones. If fortunate enough to die in the good graces of their subjects they are often deified in death; some, like the Pharaohs of Egypt or Emperors of Japan, may even be worshipped as gods before they die. If all power in the community rests in Caesar, it is understandable that the seat of such power be glorified, its occupant awed and feared. Democratic leaders, on the other hand, exercise their powers for designated periods as elected occupants of offices created by the citizens for their own ends. For having won the confidence and support of their fellow citizens in being chosen for office, honor and praise are due them—but glory not. Respect is owed them; awe in their presence is out of place; deification is absurd. The leader in a democracy has specified duties and prerogatives flowing from the post to which he has been appointed by his constituents, to be reelected or replaced in office at their pleasure. In the strictest sense he is answerable to them. In a word, the democratic leader is a public servant. Where democracy is healthy, he will take seriously his role as servant to the community, and will really be so considered by his fellow citizens. A proper admonition to the members of any democracy is given in the Gospel according to Matthew (20:25–27): "Ye know that the princes of the Gentiles exercise dominion over them, and they that are great exercise authority upon them. But it shall not be so among you; but whosoever will be great among you, let him be your minister; and whosoever will be chief among you, let him be your servant."

12.5 Flexible citizens

The citizens of a democracy need to adjust themselves to constant changes, great and small, in the conditions of their lives. Democracy requires citizens who are flexible not only in the sense that they are prepared to tolerate change, but in the more positive sense that they are disposed to approve of a changing society and are attuned for life in it. The flexible citizen sees change as natural; he expects his circumstances to be altering from year to year—even from day to day in some respects —and he is not surprised when these changes impel him to make correlative changes in his leaders, his policies, his plans, and even the patterns of his life.

Flexibility does not mean a love of change simply for the sake of change. It does involve the rejection of that irrational conservatism which stubbornly maintains fixed patterns of conduct in the face of good reasons for change. What Jeremy Bentham called "the Chinese argument"—that some practice should be maintained because that is the way it has always been done—is spurious in a democracy. The flexible citizen may respect the institutions of the past, but he does not worship them; he is prepared to alter them when alterations are called for by new developments in objective circumstances.

Intelligible change presupposes that some aspects of the situation remain unchanged; where everything changes at once there is only sheer replacement and chaos. The democratic community needs continually to be deciding, therefore, what elements within itself are really worth conserving, and what need to be eliminated or improved. The willingness to recognize needs for change, even fundamental change, and the capacity to adjust to the new life that the citizens may themselves create, is the flexibility that is a psychological condition of full democracy.

12.6 Realistic citizens

The citizens of a democracy need to be conscious of the imperfection of all human institutions; realism is the disposition to act and judge in the light of that consciousness. Standards by which representatives are judged, for example, should be high, but realistic democrats will understand that in selecting deputies or leaders a choice must always be made among differing combinations of virtues and vices. What is true of men is equally true of their work. Realists will be aware that there are no final solutions to social problems, that the process of adjusting and improving human institutions goes on without end. Reform never being completed, citizens must resign themselves to life under imperfect government if democracy is to work.

Realism manifests itself in a healthy democracy as an attitude balanced between perfectionism and despair. Despair with humankind and their works leads to the abandonment of the labors of supervision, and therewith the abandonment of the essential tasks of self-government. Perfectionism leads to the endless rejection of reasonable alternatives, until at last problems become unsolvable without violence, or until discontent with the imperfections of democracy leads to its overthrow. Between these extremes a reasonable mean must be struck. Democracy rests upon men and institutions that are never flawless. Yet any flaw may be the object of concern, and if very serious may probably be ameliorated. The disposition to behave reasonably in seeking this amelioration, to be constantly dissatisfied but never in despair, I call realism. If the members of a community cannot maintain realistic expectations in appraising their own works and the works of other men, they will not long be able to govern themselves.

12.7 Compromising citizens

The citizens of a democracy need to be disposed to compromise their differences. No condition of democracy is more important than this, for where there are no compromises there is no democracy, and there will be no compromises unless the parties concerned are disposed to reach them.

Conflicting human interests are inevitable in any community; rarely will it be possible to resolve them in ways entirely satisfactory to all. In a self-governing community it becomes the task of the members—directly when they are few, indirectly through representatives when they are many—to work out conflict resolutions that will be at least tolerable to all, if perfectly satisfactory to none. The process of forming policies and framing laws by balancing the pushes and pulls of competing interests within the community is the process of compromise. Compromise is the procedural heart of democracy; no body of men who find this procedure unhappy in principle can hope to rest content with democratic government or to make it succeed.

Members of a community who would be successful in self-government must learn that solutions to common problems can rarely if ever be simple or one-sided. Government through the participation of opposing interests requires not only that this be intellectually grasped but that participants be disposed in practice to implement this understanding, to refrain from demanding solutions that yield complete satisfaction. The disposition to compromise differences is a behavioral correlate of a realistic frame of mind.

The refusal to compromise, to accept anything less than unconditional surrender, is a trait often exhibited by the heroes of stories written specially for children. Justice Holmes once characterized the mentality that approves such conduct: "It is not enough for the knight of romance that you agree that his lady is a nice girl—if you do not admit that she is the best God ever made or will make you must fight"

("Natural Law" in *Collected Legal Papers,* 1921). Such thinking is literally childish; members of a community who so conduct themselves will not be successful at self-government, and will be treated like children by those who come to have power over them. The politically mature will seek intermediate solutions, giving some satisfaction to the several conflicting interests. Democracy requires that its members, by and large, exhibit this kind of maturity.

The contrast of democracy with autocracy is sometimes likened to that of a raft with a full-rigged sailing ship. The former travels safely but slowly, bobbing with the waves, at times moving backwards, in storms awash, the feet of its passengers often wet. The latter travels swiftly and grandly, with comfort and assurance, sometimes to encounter disaster on rocks whose passage the raft could safely have managed. The simile, though overdrawn, is quite appropriate in contrasting the modes of conflict resolution under the two forms. Dictatorial resolutions proclaimed with confidence, are likely to be neat and straightforward, their movement swift, their direction unambiguous. But the many interests in a community do not generally wish to go in precisely the same direction. The efficiency and decisiveness of autocracy is achieved at great cost; its grandeur may hide beneath the surface mounting anger and discontent, basic instability. Democratic solutions, emerging through compromise, are more raft-like. They do not resolve problems grandly and rarely with efficiency or neatness. They may not even move in one direction unambiguously. Arising from the pressures of competing interests, however, and offering some satisfaction to each, they are likely to ease the most serious tensions and to endure through crises that no absolutism could survive.

So we say of democratic communities that, while their institutions may be a patchwork and their progress uncertain, they generally manage to muddle through. Realistic democrats will be resigned to this muddling. The chief thing is that internal conflicts be resolved without intolerable sacrifice demanded of anyone or intolerable inequities imposed. That comes only through compromise.

Some hold that the conscious adoption of compromise as a political method is morally wrong. It is wrong, they say, because it is hypocrisy to compromise when one knows—or at least firmly believes—one's principles to be altogether right and just. Only by resolute support can these principles be expected to emerge triumphant, and such resoluteness is undermined by any disposition to compromise.

To this I reply: one's knowledge of the truth and justice of his principles, or his firm belief in them, is counterbalanced within the community by others who also know, or firmly believe, that other principles, in direct conflict with his own, are just and true. The uncompromising critic cannot grant the force of this just because he is utterly convinced of the wrongheadedness, if not the outright evil, of his opponents, and because he is determined to triumph at whatever cost. This stance threatens democracy. Democracy presupposes community [4.6]. No community can expect to remain united and effectively self-governing if one of its segments is determined to vanquish another, for between victor and vanquished there can be no true community. Where the unrelenting defense of irreconcilable positions is more important to the opposing parties than the maintenance of community between them, that community is doomed. Re-establishment of "union" by the force of arms may be possible, but the war is likely to be bitter, the reconstruction of genuine community slow and painful. Nothing is more damaging to a democracy than a conflict of principles so profound, with parties so intransigent, that compromise will not even be considered.

Must principles, then, be forever sacrificed to the demands of unity? Certainly not; principles need not be sacrified at all. Compromises are reached on solutions, particular programs of action. One may indeed believe that the course agreed upon is only a partial fulfillment of his demands in principle. But there is all the difference in the world between, on the one hand, accepting for the time a proposal that does not satisfy all of one's demands, and on the other, ceasing to make the demands one's principles give rise to. The principles can and very possibly should be maintained. Their firm support is entirely consistent with a course of political action which furthers partially but not perfectly the goals sought. There is no inconsistency between resoluteness in principle and cautious wisdom in action; indeed, the history of successful causes gives much reason to believe that maximal fulfillment of one's demands is more likely to be achieved in the long run by a series of compromises, than by dogmatic insistence upon one's own way at every turn. With time, education, and good will, and with continued freedom to criticize and discuss, the participant may see his principles generally —perhaps universally—accepted. Or he may come at last to see the force and value of other principles. There is nothing in a willingness to compromise that is inconsonant with the principled defense of one's position, or criticism of another's. Where compromise rather than force is the mode of solution adopted, it is the more likely that sound principles will emerge predominant at last. It is catastrophic for a democracy when a farsighted willingness to compromise is equated with hypocrisy, and resoluteness in support of principles mistakenly justifies intransigence.

The process of compromising gives special support to democracy. It is not only a way of reaching mutually satisfactory outcomes, but also of producing valuable byproducts. *Compromise* entails participation, a mutual agreement in which parties must play an active role. Genuine compromise synthesizes conflicting forces and retains in its imperfect form the verve and push of both (or several) points of view. Where it is not a guise for a forced capitulation, compromise is an active process, reinforcing the spirit of participation on all sides. It is also a rational process. Mutually satisfactory agreements are possible only when the parties are prepared to distinguish the several elements in their demands, yielding upon some in return for satisfaction upon others. Compromisers must therefore have an intellectual grasp of the issues at stake, of what they are bargaining for and what they can yield without intolerable damage. Compromise is a way of involving thoughtfully, emotionally, and concretely the several elements of the community in their joint government. It not only supports democracy but helps give it substance.

The process of compromise goes on within a community of which the several competing interests must be conscious if democracy is not to suffer. The parties must keep in mind the likelihood that an opponent in one sphere may be an ally in another and that there is very high value in reaching some agreement on the matter at hand that will at least keep things going and permit a continuing process of adjustment. To this end democratic citizens must manifest in their bargaining what John C. Calhoun calls the "disposition to harmonize," a disposition he identifies as the central, conserving principle of all constitutional governments. Contrasted with compromise is force, which Calhoun calls the conserving principle of all absolute governments. If harmony cannot be achieved voluntarily it is likely to come involuntarily, through the victory of the physically stronger. The use of force, or the threat of its use, gravely endangers the stability of a polity. The government that relies upon such threats encourages countervailing force in rebellion; the increased risk of such rebellion prompts the government to arm itself in advance to meet any armed resistance. "Hence of necessity," Calhoun concludes, "force becomes the conservative principle of all such [absolute] governments" (*A Disquisition on Government,* 1851). But since compromise is the only alternative to force, the abandonment of compromise as a deliberate technique is likely to be the prelude to violence [14.4].

Where the disposition to harmonize has never developed, democracy is unlikely to take root. Consider, as illustration, the international community. Participation by the great powers in international organizations has always been guarded and has been ultimately vitiated by the overriding commitment to national "sovereignty." Some argue that such sovereignty is the foundation of all legal rights, and that therefore relinquishing it under any circumstances undermines those rights, subverts the cause of justice. If that is so we must give up every expectation of resolving international differences democratically. Nations have been simply unwilling to sacrifice some particular advantages in the interest of the larger community of nations; among the members of that community the disposition to harmonize is largely absent. So long as it remains undeveloped, democracy in the world community must remain unrealized, or at best sharply limited in depth and range [17.4]. Nations must be prepared to compromise or be prepared for war.

12.8 Tolerant citizens

The citizens of a democracy need to be tolerant, deliberately forbearing, on three levels of progressive difficulty. First and most basic is tolerance of non-conformity. Non-conforming behavior is genuinely precious. Every important advance made by human societies is the result of some courageous non-conformity, very likely viewed with alarm or disgust by the masses. Conduct odd or repulsive at first showing may prove a valued alternative in the lives of many. Imagination, individuality, variety in perspective, all add immeasurably to the depth of participation; pressures, legal or extra-legal, to conform to custom necessarily restrict that depth, injure the democracy. Where the citizens are not disposed to tolerate non-conformity, participation in government may be wide, but it is likely to be superficial. Overall depth of participation is virtually impossible in a community where all tend to think and act alike. Tolerance of non-conforming conduct is no doubt defensible in its own right, but it is also a condition of successful democracy.

John Stuart Mill's remarks about conformity in nineteenth century

England are appropriate for all nations today and may prove unhappily more appropriate tomorrow:

> [E]xceptional individuals, instead of being deterred, should be encouraged in acting differently from the mass. In other times there was no advantage in their doing so, unless they acted not only differently, but better. In this age, the mere example of non-conformity, the mere refusal to bend the knee to custom, is itself a service. Precisely because the tyranny of opinion is such as to make eccentricity a reproach, it is desirable, in order to break through that tyranny, that people should be eccentric. Eccentricity has always abounded when and where strength of character has abounded; and the amount of eccentricity in a society has generally been proportional to the amount of genius, mental vigor, and moral courage which it contained. That so few now dare to be eccentric, marks the chief danger of the time. (*On Liberty*, 1859, Chap. III)

Protection for diversity in style of life may be sought through constitutional provisions. Justice Louis Brandeis argued, for example, that the Constitution of the United States conferred, "as against the Government, the right to be let alone—the most comprehensive of rights and the right most valued by civilized men" (*Olmstead v. U.S.*, 1928). Such formal safeguards are valuable, but the ultimate defense of privacy, of the right to be let alone, can only lie in the dispositions of community members who must do the letting.

On a second level citizens of a democracy must be disposed not only to allow others to live their own lives without interference, but to tolerate even direct opposition to beliefs and principles of their own. The freedom to oppose has already been discussed as one of the constitutional conditions of democracy [10.5]. That freedom is likely to be embodied in the constitution of a community, its organism, only if the disposition to permit it is embodied in the constitution of the individual citizens of whom the community is made. It is not merely some impersonal institutions—"the government" or "political parties"—that must tolerate opposition; so also must the individual human beings who will be tempted to put down opponents by whatever means are at hand. The unhappy story of human society over the greater part of history has been one of suppressed opposition, the suppressors invariably believing themselves justified, acting for the general good. Democracy has been rare partly because it obliges a disposition even on the part of the powerful to live with their opposition, to talk and work with them, and even to yield up power to them when the people demand it. Only a highly civilized body politic can thrive under such circumstances, and only there can democracy arise.

On a third level the citizens of a democracy must tolerate opposition even when presented by vicious or stupid men. In the heat of political strife, with important issues at stake and all one's energies engaged, it will often appear that only sheer thick-headedness could lie behind an opposition so stubborn and blind as that one faces. If one's opponents clearly are not ignorant or stupid, it is tempting to conclude that they are evil men, driven by selfishness, ambition, or other base motives. To the vigorous and honestly committed participant in democratic government, so it must often seem. Sometimes it will be so. But central to a democratic system is the general conviction that, whatever the motives or beliefs of the conflicting parties, governing decisions cannot be determined prior to the participatory process, but only through that process. And if the process itself is to go on, the several members of the community must be internally disposed to tolerate every kind of opposition, notwithstanding the irritation and anger it may cause.

This disposition is manifested through the practice, not merely the profession, of great self-restraint. A democrat believing sincerely that his opponents are thoroughly and absolutely wrong must still live and work with them, permit and even encourage their participation in the self-governing process of the whole. If he and his party hold power in the community, they may have the strength to eliminate their adversaries forcefully. So soon as they succumb to that temptation, democracy there is ended. To live constantly under such restraint is not easy, but then, democracy is not an easy system to operate.

The key point is that these restraints upon the use of force must be self-imposed. It will not suffice that there are laws or constitutional provisions protecting minorities against the oppressive use of force. The laws may be changed, the constitution amended. We are all familiar with so-called democracies in which constitutional guarantees are "suspended" in the interest of some allegedly more pressing need. The real constitution of a community, however, is not within the power of any administration to suspend; it is rooted in the character of the citizens. The only reliable guarantee that democratic procedures will be honored even under stress is the internal commitment to those procedures by the members of the community at large. Confidence that brute force will not be wrongly employed by the party in power rests ultimately only on the conviction that the citizens of the community are simply not so disposed. If they are, no formal or external restrictions will be strong enough to save the democracy.

Self-imposed restraint on the use of power is a virtue not common among human communities, which helps to explain why genuine democracy has not been common among the governments of men. The citizens must be so cultured as to feel spontaneously and naturally that, as Kipling said, "There are nine and sixty ways of constructing tribal lays, / And every-single-one-of-them-is-right." In these times, when all claim the name of democracy, few fully understand the arduous psychological conditions its genuine practice requires. Jose Ortega y Gasset calls these conditions, taken collectively, liberalism, and says (in *Revolt of the Masses*, 1937, Chap. 13) that such liberalism is "the supreme form of generosity; it is the right which the majority concedes to minorities and is therefore the noblest cry that has ever resounded on this planet. It announces the determination to share existence with the enemy; more than that, with an enemy that is weak. It was incredible that the human species should have arrived at an attitude so lovely, so paradoxical, so elegant, so acrobatic, so anti-natural. It is not surprising, then, that this same humanity should appear determined to get rid of it. It is a discipline too difficult and too complex to take firm root on earth."

12.9 Objective citizens

In an everyday sense, to be objective is to take ideas and events for what they are, without subjective prejudice, and hence straightforwardly and honestly. Objectivity in this plain sense is always a virtue; decisions ought generally be made with a careful regard for the facts of the case, and intelligent decision-makers will try to take their own biases into account, to face up to conditions realistically. Wise governors under any system require an undistorted view of the facts; where the people govern themselves and cannot be reasonably objective, the democracy is likely to soon find itself in serious trouble.

The objectivity needed in a democracy, however, is somewhat special in that it includes the recognition by the members of special facts about the different kinds of interests within the community. They must be prepared to weigh in their deliberations different levels of concern involved in any particular controversy. Personal and family interests are on one level, ethnic affiliations and economic loyalties on others, special interest groups and local associations on still others—and alongside all of these are the interests of the larger political bodies of which all citizens are part. Conflict among interests on different levels being common, citizens are often obliged to weigh private against public or quasi-public advantage [7.10].

Political philosophies holding the state supreme and the citizen subordinate are often contrasted with those holding the citizen supreme and the government subordinate. Successful democracy must avoid both extremes. It must effect a resolution of public and private interest not by damning the one or the other, but by their mutual absorption. Self-government requires that the citizens view themselves neither as instruments of the government nor as powers above the government, but as real and significant parts of it. Objectivity is the disposition on the part of an individual citizen to give proper place, in his deliberations, to the several roles he occupies concurrently. He may be father, employer, religious communicant, and so on. Whatever his several private roles he is also citizen, and as citizen of a democracy, governor. He must see himself as subject to the laws and at the same time as participant in the making and executing of the laws. Without some understanding of these special obligations imposed by democracy he is not likely to suffer the subordination of some private interests to some public ones that is on occasion indispensable. The disposition to weigh competing interests on different levels impartially, and especially to treat the interest of the larger community as a consideration of importance in its own right, may be called "civic objectivity." It is a refined trait, not easy to develop or maintain, but one essential for successful democratic government.

12.10 Confident citizens

The citizens of a democracy need to be confident of their collective capacity to govern themselves. If the members of the community view one another as untrustworthy, look upon themselves collectively as a rabble, the community (so far as there is one) will be without heart. Lacking confidence, the citizens will be seeking—especially in times of crisis—some external authority to make the decisions they cannot or will not make for themselves. So Demosthenes felt that his long struggle against the Macedonian despot, Philip, was in vain because the people

of Athens in his time had lost the confidence necessary to govern themselves. Said he to them: "You walk about the market-place asking each
other about every fresh rumor. 'Is Philip dead?' says one. 'No, but he
is ill,' says another. What difference does it make? If anything happens
to him you will soon call into existence a fresh Philip to your own
undoing." The fall of Athenian democracy cannot be blamed wholly
upon the despots into whose hands it fell.

The confidence democracy requires does not entail an absolute
faith in the wisdom of the masses—the conviction that everything the
people believe is true, or that their enactments are invariably right.
Rather, it is the disposition to trust the people to govern well over the
long run, to rely upon their competence to correct their own mistakes,
work out solutions to their own problems.

Fundamental here is individual self-confidence as well as confidence
in the community as a whole. If the individual will not rely upon his
own judgment, believing it worthy of serious consideration, he is not
likely to contribute to the decision-making process, and if he then does
contribute he is not likely to do so vigorously or effectively. Abstention
by such persons from the participatory process may result in a substantive outcome better than it would have been had all taken part, but
the process will not have been as democratic, the breadth of participation being then reduced [2.2]. The burdensome obligations of democracy are likely to be met only if all or most citizens believe that each has
something to contribute to the resolution of common problems. Individually, and as a community, the members of a democracy must have
confidence in themselves, and must be disposed to act in accord with
that self-confidence.

12.11 Concluding notes on psychological conditions

Three remarks of a general nature will bring to a close this discussion
of the psychological conditions of democracy. *First*: in laying out these
conditions I have not meant to suggest that democrats are saints or that
there is no real democracy except among saints. No one supposes that
all the members of a democratic community must, or do, manifest all
of these dispositions. But as I remarked at the outset, the success of
democracy does require that each of these traits of character be manifested in considerable degree by a goodly proportion of the community
a goodly percentage of the time. These degrees and proportions, unfor-

tunately, do not seem to admit of precise measurement, and even the roughest estimate of them could be made only within the context of a given community.

Second: of all the conditions of democracy, these are the most difficult to realize. To some degree their deliberate cultivation is possible, but such cultivation can only have impact if undertaken by great numbers of individual citizens and families. The problem is one of character formation, of encouraging the development of certain dispositions by each citizen. This is a moral problem, and a deep one.

There is no single or simple way to proceed in seeking such objectives. The inclination to be at once tolerant and critical and the disposition to compromise can be promoted by public example, by socially organized campaigns, even by the deliberate instruction of the young. With time such techniques will be improved. For the present the development of these dispositional traits must go on in the relatively hit-and-miss fashion of centuries past in the form of indirect training at the dinner table, on the job, and in recreation. Much of what was learned on the playing fields of Eton was not democratic, but some of the character developed there helped make the growth of democracy in Britain possible.

The forms of political democracy are instruments of special importance; their use requires special skills acquired only through long practice. Practice in the political sphere is sometimes painful, often hard to provide. The national democracies we consider most healthy and secure are those which have taken form gradually through generations of slow growth; they are bolstered by centuries of experience in self-government. Where the forms of democracy are imposed upon a community unprepared for them, the character and dispositions of the people are not likely to sustain it.

An excellent illustration of this principle lies in the contrast between those lands in which there has been a long tradition of local self-government and those in which that tradition is absent. The dispositional traits required for successful democracy develop most readily when the citizen participates in the government of his town or county. Here the affairs of government bear directly and immediately upon his life; in this context he witnesses not only the effect of his own participation but the vital role of compromise, tolerance, flexibility, and so on in conducting government. Local self-government is the best and surest incubator of democracy in general. Where it has been long practiced democracy on a larger scale has a good chance of success.

The psychological conditions of democracy

Many new nations, however, have experienced until a few years or decades ago only the life of a colony, or territory, or personal possession of a foreign monarch. For much of their history the government of many peoples has lain almost entirely in the hands of alien powers or their representatives, out of the control of the citizens themselves. Even where some measure of national autonomy had been achieved it was common practice to retain governmental authority in the capital city, where it had been traditionally exercised by colonial rulers. The authority of government flowed regularly from the capital to the provinces, rather than the reverse; local self-government was largely unknown. Now the citizens are suddenly called upon to govern themselves; it is not surprising that they should be dispositionally unready for the task. Lack of experience in the rough and tumble of local self-government breeds psychological deficiencies that are major obstacles to the development of a healthy and lasting national democracy.

Ultimately the habits that promote and sustain any form of government, especially democracy, are developed in the daily lives of the citizens; intellectual appreciation of their necessity is not enough. Before democracy can succeed in the larger scale, it must have been applied in the smaller. It does not follow from this that all or even most of the internal communities of a nation need to be organized democratically, but there must be significant activities in which the citizen engages directly and commonly that are so organized, giving him the opportunity to develop the necessary attitudes and dispositions. He must have personal experience in their exercise and personal proof that they can be maintained to the benefit and satisfaction of all. Where there is no experience in direct self-government the dispositions required by its indirect forms have little chance to develop.

Finally: the dispositional conditions of democracy, taken as a group, roughly serve to identify the temperament of one who is prepared to live in and make his peace with an uncertain and perilous world. The traits of tolerance, objectivity, confidence, and the rest do not by themselves constitute mental health, but they are surely indicative of good mental health, and perhaps even part of what is meant by that expression. It is not surprising that traits indicative of good mental health in the individual should be requirements for democracy, because democracy (as I argue in Part Five) is the good health of the polity. Even if that be denied, however, it is certainly the case that democratic government cannot succeed unless its citizens do exhibit the psychological characteristics herein described.

191

Chapter 13

The protective conditions of democracy

13.1 Introductory remarks on protective conditions

Democracies—especially national democracies—must be prepared to defend themselves. The experience of democracies in the recent as well as the distant past clearly shows that the other conditions of self-government, however well realized, may be to no avail if the community cannot overcome or repel its enemies. It is unfortunate that defense and preparation for defense, unproductive enterprises at best, should demand as much expenditure of human energy as they do. In some happier day, perhaps, this need will be much reduced. But circumstances must be dealt with as they are, and this means that self-protection remains, at least for national communities for some time to come, a vital concern.

The very fact that we hope for a day when the protection of democracy will not trouble us indicates that the relation between democracy and its protective conditions is not intrinsic in the way that relations between democracy and its other conditions are. Certain capacities, dispositions, and institutions are essential for the process of participation itself; the ability of the community to defend itself is not so closely tied to that process. This more extrinsic character of protective conditions does not reduce their importance however. When times of crisis come they may mean the difference between life and death for the democratic community.

The protective conditions of democracy are of two kinds—defending against attacks from without and attacks from within. I consider these in turn.

13.2 Protection against external threat

A self-governing community may find itself the victim of aggression from without, either by the direct use of military force, or by the indirect threat of such force. Then it may transpire that, however perfect the process of participation within the community, the people's government of themselves is interrupted by a foreign power they can neither accept nor overcome. The result may be war, or the subjugation of the democracy by the threat of destruction. If a national democracy expects to survive such crises it must be prepared for them.

Such preparation may take various forms. Sometimes there is no resort other than defense by military means. Awful though it is to use such means, events of recent years make it clear that there are times when a democracy must fight or die. A nation, like an individual, will find that a most unhappy dilemma and must act with forethought in the effort to avoid being cornered so. But if the choice of armed conflict is made by an aggressive enemy, the democracy may have no alternative than that of responding likewise in its own defense.

It is always open to a community in that position to submit, to choose to abandon its autonomy and democratic form, rather than make war to defend them. Democracy, after all, is far from the only human value, and an intelligent weighing of the alternatives may call for the sacrifice of it rather than life or peace or some other values. Our decision in such circumstances must depend upon the best judgments we can make of the alternatives—on the one hand the horrors of the war in prospect and the results of possible defeat, on the other hand the humiliation of surrender and the horrors of subjugation.

A man attached to democracy with all his heart might reasonably suffer its loss, and even the loss of his own freedom or life, if the only alternative were a war so catastrophic as to impose yet greater misery upon a greater number. Some argue that a resort to large-scale nuclear war is so intolerable, so unthinkable, that nothing, not even the threat of cruel tyranny, can justify it. They may be right. On the other hand there are those who hold that democracy is dearer than life itself—not only their own lives but the lives of millions of others—and that everything, without exception, must be sacrificed, if necessary, in its defense. This position requires a strong stomach, and is hardly consistent with Christian ethics, but it may nevertheless be right. Still the slogan "death before dishonor" has less than a noble ring when the death contemplated is that of others, most of them innocent bystanders. Given certain beliefs about the values of democracy and the horrors of war, it may be reasonable to conclude in some circumstances that the resort to war in defense of democracy is unwise or unjustifiable. But that decision, by a nation or an individual, commits it (or him) to the sacrifice of democracy to some higher values. If, on the other hand, that sacrifice is intolerable, the democracy must be able in the event of armed aggression, to field victorious forces.

The protection of democracy against external threat does not always entail going to war. A readiness to defend effectively with armed strength if necessary—the so-called "credibility" of military capacities —may prove by itself an adequate defense. Short of war there are an unlimited number of strategies, threats, pressures, promises, and their combinations that a democracy may use to counter external aggression. When anti-democratic forces are powerful and numerous the fullest range of protective devices, from clever statesmanship to big guns, may be needed in the arsenal of democracy. It is impossible to specify all of the kinds of instruments that may be required for defense against external threat. Among them, however distasteful it may be, the capacity to meet force with force must presently be included.

External protection imposes another difficult requirement—the capacity to respond to threat quickly. That democracies tend to move ponderously is one of their most notorious faults; the participatory machinery is cumbrous and often unable to react with the speed that rapidly changing circumstances may demand. The larger the community the more awkward the process of participation becomes, while at the same time great size may intensify the need for quick reaction. Threats from external sources may demand from the democracy so immediate a response as to rule out entirely any resort to general participation in deciding upon that response. A democracy, therefore, must devise instruments that will at least make it possible to respond to threat with the speed that adequate defense requires.

Such instruments are available but there is always a danger of their being misused. Normally, the parliament will be the body having the duty to respond to threat. In emergencies that leave not even enough time to seek parliamentary approval of action, the representative body responding must be still smaller—a cabinet or a national security council—that can act with the necessary decisiveness. Some question the reality of democracy when important decision-making power is delegated to so small a group. It is true that when a very small group acts for a large nation the voice of each citizen who participated in the selection (direct or indirect) of that group is much muted. Although the degree of representation in such bodies is very low [7.3], the government may be democratic still if the group holding emergency power is selected through a process of general participation that is broad and deep. When a large nation is obliged to respond very quickly, democratic processes must become highly indirect. World-shaking decisions made by appointed officials behind closed doors are not the product of democracy at its purest; but they may be consistent with democracy, and the life of the democracy may even depend upon them.

Delegated power may be used unwisely, of course, and even if used intelligently in the light of available information unforeseeable events may cause an unhappy outcome. But such risks are faced by every body of decision-makers, whatever the source of their authority. When that authority is derived in fact and not merely in name from the citizens at large, it will be democratic even though a very high level of representation is required for the community's protection [7.7].

The conditions of external defense are almost exclusively the concern of national democracies. Democratic communities of other kinds, especially when non-political, may occasionally need to act quickly, but their failure to do so is rarely fatal because they do not normally face any danger from physical aggression. Even among political communities, the fielding of military forces is generally the business of sovereign states, not of the communities within them. That external defense is chiefly a concern of national democracies and may be largely ignored by other democratic communities is a further indication of the extrinsic relation borne by the protective conditions of democracy to democracy itself.

13.3 Protection against internal threat

Threats to democracy from within are sometimes more serious than those from without and are much more common. All the varieties of internal threat cannot be specified, but two very general kinds may be distinguished: *(1)* attacks from within upon the conditions of democracy—constitutional, intellectual, or other; *(2)* attacks from within upon the process of participation—its breadth, or depth, or range. I shall discuss each of these in turn.

With regard to internal threats of both kinds two remarks are in order. *First*: unlike external attacks, these may endanger democracies of all kinds and sizes. *Second*: internal threats to democracy may arise from persons or groups whose ultimate aims are noble, and whose sincerely professed ideals are patriotic, perhaps even democratic. Of course there are those who do not like democracy and who wish to see it replaced by another form of government. But in most democratic communities such persons are few, and their avowed opposition to the democracy renders protection against them relatively easy. Those, on the other hand, who honestly believe that they struggle in democracy's name, but who, because of their failure to understand it or its conditions, in fact subvert it—they are the internal enemies against whom it is hardest to defend. In the last analysis there is no defense against them save the vigorous practice of democracy and the active support of its conditions.

(1) Attacks upon the conditions of democracy by the citizens of that democracy are painfully frequent, usually taking the form of proposals whose full consequences for the democracy are not understood by their authors. Of these the most common is the effort to "protect" democracy by limiting in some way the freedom to criticize, publish, or dissent. Believing in good faith that their objectives are wholesome, and that those whom they propose to silence are only the enemies of democracy, such persons think that they can safeguard an open society by closing it up just a little. The effort is misguided and can prove catastrophic [Chapter 13]. This internal threat chiefly arises from failure to understand the constitutional conditions of democracy. Hyper-patriots mistakenly suppose that the constitutional rights of a democracy need only be extended to those who share its goals, finding sedition in every strong dissent from those goals. Of all the internal deteriorations to which democracy is subject, this is probably the most serious. It has no universal remedy. The constitutional conditions of democracy grow stronger with understanding and with use, as do the psychological conditions that lie behind them. But internal defense of them clearly may not resort to the use of that very restriction of free speech it seeks to defend against. These are dangers to which democracy is naturally heir.

The case of the intellectual conditions may serve as a further illustration. If a large scale democracy of the present day is to be reasonably successful, great collective effort in support of its educational systems is essential. This support is not a luxury nor a convenience but a matter of life or death. Democrats who do not understand this may vehemently oppose the self-taxation needed to support public schools and universities, posing thereby a real threat to the welfare of the democracy. But these obstructionary efforts the democracy cannot rightly silence, and if it happens that obstruction wins the day, the citizens of that community may (by permitting its conditions to deteriorate) allow the democracy they once possessed to slip through their fingers. Short-sightedness of this kind must be combatted with rational argument and non-violent persuasion of every reasonable sort, but there can never be any guarantee that the citizens will maintain the conditions of successful democracy. It is a second-level condition of the protection against certain internal threats that the remaining first-level conditions of democracy be understood and appreciated.

(2) The second general kind of internal threat to democracy is that of the restriction, or even abandonment, of the process of participatory government directly. Most often this is the inadvertent result of measures originally devised to protect the democracy from external threat. In times of crisis the need for speed and decisiveness encourages reliance upon the judgments of leaders, and makes effective citizen participation difficult. The leaders may be democratically elected. But democratic habits may weaken, and there is always the danger that the interest of citizens in actively criticizing and influencing their elected leaders will wane. The citizens may find that even without their participation important decisions get made, often intelligently, and that the removal of the felt need to participate frees their minds and their time of the cares of government. In this way democracy may be innocently and half-unconsciously abandoned as a result of growing inactivity by its members.

Such deterioration is likely to take place gradually, the leaders first acquiring power through legitimate processes of election and delegation, and little by little finding themselves heir by default to the power that the community at large ceases to exercise. This is more likely and less noticeable when the first months or years of a new government are prosperous, and the leaders (or leader) seem wise and just. Hence the truth in the saying that nothing is more inimical to self-government than a good king. When the day comes upon which the people wish to reassume the authority once theirs, it may be too late. The institutions of democratic government atrophy quickly; the habits of critical participation cannot be called up at will but need constant practice and support. Democracy is much easier to abandon than to recapture.

Any inclination on the part of the citizens to yield their voice in government will be quickly complemented by a willingness on the part of some leaders to take advantage of the opportunities given them. Power rarely goes begging, and if the people are not willing to shoulder the burdens of governing themselves, there will always be those who are happy to govern for them. The reins of government may then fall to men of very good intentions, who honestly think themselves qualified to decide for the people when the people are not anxious to decide for themselves. Whether the intentions of usurpers be noble or base, and whether the newly developed leaders are balanced or insane, is very important for the welfare of the community, but is irrelevant to the democracy. It will have suffered in any case. Indeed, an early glimmering of base intentions or a brief show of psychological instability by aspiring autocrats may be a fortunate thing in bringing the people to their senses and to the rescue of their democracy.

Ironically, the conditions of internal defense and those of external defense often come into conflict in a national democracy. A people may be tempted to relinquish self-government under circumstances created by measures themselves introduced to protect self-government from external threats. On the one hand, insistence upon pure democratic process whatever the emergency may expose the community to fatal attacks from without; on the other hand, the concentration of authority and the rigorous discipline believed necessary to meet such attacks may result in the complete deterioration of the democracy from within.

There is no general resolution of these tensions. A successful democracy must find ways to delegate the powers needed for immediate response to external threat without yielding popular control over those to whom they are delegated. Delegations of great power must be made only when absolutely essential; they must be made with clearly specified restrictions upon the use of such power; and they must be made for clearly specified periods of time, coming up automatically for review and possible expiration. Protection against internal threats to democracy can never suffice if merely formal; atrophy can only be prevented by the active employment of democratic muscles. In one respect at least, defense against external aggression is simpler than defense against internal rot. Faced with the former the members of a democracy will readily see and understand what they are fighting and what victory requires. Internal deterioration, on the other hand, is far more difficult to recognize; once recognized it may require a defensive effort less bloody, but equally strenuous and far more difficult to organize.

13.4 Undemocratic origins and anti-democratic effects

Internal threats to the democratic process itself do not always arise from inadvertency, apathy, and the like. They may take the form of deliberate efforts by some elements within the community to limit participation directly, in one or more of its dimensions. Some persons do not want their community to be democratically governed, and are anxious to give legal force to the restrictions they envisage.

The presence of such elements within a democracy gives rise to theoretical problems at once confusing and important. One set of these problems, regarding the appropriate treatment of an anti-democratic minority, has been dealt with earlier [10.10]. Another set of difficulties arises when we seek to give a plausible and coherent account of acts or policies which seem to deserve and at the same time not to deserve the description "democratic."

Consider, for example, the principle according to which all those of a certain religion (or race) must be excluded from participation in government. Such a principle directly restricts the breadth of democracy and is patently not democratic [3.2]. Now suppose this principle of unjust exclusion were proposed as a piece of major legislation in a small community in which direct democracy is the established form of government. Suppose a town meeting is held on this issue; attendance is universal; the discussion is long, critical, and thorough, every member speaking who wishes to do so. Suppose that every procedural propriety is observed, that no reflection whatever can be cast on the democratic treatment of the proposed legislation. Suppose this legislation is then enacted, with the support of a large majority. How shall we describe these events within the framework of the theory of democracy here proposed? That the legislation is undemocratic is clear from its nature and intent. That it was proposed, discussed, and adopted democratically is true by hypothesis. It would appear, in this hypothetical case, to be both highly undemocratic and highly democratic.

A distinction is clearly called for, one not hard to draw. Laws or policies may be classified as democratic in origin, or democratic in effect, or both, or neither. In any policy-making affair of concern to the community we may attend to the procedures being employed, or the objectives achieved; very possibly we may, as democrats, approve one and not the other. In the hypothetical case proposed the bill of exclusion is unquestionably democratic in origin, and with equal certainty is undemocratic in effect. While this is an extreme case it illustrates some awkward but interesting problems a democracy may face.

To know that legislation is democratic in origin is to know that it is legitimate, that it has received formal, parliamentary adoption after appropriate scrutiny and a fair vote. This may assure us that the act represents the will of the majority (or at least of the largest minority) of the self-governing community or their representatives. To know that legislation is democratic in effect is quite another thing, being the assurance that participation, along at least one of its dimensions, has been strengthened. We may approve such consequences favorable to a democracy, but the fact that any legislation has these consequences does not by itself legitimize it.

Four hypothetical examples will present more concretely the kinds of circumstances that can arise, and which this distinction helps to clarify.

(1) An act (or policy) may be undemocratic in origin but democratic in effect. A military junta, for example, may impose legislation establishing regular elections and enfranchising all citizens for participation in them.

(2) An act (or policy) may be democratic in origin and democratic in effect. A parliament already representative in large measure, for example, may enact laws resulting in yet more universal enfranchisement.

(3) An act (or policy) may be neither democratic in origin nor democratic in effect. A dictator may, by fiat, "suspend" constitutional provisions, dissolving the parliament indefinitely.

(4) An act (or policy) may be democratic in origin but not in effect. An example (like that presented earlier) would be a town meeting or a parliament enacting legislation deliberately restricting popular participation in political affairs.

Cases of this last kind are the most puzzling since they constitute direct internal threats to democracy against which there is no general defense. Sometimes, of course, restricted participation results from democratically enacted legislation that had an altogether different, possibly even opposite aim. A poll tax might be enacted by the community, for example, in order to increase revenue, or with the hope that this direct and universal contribution to the general funds would stimulate greater interest in their expenditure. Its backers may honestly anticipate a deepening of the democracy as one consequence of such a tax. The result of its imposition in fact may be the failure of a great many citizens to qualify for the vote, by neglecting, or refusing, or being unable to pay the poll tax—a result that would sharply reduce the breadth of democracy. Or there may be a dual outcome, participation becoming both deeper and narrower—in which case democracy is weakened in one dimension and strengthened in another [3.2].

Usually, however, direct action whose main effect is the limitation of democracy in one or more of its dimensions has just that consequence as its object. Poll taxes are almost invariably imposed with the chief aim of excluding certain elements of the community from the participatory process. Literacy tests, property qualifications, and other devices are invoked with the intention of screening the citizenry so as to give only that portion of it believed fit a voice in community decisions. Without passing judgment on the long-range wisdom of such devices, there can be no serious doubt that they aim to restrict or eliminate democratic process in the government of the community. Whatever the motive behind them (as when persons or parties are silenced to "protect" the democracy) direct restrictions upon participation seriously threaten the democracy from within.

The question, "Can a democracy act undemocratically?" must be answered forthrightly; it can. By somehow restricting the number of participants, or the effectiveness of general participation, or the range of popular control, the members of a democracy may make it difficult for themselves to continue to govern themselves. Democracies may inflict serious self-damage. It is even possible for a democracy to kill itself straight out, by deciding (perhaps clearheadedly and perhaps not) that its members will be better off if they do not participate in government, but recognize instead the permanent authority of a (hopefully benevolent) despot or oligarchy. It is helpful to adopt the following semantic convention. Acts or policies whose origins do not lie in the democratic process are properly called "*un*democratic"; acts or policies whose consequences serve to restrict or injure democratic process may then properly be called "anti-democratic."

The paradoxical threat here discussed may then be accurately described thus: democracies can, and often do, adopt anti-democratic measures. Again, there is no general defense against this danger. That a self-governing community may make self-injurious or self-destructive decisions is just one of the risks that every democracy must run. The logic of the democrats' position makes it impossible for them consistently to restrict, antecedently, the kinds of decisions that they may make regarding their own affairs. It is conceivable, of course, that protective measures, genuinely democratic in intent or effect, might be imposed upon a community from without; but in being so imposed they would certainly be (in spite of their happy aim) undemocratic in origin.

One recourse is to seek to restrict the kinds of decisions a democratic parliament may make by developing a written constitution, itself democratically adopted. The prohibition of poll taxes or property qualifications for the franchise, and the like, by being thus incorporated in the democratically formulated basic instrument, might seem to safeguard against such internal threats. Such formal prohibitions, however, are very far from infallible protections for the community. They may serve to restrain an excited populace, or cool a rambunctious legislature, deterring the quick passage of anti-democratic legislation not thoroughly thought through. But every written constitution must embody (or suppose) an amending process, and if a sufficient number of the citizens of a democracy persevere in their intent to enact legislation restricting participation in that democracy, no document or formal device can block them permanently.

The only lasting protection a democracy can have against such internal threats lies in the dispositions and intelligence of the citizens who constitute it. The problem is indeed a constitutional one, but not in the legal sense, nor even in the sense of that term employed in the earlier discussion of democracy's constitutional conditions. Ultimately the outcome must be determined by those who make up the democracy—what they understand and feel about their government, and how they want to be governed. If they do not want democracy, or do not want it in some respects, it cannot be forced upon them. Protection against deliberate internal threat must be found in the political will of the citizens, in their desire for self-government, and in the maturity of their character in sustaining it. They must understand democracy and what it requires. Considering the price that must often be paid for it in time, energy, anxiety, and risk, they must want democracy badly if they hope to keep it.

Part Five

THE DEFENSE OF DEMOCRACY

Chapter 14

The vindication of democracy

14.1 General remarks about vindicatory arguments

The most difficult of the major questions regarding democracy must now be faced. It is: *why* have a democracy? For what reasons might we or should we choose democracy in preference to some other system of government in a given community? Some form of government for human communities is essential. Is self-government, government by general participation, always (or usually) the best of the alternatives open to us? That it is the best of governmental systems is now very widely believed; but this belief has been far from general in the history of political thought, many acute thinkers having rejected democracy entirely, while others, even today, accept it only with serious reservations.

However much the preceding chapters may have exhibited an enthusiasm for democracy, I have not yet, strictly speaking, argued in its defense. One may accept fully my account of the nature of democracy, its instruments, presuppositions, and conditions, and then conclude upon reflection that, for his part, he wants none of it. Or he might conclude that he wants it in some of the communities to which he belongs but not in others. However wise, such decisions are not logically inconsistent with the acceptance of the preceding account. A defense of democracy, therefore, is now in order.

That defense is a complicated affair. The arguments in support of democracy, often confusedly bunched, may take one of two very basic forms; the first of these forms I call *vindication* and shall discuss in this chapter; the second I call *justification* and shall discuss in the next.

The most effective defense of democracy is the exhibition of its merits in practice. I do not hesitate to call this defense pragmatic, but the careless and invidious uses of the terms "pragmatic" and "pragmatism" in the public press have so cheapened these words that their employment here may do more to obstruct than assist the understanding of the argument. The words used, however, are not of central importance. Defenses are pragmatic when based upon the way democracy actually functions in human life, individual and social; pragmatic arguments focus upon the consequences of democracy, what it leads to, rather than anything from which it could be derived or deduced. Such a defense of democracy has nothing to do with crass expediency; it is based ultimately upon the utility of governments so organized, but that is utility, as Mill puts it, "in the largest sense, grounded on the permanent interests of man as a progressive being." Within this defense I distinguish several parts, each based upon a distinct but important benefit self-government may yield. Taken all together I call this set of arguments the vindication of democracy.

I disclaim at the outset any effort to vindicate democracy for all communities, or for any given community under all circumstances. There surely have been, are, and will be communities in which democracy may not be appropriate or workable. The ensuing argument goes forward on the assumption that, in some reasonable degree, the conditions of democracy have been or can be realized in the community in question. Supposing that, I deliberately choose the term vindication, to emphasize that the arguments that follow are not deductive in character, but seek to exhibit the concrete advantages that flow from the practice of democracy.

Three features of all such arguments should be remarked. *First*: being utilitarian in the largest sense, they depend upon a widely shared prizing of the consequences toward which democracy tends. One could grant that democracy is likely to have such consequences, and still reject it on the ground that he does not prize those results. The persuasiveness of my arguments will rest upon the assumption that the consequences claimed for democracy are indeed highly valued. In short, these vindicatory arguments are hypothetical. They may be paraphrased crudely: "If you seek to obtain certain objectives, or maximize certain tendencies, you are well advised to establish a democracy; for of all the available alternatives, democratic government is the one most likely to accomplish those objectives or maximize those tendencies." This hypothetical character is no serious defect, however. The arguments depend upon certain goals being generally prized, but in fact they are so prized, long have been, and are likely to continue to be. Their defense may be sought in turn; and that would be a legitimate philosophical inquiry, but it is not mine here. Whether those objectives could be defended in the same pragmatic fashion, or require some absolute foundation, is a deep and important question, but it need not be answered in this context. It is wiser to undertake the defense of one philosophical ideal at a time, and it is only the part of good sense to do so within a framework of values already widely understood and shared.

The *second* general feature of these vindicatory arguments is their comparative nature. In the paraphrase of these arguments given above appears the phrase ". . . of all available alternatives, democracy is the one most likely to. . . ." There are a number of alternative systems of government that may be adopted by or imposed upon a community. The exhibition of the merit of democracy consists in a showing that it more than any other is likely to have the desired consequences.

While the number of variations in governmental patterns is very large, the number of alternative basic theories is very small. Essentially the Greeks were right in asserting that government must be conducted either by one (autocracy), by few (oligarchy), or by many. Within each category there is a great range of quality. The autocrat may be a benevolent despot or a half-mad dictator; the oligarchy may be of the wisest or of the richest; the many may constitute a rabble or a republic. What qualities each of the basic forms is likely to display can only be determined in the light of the circumstances of a given community. It bears repeating that arguments in vindication of democracy do not apply to all communities or all circumstances; if the conditions of democracy are largely absent, democracy may be no more likely to achieve desired objectives than one of its alternatives. It is where these conditions of democracy are reasonably met that arguments exhibiting the relative superiority of democracy apply.

Even under such conditions, however, democratic government may fail, in whole or in part, to attain the ends sought. Or it may attain them at the cost of certain evils that had not been fully anticipated. The vindication of any governmental forms does not require that it be shown to be without flaw. If, therefore, one could argue successfully that, no form of government being without serious failings, democracy is still the least risky or the least bad of the alternatives open, that might prove a sound defense. One might then go on to catalogue in full the evils and probable evils of autocracy and oligarchy. Such a defense of democracy, as the least of a set of alternative evils all of which cannot be avoided, can be undertaken successfully. But, although the following arguments also are essentially comparative, they deal more affirmatively with the major political alternatives, contending not merely that the consequences of autocracy or oligarchy are bad, but that those of democracy are good.

Comparative arguments are commonly flawed in the following unhappy way. In criticizing a political form we do not favor, it is all too easy to compare its actual workings with some ideal formulation of the alternative we support. This mistake—of comparing competing alternatives on disparate levels—must be carefully guarded against. The realities of democratic practice must be compared with the realities of monarchy or oligarchy, and the ideal despotism must be measured against the ideal democracy. We shall not then find that democracy suffers by the comparison on either level.

The *third* general feature of the vindicatory defense of democracy is its essentially empirical character. Each of these arguments for democracy asserts some factual connection between democracy and certain ends to which it leads or conditions it promotes. The aim is to explain why, being what it is, democracy has these consequences and tendencies; this is a philosophical task. Providing the empirical evidence needed to complete this vindication, garnered from the detailed study of the workings of democracy in human societies, is an appropriate enterprise for sociologists and political scientists. A good deal of empirical support, however, is readily available to ordinary citizens of every democracy, and any such person may make some trial of the arguments I present on the basis of his own experience in communities large and small.

It follows from these three features of the vindicatory arguments—their hypothetical, comparative, and empirical character—that their conclusions are not absolutely certain. Each harbors a degree of tentativeness and open-endedness that cannot be eliminated. This is appropriate in the sphere of political philosophy, and particularly appropriate in the defense of a philosophy of government whose successful application requires a fallibilistic disposition of its members. It does not follow from the hypothetical, empirical (and therefore fallible), character of these arguments that they are weak. Quite the reverse is true. We can and do develop reliable knowledge in many spheres relying essentially upon experimental, hypothetical arguments; in the sphere of government we can do so also. A common misconception of experimental argument supposes it necessarily tied to laboratories, controlled tests of specified duration, and the like. From this it is concluded that hypotheses and experiments are all right in their place, but that social theory is not their place, that they are too transitory and insecure for anything as important as political doctrine. In fact, hypothetical procedures have a crucial role in dealing with social and political problems as well as with those of a more technical nature. In some cases hypotheses are as solidly reliable and lasting as anything we possess. They may prove not only ideal in resolving the problems engendering them but fruitful in suggesting solutions to other problems. Good

208

hypotheses may be retained for periods longer than even absolutes can reign. They may prove ever more successful, the empirical results to which they lead giving them ever firmer support. Even the so-called "laws of nature" are hypothetical, in some degree tentative. We have every confidence in them; but we are intellectually prepared for the possibility that some better hypotheses, some better theory, may be devised to deal with or explain existing circumstances. So it is also in politics, where we may act with confidence upon principles that have solid empirical support, knowing that someday we may have to revise those principles in the light of newly developing situations.

Six arguments in vindication of democracy here follow. Each suffers from the incompleteness and tentativeness just alluded to; but each is highly persuasive nonetheless, and the set of six has overwhelming force.

14.2 Democracy and wise policy

Of all forms of government, democracy is the most likely to lead to wise policy in the long run. This is not to argue that the people cannot err or that their voice is the voice of God. The members of a community can, and often do, make serious mistakes in governing themselves. The question here is whether serious error is more likely to be avoided if policy is entirely determined by one man, or a few men, rather than all (or most) of the governed. The ideal of a supremely wise despot— one who would establish and enforce the best laws, select as his lieutenants only the best men, administer justice with supreme wisdom, and best encourage the cultural growth of his community—has often been espoused. It is, as Mill has effectively shown, ". . . an altogether false ideal, which practically . . . becomes the most senseless and dangerous of chimeras" (*Considerations on Representative Government*, 1860, Chap. III). It does not take much experience in the world, or much historical learning, to realize that such an ideal supposes superhuman faculties and energies on the part of the imagined Prince. The ideal of the all-wise despot has been prettily painted, even by influential philosophers in the twentieth century. The realities of despotic rule, however, have been cruelly disappointing. The facts of the matter are that highly intelligent and effective rule by despots has been extremely rare in history. Probably the demands made upon the despot by absolute rule are too great to be lived up to by any man.

When supreme power has been concentrated in one man or a small group, it has almost invariably been by accident (e.g., hereditary succession) or because he or they have wanted power and wanted it badly enough to fight for it. Most often that want has been selfishly motivated. As a matter of political reality, one is likely to find power of will and toughness of mind in a despot, but rarely wisdom or a well-developed sense of justice. Says Mill, "For one despot who now and then reforms an abuse, there are ninety-nine who do nothing but create them." Here is but one of the cases in which we are sometimes tempted to compare the imperfect realities of democracy with the perfect idealization of benevolent despotism.

Even supposing it possible to find one man intellectually, physically, and morally capable of governing the affairs of the whole community, and further supposing that he is successfully placed on the throne, there is little assurance that he will be succeeded by one of equal competence. The ideal we seek is not just good government in a single place or over a single stretch of time but the form of good government. One swallow surely does not make a summer. In the light of history we may have every expectation that even moderately satisfactory despotism soon degenerates. Marcus Aurelius cannot sit the throne forever, and even he may persecute the Christians.

The criticisms of autocracy apply with equal or greater force to oligarchy. A group of leaders, supremely wise and profoundly benevolent, are less likely to be found than one great man; if, among the oligarchs, there are likely to be some imbued with wisdom and justice, there is an equal probability that there will be some among them who cannot resist the temptations of power, and their corruption will infect the whole. Could an ideal set of oligarchs ever be identified, their joint elevation to supreme authority would be a near miracle. Just as in the case of the despot, their rule is likely to arise from burning ambition. Even less than in the case of the despot, if they happen to be competent, are they likely to secure equally competent successors. The oligarchs, collectively, may be more able to meet the sheer physical and mental demands of rule than is one man; but they are also sure to exhibit a wider range of personal ambitions and prejudices. All considered, good government is as unlikely under them as under an autocrat. Again, it is actual oligarchy, and not ideal oligarchy with which actual democracy must be compared. An actual oligarchy may claim the name of an "elite" (Fr. *elire*, to choose), but it is far more likely, in practice, to be "chosen" from the wealthy or the strong, than from the wise or the just.

That democracy is most likely to lead to wise policy in the long run is more than a claim of comparative merit; it rests not merely on the belief that the available alternatives, autocracy or oligarchy, are likely to result in policy infected by prejudice, ambition, incompetence, and private interest. More positively, the argument is an expression of confidence in the capacities of ordinary men. Specifically, it is the belief that such men, acting in concert upon their common affairs, where the conditions of democracy have been reasonably met, will emerge with directive decisions in the long-run best interests of the deciding community. That the many will judge more wisely than the few in every case is clearly false; but that claim the democrat need not make. The danger of error, even on matters of the highest importance to the community, is one that democracy (like every other system) cannot eliminate. The democrat nevertheless contends that directive decisions reached through the general participation of those affected by them vindicate democracy over the course of time.

This claim is founded upon confidence in the practical wisdom of plain men. There is no proving it true, or false, beyond doubt. The evidence relevant is extensive, but confused. It consists of the histories of communities in which the conditions of democracy are met, some of which have, and some of which have not permitted participation of the members in the governing process. Taken all in all, the democrat will insist, the evidence is impressively in his favor. In that he is correct; but, one must admit, the matter is not closed, nor is the evidence perfectly conclusive.

So the most fundamental issues between those who defend democracy and those who distrust it concern their conflicting views of the judgments and capacities of the citizens acting individually and collectively. In the last analysis the anti-democrat believes the people cannot be trusted to govern themselves; the democrat believes they can. Critics of democracy, from Plato to Walter Lippmann, have denied that the people have the capacity to judge wisely on crucial issues. Their arguments usually take the form of exhibiting some glaring cases of error by democratically governed communities. Such instances however, although genuine, do not establish what they aim to establish. They show only that the people do make serious mistakes; they purport to show that the people err consistently, that they cannot successfully make the kinds of judgments democracy requires of them. In discussing the role of the American judiciary Governeur Morris in 1801 asked, "Why are we here?" He answered, "To save the people from their most dangerous enemy: to save them from themselves." And to Alexander Hamilton is attributed a remark which puts very neatly the fundamental ground for distrust of democracy: "The people, Sir—the people is a great beast."

Just this conception of the people the democrat rejects. He need not deny that the members of the community are very unequal in intellectual capacity and in moral virtue; he will certainly agree that their training and experience greatly differ. What he does not admit is that such differences render the members of the community unable to make, jointly, reasonable decisions on matters that affect them jointly. To the contrary, he argues that a variety of experience, background, and interests makes possible an enrichment of the decision-making process that would be impossible without general participation. The wisdom of policy must be judged at last in light of the interests of all the members of the community; for the pursuit of such wisdom the members themselves are particularly suited. Democracy makes possible and in fact often develops a collective wisdom that surpasses the wisdom of the few. On matters of common concern it is indeed true that many heads are better than one. "Feasts to which many contribute may excel those provided at one man's expense. In the same way, when there are many who contribute to the process of deliberation, each can bring his share of goodness and moral prudence; and when all meet together the people may thus become something in the nature of a single person, who—as he has many feet, many hands, and many senses—may also have many qualities of character and intelligence" (*Politics,* III, 11, 1281). This argument is sound. It needs, however, to be enlarged and refined in three respects.

First: in applying this argument one must not fail to distinguish between directive and administrative activities [1.3]. Many functions entailing great technical skill require for this performance persons specially trained and qualified; here we carefully distinguish expert from layman. For surgery we want only the skilled surgeon; to navigate in perilous waters only a trained navigator will do. In governmental affairs, likewise, there are technical functions demanding specially qualified personnel. But decisions on matters of community policy are very different from these, and although they require wisdom, it is not a kind of wisdom any technical training can provide—nor is it likely that any full member of a democratic community is wholly without it. The criticism of democracy resting upon the supposed ignorance and incapacity of the people often springs from the failure to apply this distinction between the formation of policy and its execution. The critic wrongly concludes that, because administrative decisions require technical skill, ultimate directive authority should also rest in the hands of "experts." Of such experts, however, there are none.

This confusion sometimes arises from the improper use of a classical metaphor—that of the political community as the "ship of state," whose "navigator" is the trained statesman. The metaphor is satisfactory to a point. The endless journey of the ship of state is always perilous, and it must, indeed, be carefully steered through the many hazards that lie before it. This picture becomes seriously misleading when the vital distinction between direction and administration is obscured by an ambiguity in the concept of steering, or guidance—and upon that ambiguity one common criticism of democracy relies. On a real ship the navigator must of course be highly skilled—but however great his skill he cannot, by the use of it, determine where the ship is to go. He guides the vessel in moving to its destination, and the dangers he reports may well be considered in selecting a destination; but the choice of that destination is not his to make. In that larger sense of "guide" it is the owners of the ship who guide it. And of the democratic ship of state it is the citizens collectively who are the owners. The journey of this great ship all are making. Perilous as this journey is, it would be absurd to suggest that each has a right to keep his hand on the tiller; but it is equally absurd to suppose that any are too ignorant or too stupid to know where they wish to go, or why.

In sum, there are circumstances in which the judgment of the use of skills—even the most technical skills—is not properly the function of the technician, but of those in whose service he labors [11.4]. There are arts, Aristotle writes, "in which the creative artist is not the only, or even the best, judge. These are the arts whose products can be understood and judged even by those who do not possess any skill in the art. A house, for instance, is something which can be understood by others besides the builder: indeed the user of a house—or in other words the householder—will judge it even better than he does. In the same way a pilot will judge a rudder better than a shipwright does; and the diner—not the cook—will be the best judge of a feast" (*Politics,* III, 11, 1282).

Second: in any given case the conditions of democracy may be so poorly realized that while participation is general, it is ill-informed and incompetent. In such communities democracy will not long prosper, and the quality of the participation may be rightly blamed. Such failures do not establish native incapacity on the part of the people. They show that democracy is a form of government difficult to make succeed, and that certain conditions—intellectual, or constitutional, or perhaps psychological—are more crucial than had perhaps been thought. Every such mistake or failure offers another lesson in the importance of these conditions; if recognized as a lesson we may hope to profit from it. With broader experience in the successes and failures of democratic government we become more able to foresee the conditions essential for its success and more effective in working for their realization. The critics of democracy, ancient and modern, have much to teach us; their lessons are not why democracy is hopeless, but how democracy can be made more promising. If government by participation has broken down in this or that context, the intelligent response is not that of throwing up one's hands in despair but of finding the cause of the breakdown and doing what is possible to prevent its recurrence. There are, again, no guarantees of ultimate success. But where the government lies in the hands of the people it is at least possible for the people to act for its improvement; if the error is that of a despot, the people can do no more than hope that he will somehow come to his senses.

Third: the critics of democracy have usually ignored the central role of community interaction in democratic decision-making; it is generally the most corrupt forms that they have emphasized—bandwagon effects, or the hysteria of mobs. These corruptions are all too familiar; but they are noticeable because they stand out as exceptions from the many decisions made in democracies every day, with care and wisdom, as the result of the interplay of competing and cooperating interests rationally concerned in the outcome. It is this interaction that gives to democracy its special character. Aristotle again: "There is this to be said for the Many. Each of them by himself may not be of a good quality; but *when they meet together* it is possible that they may surpass—collectively and as a body, although not individually—the quality of the few best" (*Politics,* III, 11, 1281; italics mine). This qualification upon the actions of the many (as Ernest Barker notes in his translation of the *Politics*) is vital to Aristotle. Not as a mere heap of individual judgments is democracy superior, but as the producer of refined collective judgments, arising out of community deliberation and debate. Where this process of interchange and argument does not go on, wisdom in government by the many is not likely to develop. That is why the freedoms to speak and publish, to oppose and propose, are constitutional conditions of democracy. Where the channels of rational debate are closed, community interaction takes irrational forms, and we may witness the people passively obedient or wildly frenzied. Where these channels are open and in use, and other conditions of democracy are reasonably met, the prospects for government by general participation are good. When may the judgments of the people excel? "When they meet together."

14.3 Democracy and distributive justice

Of all systems of government democracy is most likely to secure the just treatment of the several members and segments of the community. The justice here referred to is distributive justice in the classical sense—giving to every one his due. How it is decided what and how much is due to whom (whether on bases of need, or merit, or equality, etc.) need not be settled for the present purpose; it is enough if there is general (not necessarily universal) agreement upon principles of justice, and if justice in this sense is highly prized. My aim is to show that, distributive justice being roughly agreed upon as a paramount social value, democracy is the form of government most likely to achieve it.

Because the vindication of democracy does not require that it be shown perfect, it is not the burden of this argument to prove that the outcome of democratic process is always just, any more than it was the burden of the preceding argument to prove that such outcomes are always wise. It is enough if good reasons can be given for believing that *(1)* directive decisions affecting a community are more likely to be just if all (or most) of the members participate in the decision-making process than if only one or a few do so, and that *(2)* such decisions (beyond their comparative merit) have a positive tendency toward just results. Such reasons are not hard to provide; they flow from the nature of democracy itself.

The essence of the democratic process is participation in decision-making. No member of a democracy can be sure of having his way in a controversy in which he participates, but he can be sure (if the democracy is genuine) of having a fair share of the decision-making power. He may be out-voted, but his voice will be heard. If he speaks for an interest shared by a sizeable element in the community, the combined voices of his faction or party will be influential, if not controlling, in molding the final decision. Democracy, therefore, does automatically and by its nature what every alternative system can achieve only partially, and that only by the expenditure of endless time and energy—that is, take into account the needs and desires of all the concerned members of the community. However well motivated the despot or oligarchs may be, the best that can be hoped for under their rule is that they will guess well on concerns of major importance to their non-participating subjects. That the needs and desires of all will be weighed is a practical impossibility (except in very small communities) unless all may participate.

Beyond this comparative merit, democracy has a positive tendency to arrive at just decisions. Because the interests of all participants must be given some attention, the needs and interests of the greater number, or of those able to convey more intense concern, will inevitably tend to receive greater attention. Some may not be treated fairly on occasion, but the channels for the expression of discontent will be open. The system is one whose normal operation tends to achieve a just distribution of goods and services by adjusting that distribution in response to the expressed wishes of those among whom the distribution is to be made. This positive tendency to achieve a balance between what is due and what is received flows from the nature of democratic government and is part of its genius.

The argument exhibiting this advantage has been called the "pinching shoes" argument for democracy. Its homely formulation runs like this: Only the wearer of the shoe can know precisely where and how it pinches. Therefore, if justice is the goal, the wearer must be entitled, not to decide the affair which causes the pinch, but to have a proportionate voice in the making of that decision. It is a sound argument. Lord Lindsay of Birker (in *The Modern Democratic State*, 1943, pp. 269–270) has put the argument as follows:

> [I]f we remember that the end of democratic government is to minister to the common life of society, to remove the disharmonies that trouble it, then clearly a knowledge and understanding of that common life is a large part of the knowledge essential to the statesman. But the common life is the life lived by all members of the society. It cannot be fully known and appreciated from outside. It can only be known by those who live it. Its disharmonies are suffered and felt by individuals. It is their shoes that pinch and they only who can tell where they pinch. No doubt the ordinary voter has the vaguest idea as to what legislative or administrative reform will stop the pinching of his shoes. That is no more his business and no more within his capacity than it is the

ordinary customer's business to make shoes. He may think, and often does think, that his shoes are pinching only because of the gross ignorance or perhaps because of the corrupt and evil intentions of his government; he may think the making of governmental shoes which ease his feet to be a much simpler business than it is; he may listen too easily to charlatans who promise to make the most beautiful shoes for the lowest possible price. But for all that, only he, the ordinary man, can tell whether the shoes pinch and where; and without that knowledge the wisest statesman cannot make good laws.

The same considerations were central to the arguments of Alexander Hamilton, John Jay, and especially James Madison as presented in *The Federalist Papers* in support of republican government. They greatly feared the abuse of power that can result from the development of factions in every large community. Believing that it is not possible to remove completely the causes of faction in human society, they held it essential that the effects of faction be controlled. This, they argued, could only be accomplished within a balanced representative structure like that of the Federal Constitution they were defending. The effective voice of the several factions within such a government would serve to prevent the oppression of any one group by another [6.6].

Some have maintained that what Madison and his colleagues presented in *The Federalist* was a special conception of democracy, of which the essence is the protection of minority rights. This "Madisonian democracy," it is alleged, is a system in which the powers of the several factions within a community are so balanced as to assure their mutual restraint and hence to assure the safety of each from oppression. This misconstrues the thrust of Madison's argument, which, although sound, does not present a special theory of democracy or kind of democracy. It is an argument in support of democracy, based upon its consequences in the protection of minority rights, those rights being of very deep concern. In a healthy democracy, where fluctuating majorities rule, a rough but unstable balance of forces, and the consequent protection of minority rights, will be a natural and common result. The equilibrium created by countervailing interests within the community gives to each participating minority group some leverage on the decision-making power of the whole. The Madisonian argument, properly understood, serves to vindicate democracy by showing that where participation is general and representation fair it is more likely that distributive justice will be general also.

To this argument it is objected that in some democracies large

217

minorities are quite evidently oppressed, meet with cruel and continued injustice. Does not such oppression plainly show that democracy does not have the just consequences here claimed for it? The facts of oppression cannot be denied; the case of the Negro minority in the United States is only one painfully obvious example of it. Such oppression does not, however, warrant an unfavorable judgment of democracy itself. Systematic injustices arise in communities calling themselves democracies precisely where and to the extent democracy is not being practiced within them. In the United States minorities have suffered from continued discrimination just where they have been effectively barred from participation, deliberately deprived of that leverage upon decision-making that full democracy assures every minority group. For an excluded minority the government that it must obey but in which it is not allowed to participate is no democracy at all.

Reflection upon considerations of this kind will serve not only to refute the objection, but to vindicate democracy (but not particular governments) more fully. As previously oppressed minority groups come to enjoy the rights to participate formerly denied them, we may expect to see them enjoy the distributive justice they have also been denied. If in America the breadth and depth of our democracy continue to improve, the entire nation will one day look back upon the exploitation of Negroes, and others, in the twentieth century with the same wonder and abhorrence with which we now look back upon the slavery of the century before.

The natural tendency of democracy to secure justice for its members is nowhere clearer than in the material sphere. Economic injustice on large scale takes two chief forms: *(1)* the impoverishment of the masses, in absolute terms, and *(2)* the grossly inequitable distribution of material goods, even where standards of living are generally tolerable. Democracy tends to protect its members against both of these.

(1) Maintaining a reasonable standard of economic well-being is likely to be the concern of any government. But despotic governments need not exhibit this concern, often have not done so, and are prone to fail in this regard. One indirect cause of such failures (especially where economic conditions are bad to begin with) is the despot's need to protect his power against active protest or rebellion from within. He may agree with Machiavelli that he should seek to be both loved and feared by his subjects. Sharply limited economic resources may force him, however, to choose between providing the comforts that may make

him liked, and securing the arms that are sure to make him feared. He will then be certain to heed Machiavelli's further advice to choose fear before love. Invariably the needs of the military and the police will receive his first and favored attention—as a "patriotic" response, of course, to supposed aggressors from without. Here lies one index of the effectiveness of popular participation where its superficial forms are present. If the material needs of the populace are excruciating, and the expenditures in peacetime on weaponry and military pomp are extravagant, either the depth or the breadth of participation is likely to be seriously wanting. In genuine democracies, on the other hand, the material needs of the citizens will receive the most anxious attention, at least in times of peace, and especially if the needs are great. These material concerns press themselves directly upon the attention of the citizens and will certainly be reflected in the policies of a government selected by general and unhindered participation.

It does not follow, of course, that every democracy will be prosperous, or that the citizens of every democracy will enjoy higher living standards than those enjoyed in neighboring lands. Undemocratic communities may be specially fortunate in benefitting from geographical or other accidental advantages that a given democracy does not enjoy, or a democracy may be handicapped by special disadvantages of some such kind. Moreover, democracies may gravely err in their choice of means to raise the economic level of their citizens. In spite of these possibilities, however, in a given set of circumstances material welfare is more likely to be protected and improved by community action if the members of that community genuinely govern themselves.

(2) In the elimination of gross economic inequalities the tendency of democratic government to treat its members justly is further exemplified. Some economic inequality can be tolerated in a democracy, but gross inequalities are likely to give extraordinary power to some, especially where the mean economic level is low, making possible the improper manipulation of the instruments of participation [9.8]. In a democracy, therefore, concentrated economic power is viewed by the many as a threat and is likely to be regulated, restricted, and even attacked outright by a genuinely representative legislature. Under popular government great wealth will probably fall victim eventually to schedules of taxation in which the aims of revenue collection and income redistribution are mixed. Absolute governments, on the other hand, even if humanely concerned about the welfare of the masses, are

quite unlikely to be concerned about economic inequalities as such. Indeed, some great inequalities are likely to seem proper in such governments and even to be protected as essential. In neither democracy nor its alternatives are gross economic inequalities impossible or their reduction certain; but their appearance is far more likely under autocracy or oligarchy, and their elimination much more probable under democracy.

Historical evidence that democracy does tend to result in the protection of all segments of the community is abundant. The instances in which justice for some interest group is provided by a government only after that group has won the right to participate in that government are legion. It is this objective precisely that chiefly motivated those nineteenth and twentieth-century reformers who labored to extend the franchise. The breadth of democracy is not its only important dimension, but it is crucial to those excluded; so long as their voice cannot be heard in the chambers in which the laws are made they are quite unlikely to be treated with the same concern exhibited for those who can and must be heard.

An outstanding example is the treatment of the working classes in Great Britain during the nineteenth century. So long as the laboring man had no vote, no effective voice in government whatever, his working and living conditions remained indescribably bad. Even the great reforms of the 1830s corrected only the most outrageous abuses, leaving the general condition of the working man unchanged. There was no real democracy in Britain then, and those who were excluded paid the price. In 1832 Alexis de Tocqueville wrote:

> The English aristocracy is perhaps the most liberal that has ever existed, and no body of men has ever, uninterruptedly, furnished so many honorable and enlightened individuals to the government of a country. It cannot escape observation, however, that in the legislation of England the interests of the poor have often been sacrificed to the advantage of the rich, and the rights of the majority to the privileges of a few. The result is that England at the present day combines the extremes of good and evil fortune in the bosom of her society; and the miseries and privations of her poor almost equal her power and renown. (*Democracy in America*, 1935, Vol. I, Chap. 14)

These conditions began to change very rapidly, however, with wave after wave of social welfare legislation, very shortly after the enfranchisement of the working classes which began in earnest with the voting reforms of 1867. This is but one case, dramatic and clear.

Since the great revolutions in America and France, the history of the West has been replete with similar struggles for representation in government and for the justice that only representation will in fact provide. "No taxation without representation," our forebears insisted. Of course it is all too easy to place burdens upon those who have no voice in the matter and therefore cannot complain effectively. Taxation here is only the symbol for any exercise of governmental power. Where that power is exercised over those who cannot participate in its direction its unjust use is invited. The determination to eliminate such injustice by remedying the non-representation that was its cause was "the spirit of '76."

No one has formulated this argument more eloquently than de Tocqueville, writing of the American democracy whose success he grudgingly admired in the early 1830s. His statement of it, of which a portion follows, remains essentially correct.

> Democratic laws generally tend to promote the welfare of the greatest possible number; for they emanate from the majority of the citizens, who are subject to error, but who cannot have an interest opposed to their own advantage. The laws of an aristocracy tend, on the contrary, to concentrate wealth and power in the hands of the minority; because an aristocracy, by its very nature, constitutes a minority. It may therefore be asserted, as a general proposition, that the purpose of a democracy in its legislation is more useful to humanity than that of an aristocracy. . . .
>
> It is easy to perceive that American democracy frequently errs in the choice of the individuals to whom it entrusts the power of the administration; but it is more difficult to say why the state prospers under their rule: In the first place, it is to be remarked that if, in a democratic state, the governors have less honesty and less capacity than elsewhere, the governed are more enlightened and more attentive to their interests. As the people in democracies are more constantly vigilant in their affairs and more jealous of their rights, they prevent their representatives from abandoning that general line of conduct which their own interest prescibes. In the second place, it must be remembered that if the democratic magistrate is more apt to misuse his power, he possesses it for a shorter time. But there is yet another reason which is still more general and conclusive. It is no doubt of importance to the welfare of nations that they should be governed by men of talents and virtue; but it is perhaps still

more important for them that the interests of those men should not differ from the interests of the community at large; for if such were the case, their virtues might become almost useless and their talents be turned to a bad account. . . .

The men who are entrusted with the direction of public affairs in the United States are frequently inferior, in both capacity and morality, to those whom an aristocracy would raise to power. but their interest is identified and mingled with that of the majority of their fellow citizens. They may frequently be faithless and frequently mistaken, but they will never systematically adopt a line of conduct hostile to the majority; and they cannot give a dangerous or exclusive tendency to the government. . . .

In the United States, where public officers have no class interests to promote, the general and constant influence of the government is beneficial, although the individuals who conduct it are frequently unskillful and sometimes contemptible. There is, indeed, a secret tendency in democratic institutions that makes the exertions of the citizens subservient to the prosperity of the community in spite of their vices and mistakes; while in aristocratic institutions there is a secret bias which, notwithstanding the talents and virtues of those who conduct the government, leads them to contribute to the evils that oppress their fellow creatures. In aristocratic governments public men may frequently do harm without intending it; and in democratic states they bring about good results of which they have never thought. (Ibid.)

No government is likely to be perfectly just. The most that can be reasonably hoped for is that the strong tendency of a government will be to treat all elements of the community justly. That tendency democracy may rightfully claim, for only in democracy is such a tendency naturally embodied in the structure of the decision-making process.

Finally, this vindicatory argument points up the error of those who identify democracy with some particular social objectives of their own —public ownership of industry, economic equality, private enterprise, or whatever. Making this identification such persons conclude that what helps to achieve their ends is "democratic" however it transpires. Democracy (on such theories) becomes government for the people whether or not it is by the people. This unhappy confusion obscures the essence of democracy as the process of self-government; it results in the people being told what is good for them, standards coming not from them but from above. Genuinely democratic process is subordinated to particular goals (public ownership, or private ownership, etc.) because it is assumed that those who impose the standard know better what is in the people's interest than the people themselves.

This is a crucial failing of every elitism, however well motivated. Every elite will contend that it alone can be trusted to recognize the real interests of the masses, as the masses themselves are not capable of doing. A fundamental mistake is embedded in every such contention. It is the mistake of supposing that all of the interests of the several members of the community can be known, that they are objects of knowledge which superior intelligence or education will render more readily comprehensible. In fact, while some of the members' interests are of this sort, many are not. The interests of the citizens are determined, in large measure, by their individual *decisions* regarding the matter at hand. Such interests cannot be known antecedently by anyone. What is just under the circumstances often consists not merely in doing what is good for the people, but in doing what they want, where their wants are a matter of purely personal tastes and preferences. It is characteristic of elitist theories to over-intellectualize the constituents of justice, to argue that since these are matters needing only to be known, authority should rest in the hands of those who know most and best. It is in fact doubtful that an elite can know more, even about the knowable part of the people's good, than the people know themselves. But it is a deeper mistake in principle to suppose that superior knowledge alone is sufficient for just decisions. Justice rests, in part, on the felt interests, the personal desires, of those concerned in the outcome. It is only democracy that can weigh these interests fairly.

Political extremists of both right and left are often guilty of this mistake. Both assume that social justice is known antecedently by them, and that any political process is just and democratic only insofar as it accomplishes their ideal ends. They turn things wrong side forward. What is just in the arrangement of social affairs can only be determined in the light of the needs and wishes of those affected by the resolution— and of such needs and wishes the governed are usually the best and frequently the only judges.

Government by the people *and* for the people is of course ideal; but it is as dangerous to identify the two as it is to treat them as exclusive alternatives. If, once having selected what we think to be for the people, we are prepared to scrap participatory government when it does not lead in that direction, we are likely to wind up with neither justice nor democracy. Government truly in the interest of the people is likely only where the people govern themselves. Government by the people and government for the people are indeed closely related—not logically but in fact. Democracy is one thing, justice is another; but we are far more likely to achieve the latter through the former than in any other way. That is one good reason we prize democracy so highly.

14.4 Democracy and the peaceful resolution of disputes

More than any other system of government, democracy is likely to eliminate the need for violence in the settlement of disputes within the community. This consequence flows directly from the participatory character of democratic rule, as the following considerations show.

First: the general agreement to deal with community affairs through some participatory system carries with it a commitment on the part of all participants to abide by the decisions reached, even when those decisions appear unsatisfactory to some. In any large community some governmental decisions are bound to have some adverse effect upon some elements of the community. Bitter resentment is almost inevitable, and even the best democracy cannot hope to avoid it entirely. But democracy is a form of government in which commitment to the system of decision-making is—both logically and psychologically—prior to any specific outcomes. Participants in the democratic process must recognize, by the fact of their participation, the possibility that they may lose out on some substantive issues. That participation, as well as the commitments and realistic appraisals of the risks that go along with it, create what no other form of government can create as effectively— an atmosphere and a constitutional structure in which resentment and opposition are not likely to grow into violence and rebellion. Where I have had a genuine opportunity to participate in the government, to have my voice heard and counted, I am far less inclined, however unhappy I think the result, to seek to alter it by force of arms.

To this it is sometimes replied that, if I am unjustly oppressed by the government, it cannot matter to me whether that government be autocratic or democratic—the oppression is equally real whatever its source. This objection misses the point of the argument. Of course, if I am (or believe myself to be) treated unjustly, the form of government does not affect the fact (or feeling) of injustice. But it may very well affect my attitude in the case, and my judgment of what, in these unhappy circumstances, I am to do about it. In fact I am more likely to tolerate without violence even what appears to be a bald injustice if I remember that I and others in similar circumstances participated (or might have) in the debeate leading to the decision. The outcome, I judge, is wrong; but the process whereby it arose was right, and I acceded to that process not only intellectually but also (very likely) by utilizing the opportunities for participation which the process opened to me. Now, perhaps, I hate the result and revile the stupidity or prejudice that brought it to pass. Still I cannot hate the process to which I agreed and to whose outcome I committed myself by my participation. My right to participate and my duty to abide by the decision which emerges from the participation of all are correlative. If I understand that even dimly, my subsequent course of action will very probably be affected. I may not cease to be bitter, or to express my bitterness, but I am far less likely than otherwise to defy the law or resort to brute force to change it.

Second: democracy encourages the peaceful resolution of disputes not only by developing certain commitments on the part of the participants but by creating situations in which the resort to violence to achieve one's goals is unnecessary and strategically unwise. The channels through which a dissident minority may express its resentment and continue to pursue its objectives remain open. However bitter the minority, they need not swallow their complaints silently, nor in their pursuit of redress, need they resort to revolution. The experience of most minorities in most democracies shows that the resort to violence is a foolish tactic. Redress is more surely come by and more lasting when achieved if the democratic process is protected and critical energies channeled into political opposition within that process. If their cause is just, their resistance strong, and their reasoning sound, an oppressed minority may hope to win sufficient support to achieve their goals. Even when they fail to convince a majority that they are right, they are likely to prove that their interests are genuine, and moreover, that the support they can later give to some larger party will be sufficiently advantageous to be worth paying for now with attention to those minority interests.

An allegedly oppressed minority may lose out completely in the end —but that may happen whatever the governmental form. What democracy provides, above all others, are the constitutional channels for the minority's protection of its own interests. It provides guaranteed concrete opportunities to work vigorously, openly, and respectably, for the defeat of the present leaders or the present policies. In the ongoing debate it may even turn out that they, the minority, will be shaken in their conviction that they have been unjustly treated. Violence, in any event, is likely to be avoided.

That avoidance is furthered by the consequent knowledge of those in power of their own situation. On the one hand they must be prepared to meet the arguments and the electoral influence of significant minorities with counter arguments and influence. On the other hand, knowing that the resort to force by the opposition is therefore unlikely, the government itself is not led or even encouraged to prepare to meet internal violence to protect itself. On all sides in a healthy democracy violence becomes (apart from its wrongfulness) so self-damaging as to be always unwise.

Third: democracy encourages the peaceful resolution of disputes because it tends not to arrive at decisions that might justify a minority's resort to brute force. There are times in the lives of men when rebellion seems the only course for honorable men. That, perhaps, was the case in America in 1776, and in many other revolutions before and since. "Rebellion to tyrants," said Jefferson, "is obedience to God." The safest and surest way, therefore, to avoid rebellion is to avoid the circumstances in which it appears at all reasonable or necessary. Violent rebellion is less likely to seem reasonable or necessary when community policy is determined, from the start, with a careful regard for the deeply held views of concerned minorities. In a word, democracy reduces the likelihood of internal violence because it reduces the likelihood of decisions so extreme as to make violence appear to any an appropriate means of defense.

The disposition to compromise [12.7] is one of the essential psychological conditions of democracy's success. It is through compromise that affairs are resolved so as to make the resort to violence unnecessary. The participation of the several interests; the need to gather these interests into effective parties; the consciousness of the need to go on doing this, not only on the present issue but on a thousand yet to arise; the realization that today's minority is tomorrow's majority, and today's vehement opponent tomorrow's needed supporter—all these support the hammering out of solutions which, though imperfect for all, are wholly intolerable for none. The essentially participatory character of democracy renders it more sensitive than any other government can be to the deep needs and feelings of its citizenry. The diverse instruments of participation provide democratic leaders with a reasonably clear (and constantly changing) picture of what the people and its several segments will tolerate peaceably, and what the limits are beyond which some may feel compelled to resort to violence.

The democratic politician is not miraculously blessed with a native sensitivity to the needs of the community that others simply lack. Natively he may be nothing special. But the entire process of his political education and selection for leadership—his ambitions, his need for support from diverse quarters, his desire to avoid bitter opposition from any quarter—train him well to consider the depth and intensity of feeling as well as numbers and the long run as well as the short. The very process of democratic decision-making sensitizes the participant, especially the elected representative of many, to the nature and relative urgency of conflicting needs and interests. Without cultivating this sensitivity no one is likely to be successful in democratic politics, is not likely to be or to remain an elected representative at all. It is not an essential faculty for the despot; Napoleon, Bismarck, Lenin, did not much manifest it. But good leadership in a democracy demands that sensitivity; Lincoln, Roosevelt, Churchill could not have achieved their success without it. The development and training of just such men is part of the genius of democracy; the exercise of precisely this genius renders the resort to violence unnecessary, at least in most cases.

The democratic process reduces the likelihood of violence even more profoundly by assuring the disclosure of what no governing power, however wise or powerful, could discover by external investigation—the real limits of the toleration of the several segments of the community. These limits are not simply facts to be discovered. The conflicting parties themselves may not know the limits of their own toleration until the pressure of the political process forces them to formulation and decision. Until that ordeal is gone through, the citizens themselves might not say certainly how far in a given direction they will go, or submit. The process of defending their interests is a process of clarifying their interests to themselves—of finding out what compromises are acceptable, what decisions they can live with. Only democracy, by obliging its several elements to defend themselves, can determine accurately what each is prepared to accept without resorting to violence.

Fourth: rapid and major changes, faced periodically by every political community, are less likely to meet with violent reaction where the community is governed democratically. Democracy can tolerate change more calmly partly because such organic changes as take place must arise out of general concern and debate and majority decision. Not all citizens will approve any given change, of course; but all having had a voice in the process that results in its adoption, it is likely that most will understand it and that all will find some way to get along under the newly created conditions.

227

More fundamentally, the citizens of a democracy are more likely to be favorably disposed toward change in general [12.5]. Conservatism in its honorific sense—concern for the preservation of past gains—is naturally embedded in all communities, democracies included. But in another sense democracy is likely to be less conservative than its alternatives because it is necessarily developed and maintained by citizens who recognize the inevitability of social change, and are psychologically prepared for it. If the psychological conditions of flexibility and experimentalism are realized, the felt need of the citizens to combat change with force is much reduced.

14.5 Democracy and loyalty

Every community requires some measure of loyalty from its members; democratically governed communities are most likely (other things being equal) to develop among their citizens loyalty that is deep and lasting. The argument applies most clearly to political democracies and especially national democracies, for it is in these spheres that loyalty is most likely to be of high concern. Indeed, loyalty has come for many to mean only loyalty to country.

Obviously democracy is not a prerequisite for strong national loyalty; all forms of government have enjoyed it. What distinguishes loyalty in a democracy is its depth, its rationality, and the sureness with which it is evoked. The reasons for these advantages are important. The causes espoused by a democracy are the causes of its members. Not by imposition, or by happy accident, or by appearance only, but truly and concretely the objectives to which the citizens of a democracy are committed are the objectives they have chosen for themselves [4.2]. The relation between a citizen and the purposes of his democracy is intrinsic, for although his influence in determining those purposes may be small, it is genuine and proportionate to the size of the community. No matter how honorably administered, no other form of government can guarantee this policy-making role for its citizens. Even where the goals selected by undemocratic governments are truly in the citizens' interests, they will be selected for the citizens rather than by them. To a community whose unifying aims are thus externally imposed, citizen loyalty can never be complete.

This is a homely but powerful argument. In a democracy the government is my government—not only in the trivial sense that it governs me, but in the deeper sense that I am an integral part of it. And I am an essential part of it because the essence of democracy requires that I have with all citizens an equal right to participate in the directive decisions of the community. Democracy wins, therefore, a natural and rational loyalty from its citizens. One need not be forced or begged to support his own causes and seek his own ends. The structural relations between the democratic government and its citizens render the loyalty and devotion of the latter very likely and very widespread.

What of the cases in which, although I participate in the decision-making process, my party is outvoted and overruled? The policies then adopted by the government are not my policies. Am I likely to remain loyal to a community whose policies I believe to be unwise or even unjust? Such conflict can arise between a citizen and his government whatever its form. Where I have participated in the decision-making process, however, I have made a tacit commitment to abide by the decision reached [14.4]. The laws may be bad laws (and I may still oppose them) but the process of making them in which I participated obliges me to recognize their legitimacy and to obey them. That obligation to remain loyal to the community is not weakened by the errors community government may make. It is not an obligation imposed upon me by any higher authority, nor does it last only so long as I get my way. The obligation arises from the fact that in part I constitute that community; its laws are my laws; I helped to forge them. If the laws are just I may take rightful pride in them; if not just I have a continuing obligation to work for their improvement. The acts of a democracy are the acts of all its citizens; they are the products of the citizens' common concern (or lack of it), and they bind the members of such a community as can the acts of no other kind of government.

I am obliged, therefore, sometimes to abide by rules I think wrong. I cannot say honestly that simply because of their democratic enactment I find them right. But I can say that given their democratic enactment I will stand by them, as the legitimate instruments of a community whose ultimate aims I share and help to determine. It is this community to which I owe my first allegiance, an allegiance in most cases far higher than that owed to the interests these bad laws may injure. That allegiance is partly due to the right given me by the community to participate in its government; it is strengthened by my knowledge that as citizen I may work vigorously and publicly to repeal bad laws and have better ones enacted. That my country is a democracy gives me strong reason, therefore, to obey its laws, to support its highest objectives, and to remain deeply loyal to it—reason which under any other form of government I cannot have.

Here loyalty and patriotism merge. De Tocqueville remarks that there is one kind of patriotism that arises in the human heart instinctively, a love for the land of one's birth however it happens to be governed. But, he continues, "there is another species of attachment to country which is more rational than the one I have been describing. It is perhaps less generous and less ardent, but it is more fruitful and more lasting: it springs from knowledge; it is nurtured by the laws; it grows by the exercise of civil rights; and, in the end, it is confounded with the personal interests of the citizen. A man comprehends the influence which the well-being of his country has upon his own; he is aware that the laws permit him to contribute to that prosperity, and he labors to promote it, first because it benefits him, and secondly because it is in part his own work" (*Democracy in America,* 1835, Vol. I, Chap. 14).

One important consequence of this rational loyalty is the greater stability of democratic communities, well manifested by orderliness in the succession of leadership. Every political community is strained when leadership changes hands; it is a special virtue of democratic process that it greatly mitigates these strains. It eliminates that critical period in the succession of non-democratic leadership when the locus of authority is uncertain and its possession tantalizing. When power is "up for grabs" the grabbing cannot be orderly and may not be peaceful. In the absence of established democratic process, the stability of the entire community is threatened by the disintegration of a clique or by the death of one man. History presents copious record of chaos and bloodshed following the death of tyrants or the downfall of despotic governments. Even before that climactic event a silent question may constantly unsettle such communities: after this leader (or these leaders), what?

The orderly succession of administrations in a democracy is an object of rightful pride for its citizens. Losing an election is no cause for pride; still much satisfaction may be taken in the system within which that loss is but one event, and one's orderly return to office may yet be in store. The act of handing over the reigns of governmental power to one's opponent in accord with the expressed will of the electorate is among the noblest manifestations and surest proofs of democracy. It is only what the members of a democracy have a right to expect. Authority is held through office; the office is created by the people, and the power to fill it rests with them. Authority rests ultimately in the people, therefore; where this principle is reasonably honored in practice, the succession of leadership need never be wanting in peace or decorum. Loyalty to a democracy takes the form of loyalty to its properly constituted offices, rather than to persons, and results in an orderliness and stability in community life not otherwise likely.

14.6 Democracy promotes freedom of speech

In this and the following sections I shall argue that democracy tends to support and promote the conditions it requires. This tendency will serve as a further vindication of democracy in each case insofar as the condition concerned is accepted as an end worth seeking in its own right. I have argued earlier [Part Four] that certain constitutionally guaranteed freedoms, a certain degree of intellectual development, and so forth, are, in practice, conditions of the success of democracy although logically independent of it. These conditions are means where democracy is viewed as end. In the arguments that follow, however, the focus of attention is shifted. Democracy remains our concern, but now in the role of instrument rather than end. The correlative shift in the role of the previously discussed conditions must also be expected; where earlier they were treated as instruments they will be treated now as ends. This reversal of position is entirely reasonable. How we conceive any social institution or state of affairs—whether as end, or means, or both—depends upon our circumstances and our aims. Our aim at this point is to see what democracy is good for.

Often, in the affairs of society, institutions and the conditions that foster them provide mutual impetus and support. Of associated elements each may function now as partial cause, now as partial effect, often in both capacities at the same time. So it is in the case of democracy; what previously were viewed as conditions of its success are now to be viewed as consequences of its practice. I do not here defend these conditions but assume them desirable in their own right. Conceiving them as ends I argue that democracy has a stronger tendency than any of its alternatives to promote these intrinsically worthy conditions. Relations here are not logically strict or exclusive. Non-democratic governments can and sometimes do protect important freedoms or exhibit real concern for the intellectual development of the masses, while democratic governments may fail to exercise forethought on such matters and sometimes may even subvert the conditions of their own success.

231

But by their nature autocracy and oligarchy do not, as by its nature democracy does, tend to protect and promote these and like conditions.

Especially with respect to the defense of its citizens' freedom to speak, write, and criticize freely democracy has a better record than does any of its alternatives. It is reasonable to infer that its performance in this regard will be better than its competitors in the future too, although this argument for democracy is not so strong as one could wish it were. Although democracy requires that freedoms of speech be embodied in the constitution of the community, the citizens of democratic communities have often failed to appreciate this requirement, legislating (or otherwise acting) in ways that eroded the conditions of their own success. Democracies sometimes do injure themselves; restriction of the freedom of speech in the supposed interests of self-defense is one way of doing so. But where citizens understand their democracy, appreciating its demands and the dangers it faces, they are very likely to give constitutional protection to the freedoms of speech and dissent.

The argument here is essentially one of relative merit, for although the record of democracies on this score is blemished, their comparative performance is bound to be good. Under any autocratic or oligarchic government the freedoms to criticize and oppose are clear threats to the security of the instituted powers. Some freedoms of this kind may be offered by these powers in order to avoid the appearance of harshness and the danger of revolt that such an appearance might breed. But the natural interest of the autocrat or oligarch is to appear liberal, not to be so. On any issue of real importance, the appearance of liberality will be readily sacrificed if that is necessary to secure the power of the existing regime. Constitutional freedoms—of speech, publication, dissent, assembly, and the like—are window dressings in authoritarian governments. They are pleasant to display and may even be promised with the sincere intention of maintaining them. But they can be nicely done without. Should the object of vigorous and justifiable criticism become the authoritarian regime itself, the superficial character of these freedoms will soon become evident. The constitution (if there is one) may be "temporarily suspended" or simply ignored. Where such an eventuality is even possible these freedoms are not part of the constitution at all. The system thereby exposes itself as one that treats freedoms as privileges to be extended and withdrawn at the pleasure of those who really rule.

Such considerations show that, speaking strictly, the constitutional conditions of democracy cannot exist under authoritarian governments.

Even if apparently extended there, such freedoms are not and cannot be built into the organic structure of such communities. But it is just these constitutional conditions of democracy that are here being viewed as ends. If democracy does not guarantee them, it is at least far more likely than its alternatives to defend them.

14.7 Democracy promotes intellectual growth

The free flow of information and opinion on all community affairs, and the development of the citizens' capacities to understand and apply these materials, treated earlier [Chapter 11] as intellectual conditions of democracy, are also likely to be democracy's result. Any form of government may promote these conditions, but there are often good reasons for an authoritarian regime not to do so, while there is every reason for a democracy to do so assiduously.

Full publication of the facts and arguments that bear on major issues confronting the community will be permitted by a despotic government only if giving that permission suits the purposes of the leader or leaders. The decision lies with them alone, and it is frequently true that secrecy and widespread ignorance of the facts will be in the interest of the autocrat, or will seem so to him. Sometimes as a safeguard against an external enemy, but often too in the effort to secure their own power within the community, despotic rulers will think it best to keep their subjects uninformed or to inform them on one side of the issue only.

There is, moreover, nothing about authoritarian structure that renders the wide dissemination of information naturally useful or valuable to the rulers, or that is likely to cause them to view that dissemination as an important instrument or objective. On the contrary, if there is a single principle in this sphere likely to be acted upon by an authoritarian government, it is that labelled "information on a need-to-know basis." However benevolently motivated, the despot will see no reason to distribute information to those who have no need to know it in the conduct of their work. What is likely to be provided, therefore, to each of the several echelons in the society, is just that body of information needed to perform efficiently on that echelon. This tends to result in the general distribution of very little. Regarding key issues of community policy the distribution of information is likely to be specially selective, since the formation of such policy lies—by the nature of the system—in the hands of very few.

Under autocratic and oligarchic governments, in short, the principles determining what shall be published, and how widely, will be principles devised in the interests of the rulers, not the ruled. Under such governments, therefore, the general public will have ready access only to those facts and opinions that tend to support the policy of the rulers. To expect otherwise would be naive. Hence authoritarian governments tend not to encourage the full and free flow of information and continue to permit that flow (if they permit it at all) only so long as their own security is not endangered.

The case of genuinely democratic governments with regard to information flow is precisely the reverse. Publicity is the essence of public control [11.3]. It is not only a requirement, but a natural consequence of that control because the membership ultimately determining information flow is the same membership benefitted by its increase and deprived by its diminution. A democratic society, therefore, even if its citizenry is rather unsophisticated, is much more likely to promote the flow of fact and opinion than a society otherwise organized.

This is not a necessary consequence of democracy, of course. In this as in other matters important to them, the members of a democratic community may err in judging their best interests, and the community as a whole may fail to understand the conditions of its own continued success. Further, the representatives of the democratic community may decide in some circumstances that keeping certain information from external enemies is so essential that tight secrecy is justified, self-protection outweighing an acknowledged internal need for openness. Such reasoning is common, but creates the serious danger that the people, in whom the power to make policy ultimately rests, will be rendered incompetent to make the needed directive decisions.

Wide dissemination of information in a democracy may therefore also be viewed as a consequence of the "need-to-know" principle. Where issues are of general concern, and their resolution is achieved ultimately by general participation, everyone needs to know the relevant facts and knows that they need to know them. Any restriction upon the flow of information in a democracy is therefore sure to meet with irritation, anger, opposition. Once operating effectively a democratic community is likely to protect the knowledgeability of all its members, and to increase it, in its own best interests. If the wide-spread publication of fact and opinion be a worthy objective in its own right, it is a strong argument in behalf of democracy that it, more than any other governmental form, is likely to pursue that objective with vigor.

Essentially the same reasoning process applies to the tendency of a democracy to encourage the development of the intellectual capacities of citizens, to support their education. In an autocracy education is simply an instrument in the service of the autocrat. So long as improving the capacities of the citizens serves to keep the ruler more secure, or make him stronger or richer, that improvement may be pursued industriously. But when the capacities of the citizens are developed beyond a certain point, or in ways other than those the regime may have intended, that very process of education may subvert the authority that initiated it. Once having learned to solve problems and administer affairs assigned to them, human beings will not be content if forbidden to solve their own problems and administer their own affairs, individually and collectively. It is virtually impossible to develop the intellectual capacities of the citizens without limit while continuing to refuse those citizens the right to conduct their own business, the business of their life in the community. So the autocrat may give lip service to the value of education, but his circumstances frequently oblige him to restrict both its extent and kind.

Under despotic governments a show of enthusiastic support for education is likely to take the form of increasing dramatically the number of technically skilled persons graduated each year. The value of technical and professional education is indeed great, but it is likely there to get more than its share of support because extending education along such lines poses little threat to the despot. The education dangerous to him is not that which develops the citizens' capacities of technical control but that which develops the citizens' capacities of moral control —their ability and determination to decide what things they need or want, how badly, and in what order of priority. These are precisely the capacities required for self-government [11.4]; once developed their possessors will not be managed from above with ease.

One of the most painful lessons of the twentieth century regarding authoritarian rule is this: the autocrat most easily comes to power and most effectively works his will when the education of the citizens is carefully managed, their choice of social goals manipulated by thorough and systematic indoctrination. A generous measure of irrationality in their education will be valuable if not essential in rendering them more malleable. Widespread study, therefore, in the rational evaluation of social means and ends is not in the interest of the autocrat;

that evaluative task he reserves for himself. Autocracy and oligarchy—over the long run—cannot tolerate the humanistic education of the citizenry.

Under democracy, on the other hand, evaluative studies being essential, their pursuit tends to receive warm support. Where the citizens themselves ultimately determine policy, their education is the more likely to be extended beyond technical matters to questions of policy judgment. And because the making of these judgments is a general responsibility, such education is more likely to be encouraged among the many, and to be the pride of the many.

In this, too, democracies prove far from infallible. Foolish economizing, mistaken over-emphasis on military defense, sometimes plain short-sightedness, may result in a failure to give adequate support to educational institutions, or to cause the misdirection of their efforts. But so long as the government is genuinely in the hands of the people, we may reasonably expect that the intellectual growth of the people will be a central concern, as under other forms of government it may but is not likely to be.

The practice of democracy, as well as its policy, supports the well-rounded education of its citizens. Even where the value of that education for the community is not fully appreciated by the members, the process of participation itself will effect an intellectual growth among them of a kind not otherwise possible. The knowledge that, as citizen, one has a voice, even if a very small and indirect voice, in forming policy on large issues naturally brings about some degree of self-education. In democracy as under no other form of government one takes on and is likely to recognize an obligation to inform himself, to prepare himself by reading and listening, and to express reasonable opinions on matters of local or national concern. Public affairs being each citizen's affairs, he is very likely to take a more active interest in them. Such interest and preparation do not replace formal schooling, of course, but they do help to produce educated men.

With regard to the role of intellect generally there is a striking contrast between authoritarian and democratic communities. This contrast provides strong reasons for believing that democracy will encourage intellectual development as authoritarianism will not. Under any form of government intellectual capacity may be viewed as an instrument, the ends to which that instrument are put being a function of the structure of that government. Where authority rests ultimately at the top, flowing downward through the levels of the hierarchy, the role of intellect for the vast majority is merely an auxiliary one. It is an important tool, but its function is that of helping one to perform tasks assigned to him by his superiors in the system. In an authoritarian structure, ideally, every person and unit is answerable to a specified superior person or unit, and each is responsible for the proper performance of specified inferiors under his command. So the principle that unifies the whole is that of "the chain of command"—a principle understandably emphasized in military organizations, since they most perfectly exemplify this strict hierarchical structure.

Within such structures the optimal amount of knowledge and intelligence for each element is the minimal amount required to perform its mission well. Anything beyond that threatens possible disruption of the system. One of the serious problems of personnel management in the military (and in every similar authoritarianism) is that of dealing with those on the lower echelons who possess too much intelligence to be happy in the work their position requires. Excess intelligence at any lower level is unfortunate; it does not increase effectiveness and is likely to cause dissatisfaction and disobedience. Supposedly unquestioning subordinates ought not think too much. Hierarchical organizations operate most efficiently when, on each level, there is just the training and intelligence needed to do the job, but no more. Too much ability, too much intellect, can actually weaken some link in the chain of command. An inquiring mind may raise embarrassing questions, may criticize or contest commands from above—conduct that will reduce the effectiveness of the command structure and may cause a serious breakdown in the hierarchical machine. The essential character of authoritarian rule entails that intellect will be unrestricted only at the top, and it supposes that that is always where the best brains are. Where the work of a man is essentially assigned, set for him by superiors, his intelligence can be excessive and its use disruptive. Authoritarian regimes, therefore, are unlikely to encourage unrestricted intelligence, nor will they permit the instability that its free application from below may engender. In sum, hierarchical systems operate best with personnel of the lowest level of intelligence adequate for the tasks assigned.

In contrast, the citizen's functions in a democracy cannot be assigned to him by another; he cannot, in principle, be given a "mission" by a "superior." What his role in the community may be, and how well he may perform it, will be limited only by material circumstances and his native abilities. In such a system the very idea of excess intelligence is absurd. Every human talent—especially intellectual talent—will be maximally encouraged and rewarded if it can contribute (even in sometimes disruptive ways) to the improvement and enrichment of life in the community. Democracy relies upon the cooperative and vigorous employment of all available intelligence, most certainly including the highest attainable level of intelligence of the ordinary citizens in whom power ultimately rests. Democratic government does not only tolerate unlimited intellectual and critical activity (as authoritarianism cannot), it encourages such activity, thrives upon it, demands it.

Behind this contrast in the roles of intellect lies a still more profound opposition between the two kinds of systems—an opposition of their fundamental conceptions of the proper duties of the citizen. Ultimate authority lies at the top of a hierarchical government, and flows downward; consequently, the overriding obligation of every member of such communities is to follow orders. That is his place, his function in the system. He may be commanded wisely and even gently, but his role is that of an inferior and his duty is to obey. The democrat also has an obligation to obey the laws, but his duties are more comprehensive and more profound than mere obedience. The laws serve to execute a policy that the citizens themselves help to determine. Any citizen, therefore, may sometimes have to perform tasks assigned to him by others, but that assignment takes place within a system in which he is called upon to help decide what kinds of tasks are worth accomplishing, and why. His most fundamental duty is to participate thoughtfully, not to obey, and to do so regarding ends as well as means. Therefore, to develop the capacity of its citizens to think well—to question, to reason, and to evaluate—is a democracy's natural and continuing concern.

14.8 Democracy promotes its psychological conditions

Certain traits of character—fallibilism, tolerance, flexibility, the disposition to compromise, and the like—must be widespread in a community if democratic government in it is to succeed. Viewing these traits [called the psychological conditions of democracy in Chapter 12] as ends of intrinsic worth, I submit that they are far more likely to be developed and encouraged by democratic than by non-democratic governments. Democracies have no monopoly on good character, of course, nor are these traits the whole substance of healthy personality —but these are valued dispositions and democracy is the form of government most likely to support them.

Dispositional traits are learned by practice. Aristotle wisely remarks that virtues, like skills in the arts, we first acquire by exercise. "For the things we have to learn before we can do them, we learn by doing. . . . Thus states of character arise out of like activities" (*Nicomachean Ethics,* II, 1). One can say simply that democracy encourages those traits of character that its operation obliges its members to practice in their everyday lives and that become thereby habitual.

Common experience strongly reinforces this conclusion. He who learns the value of compromise as a child is the more likely, when mature, to recognize its need and value in larger issues, and is more likely then to accept compromises as reasonable solutions. One who matures in an intellectual atmosphere in which candid advocacy of competing positions is encouraged is the more likely, when adult, to tolerate opinions conflicting with his own and to recognize the wisdom in free advocacy and free expression. Again, vigorous participation in club or school elections is invaluable training in the need to criticize leaders and even to distrust them. Further, one needs to have been wrong himself, and to have been corrected, in the government of small affairs, to appreciate fully his own and others' fallibility in large affairs and thus to value fully an experimental approach to unresolved issues. And so on, and on. Democracy is vindicated, in part, by its strengthening of those priceless dispositional traits the development of which its practice continually demands.

Similarly, authoritarian government, in the military or elsewhere, promotes those behavioral traits naturally associated with its successful operation. At any post in "the chain of command" a person has little need to compromise with his subordinates, little opportunity to compromise with his superiors, and little reason to cultivate the art of compromise with either. As commander he works his own will and not another's; as subordinate his duty is obedience above all. Virtually all of his official functions are either in his capacity as commander or commanded, and in none of these dealings with other levels in the hierarchy is compromise needed or appropriate. In like manner, the toleration by a commander of critical opposition within the ambit of his command can neither be demanded nor expected by his subordinates; neither have they any right to expect flexibility on his part in the imposition of duties, or an attitude of fallibilism in the evaluation of their performance. The commander, in his turn, has no legitimate complaint against his inflexible or intolerant superior.

It is not that all members of an authoritarian chain of command are by nature inflexible, intolerant, or unwilling to compromise. Rather, the point is that the operation of authoritarian government encourages and reinforces such patterns of behavior, while strongly discouraging criticism and that independence of thought and action which the operation of democracy promotes. The vigorous criticism of leadership in an authoritarian system ordinarily meets with punishment, perhaps in the form of the loss of one's job in an authoritarian business, or a solid spanking from an authoritarian father; in the military the criticism of leadership is literally a crime and may result in imprisonment at hard labor.

Another variant of this argument Mill presented (in *Considerations on Representative Government*, 1861) as one defense of democracy. Participation in the government of one's community has, he rightly contends, an invigorating effect upon character. Lives otherwise routine are enriched, enlarged by having public duties. Still more salutary, Mill continues,

> . . . is the moral part of the instruction afforded by the participation of the private citizen, if even rarely, in public functions. He is called upon, while so engaged, to weigh interests not his own; to be guided, in case of conflicting claims, by another rule than his private partialities; to apply, at every turn, principles and maxims which have for their reason of existence the common good; and he usually finds associated with him in the same work minds more familiarized than his own with these ideas and operations, whose study it will be to supply reason to his understanding, and stimulation to his feeling for the general interest. He is made to feel himself one of the public, and whatever is for their benefit to be for his benefit.

Democratic participation—especially when intense, and when the community is not too large—can serve as a school of public spirit, uplifting the moral standards of citizens in both their public and private roles. It does not do so invariably, of course, nor does authoritarian rule invariably do the reverse. Under both forms, however, there are marked tendencies to develop in the citizens character traits of certain types. Every form of government promotes and supports those traits of character its operation requires, and which it thereby causes its members to develop in practice. To the extent that the dispositions encouraged by democracy are prized, they are good reasons for democracy's defense.

Chapter 15

The justification of democracy

15.1 Justification and vindication

Democracy may be justified as well as vindicated. Its vindication consists in showing that certain states of affairs, desirable in themselves or relatively desirable, are its probable consequences. Its justification consists in a demonstration of its rightness, based upon some principle or principles whose truth is evident or universally accepted. This demonstration may not be rigorous, but the aim of a justificatory argument is to show that democracy is in some way rooted in general truths not likely to be seriously questioned.

The contrast between vindication and justification, then, is one between arguments *pro*spectively and *retro*spectively oriented. Vindication focuses upon the results of democratic practice; justification looks to some theoretical structure within which democracy may be grounded antecedent to its practice. The former attends to what democracy implies; the latter to what it is implied by. The one is essentially empirical in tone and relies upon the strength of factual evidence; the other is essentially rationalistic in tone and relies upon the strength of general principles and inferences drawn from them.

The contrast between these types of argument is manifested also in the differing ways the critic of democracy is likely to attack them. In reply to the vindicatory defense he may dispute the actual tendencies of democracy; or he may admit such tendencies but hold them undesirable. In reply to the justificatory defense the critic may question the reasoning process; or he may allow that the reasoning is valid but contest the principles from which it begins.

The vindication and justification of democracy are logically independent of one another. Because they lie in quite separate spheres, the strength of neither is affected by an alleged weakness in the other. Without inconsistency it is possible to accept one while rejecting the other; depending upon one's philosohical outlook such preference could go either way. But it is also possible to accept both the vindicatory and the justificatory defenses of democracy without contradiction.

15.2 The argument outlined

The defense of democracy that follows proceeds in two phases. In the first I shall try to show what would be required to justify democratic government in *any* given community context. This I call the justifiability of democracy in general. In the second phase I shall try to show how democratic government can be justified in the context of the *political* community. This I call the justification of democracy in the body politic. The expression "the justification of political democracy," I avoid because the phrase "political democracy" suggests, incorrectly, that there are kinds of democracy of which the political is one. In fact there are different spheres in which democracy may be operative, of which the political is one [9.6].

The justifiability of democracy in general rests essentially upon one moral principle likely to meet with universal acceptance: that equals should be treated equally. This is a formal principle purely; it says nothing about who are or are not equals. Therefore, any effort using this principle to justify democracy in a particular community or kind of community needs to be supplemented by argument showing that the members of that community (or kind of community) are indeed equal in the necessary relevant sense [15.3].

The justification of democracy in the body politic requires that this supplementary argument be provided specifically with reference to the political community. To do this it will be necessary to maintain that there is some fundamental respect in which all men are equal—all men because, in principle, any man may be a member of the body politic. And it will be necessary to maintain further that that respect in which all men are equal is so related to the political community that it serves to justify democracy in that community [15.4].

Three key principles, then, will be discussed in the following two sections; each is crucial to justificatory arguments used in defense of democracy. They are: *(1)* That equals should be treated equally. *(2)* That all men are equal in one fundamental respect. *(3)* That the respect in which all men are equal is precisely that necessary to justify democracy in the body politic.

15.3 The justification of democracy in general

That equals should be treated equally is a basic principle of distributive justice. So fundamental is this principle, and so universally accepted, that it is likely to be thought of as least part of what is normally meant by justice, part of what is meant by "giving to everyone his due." It is not my present purpose to defend this principle. Rather I aim to show that, supposing its truth, democracy is generally justifiable for those communities in which certain equalties are realized.

From the time of Aristotle, at least, there has been wide agreement that "persons who are equal should have assigned to them equal things." But a principle so general in formulation cannot be applied until supplemented by specific claims about actual equalities, and about what equalities are relevant in a particular context. No sooner do we assert the general principle than, as Aristotle continues, "there arises a question which must not be overlooked. Equals and unequals—yes; but equals and unequals *in what?*" (*Politics,* III, 12, 1282b).

It is largely the result of fundamental disagreement on these questions—who are equal, and equal in what—that attitudes toward democracy and social policy in general have varied so over the ages. In the assignment of any given set of goods, tangible or intangible, justice requires that equals be assigned equal portions. But for the just assignment of a particular set of goods some equalities and inequalities will be important and some will be irrelevant. Aristotle makes this point crisply:

> It is possible to argue that offices and honors ought to be distributed unequally [i.e., that superior amounts should be assigned to superior persons] on the basis of superiority *in any respect whatsoever*—even though there were similarity, and no shadow of any difference, in every other respect. . . . If this argument were accepted, the mere fact of a better complexion, or greater height, or any other such advantage, would establish a claim for a greater share of political rights to be given to its possessor. But is not the argument obviously wrong? To be clear that it is, we have only to study the analogy of the other arts and sciences. If you were dealing with a number of flute players who were equal in their art, you would not assign them flutes on the principle that the better born should have a greater amount. Nobody will play the better for being better born; . . . If our point is not yet plain, it can be made so if we push it still further. Let us suppose a man who is superior to others in flute-playing, but far inferior in birth and beauty. Birth and beauty may be greater goods than ability to play the flute, and those who possess them may, upon balance, surpass the flute-player more in these qualities than he surpasses them in his flute-playing; but the fact remains that *he* is the man who ought to get the better supply of flutes. (Ibid.)

The point is that where an equality (or inequality) among men is not properly relevant to the use of the goods to be distributed (as noble birth is irrelevant to flute-playing ability) that equality (or inequality) ought not affect the allocation.

Furthermore, Aristotle argues, it must be the case that some equalities (or inequalities) are relevant to a given allocation while others are not. For if we could not distinguish the relevant from the irrelevant we should have to weigh all equalities and inequalities in making the allocation. But to suppose that we can weigh them all is to suppose that every quality of a person is commensurable with every other—and that is plainly false. One man exceeds another in height but is exceeded by him in wealth. Now if it were possible to say in the particular case that A excels B in height to a greater degree than B excels A in wealth, we seem committed to the position that, in general, it is possible to measure the relative merits of height and wealth. But this is absurd. There is no degree of height equal or even properly comparable to a degree of wealth. So, depending on the goods to be assigned, it may be the one, or the other, or neither of these respects in which the equality or inequality of A and B is to be measured.

These arguments are compelling and their conclusions correct. To achieve a just distribution of a given set of goods in a given community we must distinguish relevant from irrelevant equalities and inequalities, and weigh only the former in making the allocation.

Selecting the justest form of government for a given community may also be viewed as a problem of distributive justice within that community. The task is one of deciding to whom, and in what degree, the right to participate in making decisions which affect the whole should be allocated. Alternative governmental forms may be conceived as alternative patterns of distribution of a special good—that good being the right to a voice in community decision-making.

A democratically governed community is one in which that right is distributed to all members equally. What would justify this pattern of distribution for any given community? Two claims would have to be made good: first, that equals should be treated equally; and second, that all members of that community are equal in the respect(s) properly relevant to the allocation of the right to participate in government.

To show that these are the claims the justification of democracy requires (and to make clearer what is involved in them) we may suppose a genuine community—Xcom—of which nothing is at first known save that it has a specified membership. If now we must choose a form of government for Xcom, nothing further being known about the members of Xcom, there is a strong presumption in favor of democracy. By hypothesis we have no information that could justify the unequal distribution of rights of participation. So far as we know, the members of Xcom are equals; at least they are equals in being members of Xcom. Regarding the right to a voice in the affairs of Xcom we have no rational way to justify any preference being given to some over others; upon him who would give such preference lies the obligation to justify such preference.

How might one seek to meet that obligation? Were one to deny that all the members of Xcom have an equal right to a voice in its affairs, he would be forced to claim either that the members of Xcom are unequal in some fundamental and relevant respect, or that, although equal, they should not be treated equally. The latter claim no one is likely to make or to accept. The denial that democracy in a given community is just will be defended by trying to show the important and relevant inequalities among its members. Where such claims of inequality cannot be made good we reject the denial, and view the preference of some to others as ungrounded and unjust. All of which is to say that we invariably do believe that equals ought to be treated equally. And we are likely to act on the presumption that where important and relevant inequalities cannot be shown, the members of a community are entitled to equal treatment with regard to the right to participate in common affairs.

There are two kinds of inequality that might be used to justify the denial of the equal right of members of a community to participate in their government. These are: *(1)* inequalities of *concern* and *(2)* inequalities of *standing*. I discuss these in turn.

(1) Inequalities of concern. Every member of a community, by virtue of being a member of it, has a stake in the outcome of the decisions of that community. He is concerned in the result; if it affects the community it affects him as one of its constituents. But, of course, the outcome need not concern all members equally. Each member (inequalities of standing aside) is entitled to some voice in the outcome in which he has a stake; each would be entitled to an equal voice only if the stake of each were equal or nearly so. Where it is clear that some members have a much larger stake in the outcome of the decision-making process than do others, we are faced with inequalities of concern. In such cases the basic principle, that equals should be treated

245

equally, calls for a stronger voice to be given to those more greatly concerned in the result. The classic illustration is that of shareholders in a private corporation to whom votes are assigned on the basis of the number of shares owned. If equals are to be treated equally, one's voice in the government of any community of which he is a member should be proportionate to his relative stake in the outcome of its decisions.

A vital qualification must accompany this conclusion, however. There are many cases in which inequalities of concern must, as a practical matter, be disregarded. Sometimes it may seem clear that some in the community have a greater interest (material or spiritual) in the outcome of certain decisions than do others. Yet it may be impossible or wholly infeasible to identify those having a greater interest, or to measure the differences of interest, and hence it may be impossible to assign differing rights of participation justly. The only practical course in dealing with such cases is to treat as a class the many decisions facing the community, then to attend to those equalities and inequalities that can be pretty clearly determined and which are relevant to that whole class of decisions. Therefore we normally and properly weigh such factors as registered membership in the community or the number of shares owned, while ignoring equalities and inequalities we cannot reasonably decide upon.

(2) Inequalities of standing. The claim of a community member to an equal voice in the government of that community supposes not only that his concern in the results of its decisions is roughly equal to that of all other members, but supposes also that the nature of his membership in that community is fundamentally the same as that of every other membership. The large shareholder in a corporation may claim a voice proportionate to the number of his shares just when all shareholders are shareholders in precisely the same sense. If that is in doubt we must look to the nature of the claimant's shares, to their "class," and should they differ in kind from the rest his claim to a voice proportionate to the number of his shares may not prove valid. The claim to equal treatment supposes equality of kind as well as equality of interest. But many communities have members in different categories, memberships of different kinds. Where these different categories of membership can be specified, and the differences are relevant to the right to participate, the principle that equals should be treated equally will not serve to justify participation proportionate to interest only. In such communities, even

supposing equality of concern, democracy may not be justifiable because of inequalities in standing.

Some illustrations from everyday experience will serve to confirm this analysis. There are communities in which we recognize an essential inequality with respect to the nature of the membership of their members; in these we are likely to think democracy inappropriate or applicable only in limited degree or special cases. The family community is an excellent case in point. Minor children are likely to have a stake at least equal to that of the parents in the outcome of many decisions that the family must make. But while parent and child are both members of that community, their memberships are of different category, and it is rarely believed that important family decisions should be reached by majority vote. Where the obligations which arise out of such decisions fall chiefly on the parents, children may be listened to with respect and may be properly overruled. On the other hand, there may be circumstances in which all the members of the family have not only an essentially equal stake, but have as well an essentially like membership with regard to the issue to be decided. What shall be the destination of a day's outing? What kind of dog shall the family acquire? On such questions we may deem it appropriate to count the vote of parent and child equally.

Classroom situations exhibit similar disparities of standing in a community. We do not normally permit full democracy in the classroom, even though the stake of the pupil in some of the decisions made may be as great or greater than that of the teacher. The clear inequality of status in that community justifies unequal voice in its government. Where this difference between instructor and student is enormous—as in primary school classes—we think democracy largely absurd as a way of making classroom decisions. Where the gap between instructor and student has greatly narrowed—as in a graduate seminar in philosophy —we are likely to think that a good measure of democracy can be justified.

Turning the matter about, whenever we begin with the assumption that a community, whatever its size or function, is essentially a community of equals, all having an essentially equal stake in its affairs, we are likely to insist upon an equal voice for each in the making of its directive decisions. The members of a chess club have precisely equal standing within that community and a concern roughly equal in its joint affairs; each may therefore claim, as a matter of justice, an equal voice in deciding whether the club shall hold a tournament or not. Fraternal orders tend to be highly democratic internally (however discriminatory they may be in choosing members) just because the significance of membership is confraternity—equal status in a social group. In any group so organized the equality enjoyed by members as members is a paramount feature of that community. This is often the reason membership in some "exclusive" club is prized; believing the members of that club superior to the mass, the member (or potential member) regards membership in it as a badge of equality with its other members. In treating membership as a symbol of equality within that community he is correct. Therefore democracy is readily justified within fraternal communities and is almost universally practiced internally by them.

To this point the argument has been concerned only with democracy in general—with what would have to be established regarding any community to justify democracy in it. In general we may conclude that: *First*: in any community, if the members have an equal concern in the outcome of community decisions, and have an equal standing as community members, they are equal in the respects relevant to the assignment of the right to participate in the government of that community. *Second*: if the principle be accepted that equals should be treated equally, and the members of any community are equal in the respects relevant to the assignment of the right to participate in government, democracy in that community is justified.

The principles employed here are principles of justice. Their application to particular communities requires knowledge or beliefs about where the relevant equalities or inequalities lie. The argument so far has involved no claim (save for those implied in the illustrations given) about actual equalities or inequalities, and hence no claims about the justifiability of democracy in specific contexts. Of course, what constitutes equality of concern or equality of standing cannot be settled for all communities in the same way. Each community or kind of community must be examined separately. But with regard to any particular community these principles indicate how we might justify, or show unjustifiable, democracy in it.

15.4 The justification of democracy in the body politic

There is one kind of community in which the rightness or wrongness of democracy is of special interest and importance, and that is the political community. So closely do we associate democracy with the body politic that, for many, democracy means only a form of government in that body. This is an unreasonably narrow conception of democracy [4.1], but the concern for democracy in this sphere is understandable enough; and in just this sphere the most fundamental disputes concerning its justifiability arise.

The justificatory defense of democracy now enters its second phase. In the preceding section I indicated what kinds of claims regarding equality would have to be defended to justify democracy in any given community; here I shall argue that claims of just these kinds can be defended with respect to the political community, and that therefore democracy can be justified in it.

The political community encompasses all persons (or virtually all) who reside in a given geographical area. This does not define such communities but does indicate their essentially universal scope. With certain possible but minor exceptions, every sort of person could be a citizen of a body politic. Therefore, to justify democracy in this body one must be prepared to maintain: *(1)* that all men are equal in some fundamental respect; and *(2)* that the respect in which all men are equal does justify the equal assignment of the right to participate in the government of the polity. That the claim should be made for all men may appear unnecessarily strong, since all men would be citizens only of a world-state; but if, in principle, any man could be a member of a democratic state, it is the equality of all that the democrat is obliged to maintain.

(1) That all men are equal. I disclaim at the outset any effort to prove that all men are equal; it is unlikely that it can be proved. I begin here with the assumption that it is in some important sense true. My aim is chiefly to explicate the sense in which this claim is commonly believed true and to show that its truth is, if not certain, at least plausible.

I begin with two denials, both important. *First*: it is commonly and correctly pointed out that one may believe all men are fundamentally equal and consistently deny that they are equal in every or even in many respects. The principle of human equality is not concerned with the empirically determinable characteristics of men—their size or strength or color or intelligence or temperament, or with any other of those innumerable features that the most ordinary experience tells us vary so greatly from person to person. If such equality were being claimed for all men the principle would be patently false, and of no use whatever in justifying democracy. In many important respects men are obviously not equal, nor would one wish them to be, nor does any sensible person claim them to be. Democracy in the body politic does not suppose men to be equal in empirical respects; it is entirely consistent with the facts of human variety and uniqueness.

Second: it is not necessary, for the defense of democracy, to provide some more ultimate ground upon which human equality must be founded. The attempt to do so is likely to lead to an infinite regress in the quest for ultimacy. But even those proposals which claim to avoid this regress by specifying some absolutely ultimate foundations are not likely to enhance the justification of democracy. Such solutions inevitably take the form of some theological or metaphysical claims about the nature of the world (and/or God) that are sure to meet with less universal acceptance than the principle of human equality itself. For example, this principle has often been defended as a logical consequence of the common fatherhood of a divine being. But that this filial relationship does certify human equality appears very doubtful when we recall that, historically, the same belief in divine fatherhood has most frequently been used (and often is still) to justify sharply stratified social systems and to defend the fundamental *in*equality of persons, classes, castes, and races. Quite apart from the difficulty of establishing the truth of religious doctrines, the resort to them adds nothing to the argument for equality. Nothing I shall say, however, is logically inconsistent with the possible further claim that human equality somehow stems from the fatherhood of God. Similarly, one may resort to some set of metaphysical principles of a non-theological character to provide an ultimate foundation for human equality. But any such set is at least as disputable as the principle of human equality itself. In the present context, therefore, nothing is to be gained by such a metaphysical quest. It will not strengthen the defense of democracy, and is likely to detract from it in suggesting that this defense presupposes the adoption of some single metaphysical viewpoint. Still, there is nothing in this argument for democracy that is logically inconsistent with the claim that the principle of human equality it employs has some more ultimate metaphysical ground.

I turn now to the core of the matter. What is the sense of the principle of human equality upon which the justification of democracy in the body politic depends? It is, simply, that beneath all the undeniable differences among men there is in every human being an element, or aspect, or essential quality that justifies our treating him as the equal of every other in the largest sphere of human life.

The justification of democracy

In the *Fundamental Principles of the Metaphysics of Morals* (1785), Immanuel Kant distinguishes the possession of value from the possession of dignity. "Whatever has a value can be replaced by something else which is *equivalent* in value; whatever, on the other hand, is above all value, and therefore admits of no equivalent, has a dignity." So commodities that satisfy human wants and needs have a market value; what appeals to human tastes (even in the absence of need) may be said to have emotional or imaginative value. But some things in the world cannot be measured on any scale of values; they are invaluable, priceless. That is the case with every human being. One man may be a better cook than another, or a better student or legislator, and in restricted spheres of conduct we may and often must appraise their relative merit. But *as men* they do not have relative merit; for what has relative merit may, insofar as it has that merit, be replaced by another like entity with equal or greater merit. A good cook may be replaced by a better cook; a good legislator by one at least equal in legislation. As a person, no human being can possibly be replaced by another. What entitles him to a place in this sphere is simply his having human dignity; it is a quality intrinsic to his being. Just this thought is expressed in the now commonplace remark that the dignity of every human being must be respected. Dignity here connotes not pride or manner, but the intrinsic worthiness of every human being, without regard to his intelligence, skills, talents, rank, property, or beliefs. Who affirms the principle of human equality normally asserts the universal possession of dignity in this sense.

A paradox arises here. It seems to be a feature of things equal to one another that they are mutually substitutive, interchangeable. But if all men are equal in possessing dignity just that interchangeability is being denied with respect to them. The paradox is resolved simply by distinguishing the sense of equality here employed from the sense in which equal things are verified as equal by measurement. In this latter sense replaceable elements in a machine or system are equal to their replacements. If human equality were of a kind to be so verifiable we should be rightly astounded if some, at least, did not measure out different from others. But it is an irrelevant objection to the principle of human equality that there is no empirical respect in which all men measure out the same. If true it would only show that this equality must lie beyond or beneath any qualities empirically measurable. If all men are equal they are so in possessing an intrinsic dignity that does not admit of any relative evaluation.

THE DEFENSE OF DEMOCRACY

John Dewey wrote:

> In social and moral matters, equality does not mean mathematical
> equivalence. It means rather the inapplicability of considerations of
> greater and less, superior and inferior. It means that no matter how
> great the quantitative differences of ability, strength, position, wealth,
> such differences are negligible in comparison with something else—the
> fact of individuality, the manifestation of something irreplaceable. It
> means, in short, a world in which an existence must be reckoned with on
> its own account, not as something capable of equation with and trans-
> formation into something else. It implies, so to speak, a metaphysical
> mathematics of the incommensurable in which each speaks for itself
> and demands consideration on its own behalf. (*Characters and Events*,
> 1929, Vol. II, p. 854)

And Walter Lippmann has put the matter more colloquially:

> There is no worldly sense in this feeling [of ultimate equality and
> fellowship with all others], for it is reasoned from the heart: 'there you
> are, sir, and there is your neighbor. You are better born than he, you
> are richer, you are stronger, you are handsomer, nay, you are better,
> wiser, kinder, and more likeable; you have given more to your fellow
> men and taken less than he. By any and every test of intelligence, of
> virtue, of usefulness, you are demonstrably a better man than he, and
> yet—absurd as it sounds—these differences do not matter, for the last
> part of him is untouchable and incomparable, and unique and universal.'
> Either you feel this or you do not; when you do not feel it, the superior-
> ities that the world acknowledges seem like mountainous waves at sea;
> when you do feel it they are slight and impermanent ripples upon a vast
> ocean. Men were possessed by this feeling long before they had imag-
> ined the possibility of democratic government. They spoke of it in many
> ways, but the essential quality of feeling is the same from Buddha to St.
> Francis to Whitman. . . .
> There is felt to be a spiritual reality behind and independent of the
> visible character and behavior of a man. We have no scientific evidence
> that this reality exists, and in the nature of things we can have none.
> But we know, each of us, in a way too certain for doubting, that, after
> all the weighing and comparing and judging of us is done, there is some-
> thing left over which is the heart of the matter. (*Men of Destiny*, 1927,
> pp. 49–50)

This passage catches well the spirit of human equality; but in suggesting that the real differences among men "do not matter" too strong
a claim is made. These differences do matter; they make life worth

living; they are the frequent objects of our attention and deserve to be. What is true is that these differences can be fully understood and appreciated only against the background of an underlying equality.

A rough analogy may be drawn between this problem and the metaphysical problem of change for pre-Socratic Greek philosophers. Heracliteans are said to have suggested that all is flux, that everything in the world is constantly changing in all respects. But Heraclitus himself well realized that everything cannot be always changing in every respect. A completely universal flux would be nothing but chaos; some regularity there must be if change is to be understood as change. So he relied upon reason as that which is permanent in a world of becoming, supposing an order that underlies all change; and so also he chose fire as a symbol of the universal stuff—a thing which changes constantly and yet remains itself. His student Cratylus, not so perceptive, is reputed to have denied all stability whatever, and was thereupon forced to deny that any meaningful communication can take place. Since he could not consistently communicate this denial, of course, he was reduced, according to the legend, to the waving of his little finger. The lesson is clear; the reality and significance of change can only be grasped against a background of at least relative permanence. If nothing whatever is stable the world is reduced to a flashing chaos of scenes of which no real sense can be made. Change and stability imply one another; the one without the other would be unintelligible.

So likewise in the case of equality and difference among men. That all men are equal in every way, or should be, is as false and foolish as the claim that nothing ever changes, or should change. But as change requires a backdrop of stability to be understood, so also do the differences among men require a backdrop of essential equality if they are to be understood and dealt with intelligently.

Here Lippman's metaphor—that the differences among men may be treated as mountainous waves or slight ripples—may be pressed instructively. It is incorrect to suggest that whether a real difference among men should be dealt with as a wave or a ripple depends wholly on whether we feel an ultimate equality with our fellows. Our feelings have no effect upon the sea, real or metaphorical. But it is correct to assert that the same phenomenon may be of major or minor importance to us, depending upon the nature and object of our activity. Waves don't become less mighty by thinking them so; in the task of making our way from place to place on the ocean's surface they can be awful obstacles, and each may have to be dealt with individually, as the sailor rounding the Horn can testify. For the oceanographer, however, whose attention is directed at the ocean as a whole, and whose aim is the understanding of its behavior in general, the differences among particular waves fade into insignificance, their common features being the focus of his interest.

So likewise with human differences and equality. Differences among men are real and enormous; no attitude on our part will alter that. In the task of accomplishing practical objectives, as individual persons moving in a world of persons, we encounter these differences as helps or hindrances in the most forceful ways. They must often be dealt with individually; they can be serious obstacles at times, and some may even prove insurmountable. The differences among men, in a human world, make all the difference. But when we change the nature of our interest, when our object is not the accomplishment of particular ends but the understanding of the whole community of men and their common problems, it is the features common to humanity that command attention, while the particular differences among men fade in significance. Whether it is the inequalities among men, therefore, or the equality they share that ought to be the focus of our attention must depend largely upon the nature of our interests and aims. Human differences important in one context may be insignificant in another; human equality entirely unnoticed in some contexts may be crucial in others.

(2) That the equality all men enjoy justifies their equal possession of the right to participate in their own government. We come now to the second hurdle in justifying democracy for the body politic. Supposing that the possession of dignity is the fundamental respect in which all men are equal, does equality in that respect justify the equal right of men to participate in their government? Allowing that equals should be treated equally, does this kind of equality justify that kind of equal treatment? Showing that it does requires two stages [15.3]. I shall argue that human equality as described above gives to every man an equal *concern* as well as an equal *standing* in the political community.

Stage one: every community has some reason for being. The common pursuit of some objectives held in common is the unifying principle of every community, and hence of every political community. But the political community is importantly different from all other communities in being, within its domain, universally inclusive. Within it all other communities of interest are organized and all other human ends are pursued. Because of this inclusive nature the objectives of every political

254

community are of the most general sort. It aims to achieve what is in the interest of all its members; particular ends arise only out of this general service function. When, therefore, it appears necessary to formulate the purposes of the body politic, the most general concepts are employed—the public interest, the common weal, the general good. So the Constitution of the United States was ordained to ". . . establish Justice, insure domestic Tranquility, provide for the common defense, promote the general Welfare, and secure the Blessings of Liberty. . . ." In short, the purpose of the political community is to help meet the universal needs of men living together.

Precisely because these needs are universal every man has an equal concern in the effort to meet them. Every man has an equal concern in the establishment of justice, the protection of liberty, and the promotion of general welfare, because these goals are crucial to the pursuit of all his other ends, and hence crucial to the conduct of his own life. Every man has a life to lead; it is a life unique, irreplaceable, having dignity but no price. In living such a life all men are equal, and that is why they have, every single one, an equal stake in the decisions of the community whose general purpose is the protection and improvement of the lives of its members. In sum: the special and inclusive nature of the political community gives to every man an equal concern in the outcome of its decisions.

On precisely this ground we deny (in a democracy) that some have a right to a stronger voice in government than others. We may admit that in some respects the interests of one segment of the community may be more seriously affected than those of other segments by certain decisions. So it was long believed, even in countries now professing democracy, that the right to participate should be the prerogative only of those with property, or other significant economic stake in the community. Now it is generally agreed that differences in economic interests do not justify such discrimination. However great these differences may be they are relatively unimportant when compared with the interests shared equally by all. Whatever his rank or wealth, every man has not only a stake in the political community but equally with all others the highest stake; for it is his life which is under that government, and that is a matter that concerns no citizen less than any other. Insofar as his having a stake entitles him to a voice in the outcome, his having an equal stake entitles him to an equal voice.

In the Putney Debates of 1647, concerning the award of the franchise to English soldiers, Colonel Rainboro argued eloquently: "Really,

I think the poorest he that is in England hath a life to live as the richest he, and therefore truly I think it is clear that every man that is to live under a government ought first by his own consent to put himself under that government, and I do think that the poorest man in England is not at all bound in a strict sense to that government that he hath not had a voice to put himself under."

Stage two: not only an equal stake, but as well an equal standing in the political community must be shown if democracy is to be justified within it. It is precisely upon this issue that much of the traditional debate over the rightness of democracy has centered. As the most inclusive of organized human communities, the political community must comprise all, or virtually all, of the human inhabitants of a given geographical area; occasional exceptions to this are given special justification. [For a discussion of the status of aliens, minors, convicts, etc., see 4.7.] Within its physical domain the political community is essentially universal. Every man, by virtue of his being a man, is entitled to membership in some polity; the man without a country is a puzzling anomaly. Furthermore, one's membership in his polity has no ground other than that he is a man. The origin and foundation of his membership is—equally with all others—the simple fact that he was born or lives there, just as the others do. Our common practice is silent testimony to this principle of universal membership. Barring deliberate changes, we say everyone is a citizen of a state who is born on its territory, or (where patrimony takes precedence over domicile) we may say that he is a citizen who is born the son of a citizen. We do not require that he be born rich, or healthy, or clever, but only that he be born there or in that family, and that when he comes to maturity he be not lacking in essential human characteristics. These established, his citizenship, his equal membership in the political community, is unquestioned.

This is why the respect in which all men are equal does justify their equal standing in the political community. That standing is their standing as members, and as a member of the polity each man is exactly the equal of the rest. The dignity and irreplaceability of his human life entitles him to a membership in the body politic essentially no different from the membership enjoyed by any other citizen.

Earlier illustrations may be recalled to advantage. Communities in which membership arises from different sources—the family consisting of parents and children, or the classroom in which sit students and teachers—exhibit a fundamental dissimilarity in the nature of membership enjoyed by their members. Student and teacher are both members of the classroom community, but they are not members on the same ground; they acquire their membership in very different ways requiring very different qualifications; even the authority that certifies their membership is likely to be different. Members of chess clubs or fraternal orders, on the other hand, however different in some respects, are exactly equal with respect to the nature of their membership in that club or society. Whatever their playing skill or social graces, they are of equal standing.* The political community, although of incomparably greater importance, is essentially of the latter sort. It is one whose members are members equally and whose membership rests upon a common foundation. In the case of the political community the chief element of that foundation is their common humanity.

15.5 Objections and replies

Three objections to the foregoing justification of democracy in the body politic must now be discussed.

The first objection: that men are not all equal in the sense described, but are in fact fundamentally unequal. This position, if substantiated, cuts the ground from under every justificatory argument for democracy. If the essence of some men is gold, and that of others iron, then equality of standing in the polity cannot be defended and membership in it must be of fundamentally different kinds. The principle that equals should be treated equally cannot then justify universally equal rights of participation. If, as Aristotle claims, "It is clear that, just as some men are by nature free, so others are by nature slaves, and for these latter the condition of slavery is both beneficial and just" (*Politics*, I, 5, 1255a), then the relation of the slave to the political community must be essentially different from that of the free man to the same community. To treat them as equals if basically they are not equals is clearly not justifiable. On this view, therefore, democracy might prove a reasonably satisfactory expedient in some circumstances, but it cannot be defended as a just ideal.

This objection is not likely to be persuasive in these times, but I do not know how it can be refuted absolutely. I think that men are equal

---

*It is noteworthy that in some communities of equals, the founding members, or "charter" members, maintain certain privileges, by dint of the special category of their membership. "All are equal," as in George Orwell's *Animal Farm*, "but some are more equal than others."

in the fundamental sense described above, and I certainly believe that men ought to be treated as though they are; but I do not know how to demonstrate that equality, nor do I think it can be demonstrated to the satisfaction of one who begins with a hierarchical view of the world and a metaphysical commitment to basic inequality among men. I do not see how those who assert and those who deny the fundamental equality of men can (while such disagreement prevails) reach any accord regarding the justifiability of democracy. They start from opposed foundations. As Plato remarks of another fundamental conflict, "those who are agreed and those who are not agreed upon this point have no common ground and can only despise one another when they see how widely they differ" (*Crito*, 49). He who denies this ultimate equality may yet be persuaded to accept democracy on pragmatic grounds, but for him no argument for democracy that is justificatory in the strong sense can succeed.

This is understandable. Traditionally the differences between democrats and anti-democrats have been traceable to differences of view regarding the nature and capacities of men. Insofar as a commitment to the fundamental equality of men is now more widespread than ever before, and more than ever an inspiration for social reform, we may expect that the foregoing justification of democracy, and democracy itself, will be now more widely and more intelligently defended.

The second objection: that although men may be equal in some fundamental sense, they are nevertheless unequal in respects crucial to their right to participate in government. This objection is more serious than the first because more moderate and more plausible. In one form or another it is presented by almost every defender of government by an elite. The classic statement, again, is to be found in Aristotle. "Claims to political rights must be based on the ground of contribution to the elements which constitute the being of the state. There is thus good ground for the claims to honor and office which are made by persons of good descent, free birth, or wealth" (*Politics*, III, 12, 1283a).

This objection need not rely upon the claim that some men are, *by nature*, better than others. Aristotle and many others have believed that. But differences of wealth and intelligence, whether natural or not, are certainly real. The question raised here is whether such real differences can justify preference in the government of the political community. Are the rich, the well-born, and/or the intelligent, entitled to a stronger voice in the community? Note that the preference here at issue is not merely preference arising out of public esteem or community choice, but preference by right.

Aristotle and his followers could argue straightforwardly that inequalities of birth, wealth, or intellectual capacity do justify political preference by right. For them the being of a state and its goodness are constituted by such elements as culture, economic power, and nobility. Hence those who excel in the possession of these can contribute most to the well-being of the state, and are therefore by right entitled to a stronger claim on the honors and offices which make that contribution possible.

The mistake in this view is fundamental and, unfortunately, pervasive. It is the underlying premise (explicit in Aristotle) that what is chiefly to be considered in assigning political rights is the individual's capacity to contribute to the welfare of the community. This premise is essential to most elitist argument—Aristotelian or modern—because if it were not true there would be no rational ground for choosing the chosen few.

The adoption of this premise has two serious consequences. First, viewing political rights as ultimately justified by contribution to the state seems to suppose the prior and independent existence of the state to whose welfare contribution may be made. The logical priority of the community to the individual may be implicit, or again as in Aristotle explicit, but it appears in any case to underlie this not uncommon approach to political right. But the notion that the state has an independent welfare, a reality and purpose separable from the reality and purposes of its human citizens, can be dangerous. While there are important insights provided by this organic view of the political community, it tends to suggest that the state is somehow "out there," a body of higher order than its citizens and one whom they must serve. As a practical matter this belief can lead, where democracy is practiced, to much groundless fear of community action. Where democracy is not practiced, the conception of the state as a higher body, assigning political rights on the basis of contribution to its own welfare, has often led to outrageous oppression and abuse.

The second consequence of the view that contribution to the state's welfare should be the ground of political rights is that some persons, at least, must be supposed to know what the state's welfare is, to know what the state is for and what is good for it. The premise supposes, that is, knowledge of what the state ought to be and how it can become so—

antecedent to the operation of political processes. Supposing all that, it might indeed be reasonable to give much stronger voice to those in the community who have this knowledge and can thereby best further the state's objectives.

I submit, however, that the knowledge thus supposed is impossible to obtain. In order to know which members of the community have the greatest capacities to contribute to the common good we must know with some concreteness the forms that the common good will take. But what those forms will be cannot be known prior to the expression of the interests, needs, and desires of the members generally, and therefore knowledge of the common good cannot be used in allocating the right to express those interests, needs, and desires, and have them fairly weighed. It is only after the general exercise of these rights of participation that knowledge of the community's particular aims can be acquired. Before their exercise we may, perhaps, formulate the purposes of the political community in very vague and general terms; but so unspecific must these notions be that they can give no ground for discrimination among its members. Prior to the participation of the membership, therefore, it cannot be adequately known what the ends are to which contribution may prove valuable. The selection and re-formation of particular community objectives is the outcome of the political process, not its ground. In sum, the well-being of a body politic cannot be ascertained in advance of the directive decisions made by its members, and therefore contributions to such well-being, or the capacity so to contribute, cannot be used to determine who shall have a right to participate in those fundamental decisions.

After the specific objectives of a political community have been selected, its members may indeed choose to give office and honor to those believed best able to forward those objectives. Perhaps the wealthy or the intelligent will be elected to serve as legislators or administrators, as in a democracy they often are. That election itself is the chief means available to the community membership to express its directive choices. But the very general and inclusive nature of the political community requires that these choices be made by the membership of the community at large. These choices inevitably result in preference to some over others, but no preference can rightly be given to any elite in the process of making the choices themselves. In that fundamental process the standing of every constituent is equal to that of every other.

The critic whose objection to the defense of democracy rests upon the conviction that the greater capacity of some to contribute to the good of the state entitles them to antecedent political preference may hold this conviction without realizing that a judgment concerning what the state's good is has been presupposed. He may, on the other hand, acknowledge that presupposition explicitly and claim direct and certain knowledge of where the good of the community lies and who the best contributors to it will be. In the latter case, again, anti-democrat and democrat reach a fundamental parting of ways, the one claiming knowledge and knowledge channels that the other does not recognize or accept. I do not see how it could be proved beyond doubt that such antecedent knowledge is impossible. But beside the argument registered above, there are two considerations that weigh heavily in favor of the democrat on this issue. The first is that where the anti-democrat claims (or presupposes) such knowledge, the burden of establishing the validity of this knowledge claim rests upon him. If he fails to sustain this burden, the objection to democracy which presupposes the possession of such knowledge must be discounted. The second consideration centers about a misconception discussed in the preceding chapter [14.2]. This claim that the greater knowledge or intelligence of some entitles them to a stronger voice in the direction of the community seems to suppose that the real interests of a community's members are subject to discovery in just the way any set of public facts is discovered. Hence the more intelligent or more well-educated are thought likely to choose community objectives more wisely. But this misapprehends how community interests take shape. In some degree they may be simply knowable. But in large measure the interests of the members congeal and become known, even by the members themselves, only in the very process of their choosing. Many community interests, therefore, are impossible to know prior to such choosing. To this degree antecedent knowledge of the community's good would have to be supernatural, or is impossible.

Objections of this second sort generally aim to show that real inequalities among men justify unequal allocation of rights in the political process. They do not succeed in showing that. What they do show in fact every democrat may readily allow—that there are human inequalities that may properly be considered when, as participants, we make political decisions. But what may reasonably affect our judgments as participants need have no bearing whatever on our equal right to participate. Differences among men are indeed relevant to political judgments, but cannot be shown relevant in determining who shall have the primary right to engage in the process of community direction. Such a right is enjoyed by every citizen by virtue of his being a member of the polity, having a life to lead within that community. And in living such lives all citizens—without regard to attainments or intellect—are fundamentally equal.

The third objection: that this justification of democracy is not absolutely conclusive. Here the truth of the premises is conceded, but question is raised concerning the rigor of the argument. Granting all that I say about the equality of men, and their universal possession of dignity, does the rightness of democracy in the polity follow with necessity? Or might some other form of government also prove consistent with these principles of justice?

My reply is in three parts. *First*: it is not appropriate to demand absolute rigor from arguments in political philosophy. In this sphere the concepts with which we deal are necessarily open and blurred at their edges; the principles we develop are elastic, and the range of their application necessarily uncertain. Tight arguments, having the form of mathematical reasoning, cannot reasonably be expected in this area, therefore, and if that sort of conclusiveness is absent I do not think the fault is grave. If, on the other hand, we approach problems in political philosophy with more moderate hopes and expectations, as we ought, the justificatory argument presented here may go far to realize them. If it does not provide a deductive proof of the rightness of democracy, it does clearly show how democracy is based upon some fundamental and universally accepted principles of justice.

Second: I would agree that the justificatory argument presented here is not absolutely conclusive in the sense that it must outweigh all other argumentative considerations. I have already introduced [in Chapter 14] a number of vindicatory considerations that certainly are relevant to the defense of democracy overall. Were these considerations of its consequences to weigh against democracy in the end, the several arguments pro and con would have to be evaluated and some balance struck, perhaps one not so favorable to democracy. But in fact these pragmatic arguments weigh heavily in democracy's favor; the vindicatory and justificatory arguments complement one another.

This point can be made in another way. The justificatory arguments may be viewed as establishing a prima facie case for the rightness of democracy in the political community. We may then conclude from these arguments not that democracy is absolutely right, or right everywhere and always, but that, considerations concerning consequences aside, there is an appropriate presumption of the rightness of democracy in political communities, a presumption derived from fundamental principles of human equality. It would then follow that one who would defend any non-democratic government in the polity necessarily assumes the burden of vindicating that form of government. Should that burden not be sustained, it would be entirely reasonable to rely upon these justificatory considerations. The arguments in this Chapter, in other words, present the a priori foundations for democracy; beyond these, there are a host of a posteriori arguments that are also appropriately considered.

Third: for those who find the argument—even as an effort to establish only a prima facie case for democracy in the polity—insufficiently conclusive, I suggest still another perspective from which the claims made here can serve an important philosophical function. Even allowing for the sake of this discussion (what I do not in fact admit) that the rightness of democracy does not follow from generally accepted principles of justice, we may still agree that democracy in the polity—in giving to every man an equal right to participate in his government—is at least consistent with these principles, and is one political form that realizes them in practice. There the matter might be left, with the question of whether any other form of government is equally consistent with the principles of justice, and equally realizes them in practice, remaining undecided. This view of the justificatory argument takes it as supporting a conclusion much weaker (and therefore more readily acceptable) than that the argument could be used to support. But even this weaker conclusion—that democracy is at least consistent with principles of justice—is worth emphasizing, for whether other governmental forms are equally consistent with principles of justice is at least doubtful and remains to be shown.

15.6 Equality as an Hypothesis

The argument justifying democracy in the body politic depends upon universal human equality of a fundamental kind. I have specifically disclaimed the attempt to prove this equality; even if real it is probably not confirmable by empirical evidence. Therefore, he who doubts the ultimate equality of human beings and will act on it only if empirically established, is likely to find this (and every) effort to justify democracy incomplete and ineffective in achieving its stated aim. But it does not follow even for the doubter that the argument accomplishes nothing. It demonstrates at least that democracy in the political sphere is justified *if* human equality be granted.

Then we may employ the justificatory argument hypothetically. Are all human beings known to be equal in embodying a priceless dignity? Perhaps not. We may be receptive to empirical support for ultimate human equality while remaining, in the absence of such support, genuinely in doubt. Nevertheless we may treat universal human equality as an hypothesis. If we accept this hypothesis and act upon it, then we will have reason to defend democracy in political communities. This surely might be a reasonable procedure. Not knowing that human beings are ultimately equal or that they are not so equal, I may decide to proceed by treating them as equals for the purposes of dealing with pressing problems in some sphere, while recognizing that I am acting on that assumption.

Is there an obligation to assume the equality of men in the absence of knowledge to the contrary? This is a difficult question; essentially it asks where the burden of proof on this matter should lie. Must the equalitarian first refute the claims for inequality among men, and then provide additional positive evidence for their equality? Or does the burden lie chiefly upon the inequalitarian to support his case, failing which equality is reasonably assumed? Traditional defenses of the equality of men have generally supposed the latter approach correct, although the frequent adoption of a "natural rights" terminology has given the appearance that some were willing to accept a heavier burden. The normal procedure of classical democratic philosophers—Rousseau and Locke are good examples—was reasonable enough. They argued, in effect, that if the reasons usually given to legitimize moral and political inequality can be discredited, equality is properly supposed.

Whatever Rousseau and Locke might have said or believed concerning this burden of proof, it does appear that there are but two alternative procedures in this area, and that there are good reasons for choosing a specific member of the pair. When we face the question of who shall have (and have to what degree) the right to participate in the political process, we cannot suspend judgment on the question of equality. Either we will treat all members of the polity as equal or we will not. Concerning the burden of proof, then, we must proceed using one of two principles. *(1)* In the absence of good grounds for discriminating among men it is reasonable to treat them as equal. *(2)* In the absence of good grounds for treating men as equal, it is reasonable to treat them as unequal. While it is doubtful that the burden of proof can be conclusively shown to lie on one side or the other, I suggest that the former of these operating principles is the more plausible and the more natural, for two reasons.

(1) In any real political community political rights have got to be allocated in some fashion. Inevitably this allocation will take place in the light of such knowledge and beliefs as are common or in authority at the time the basic decisions are made. Now if, to the best knowledge and belief of those who must act on this matter, there is no good ground for discriminating among men in a given context, those men are, in that context of action and belief, equal to one another. This is not equality positively shown, but it is a real equality from the point of view of those who must decide either to discriminate or not to discriminate.

(2) With no good grounds to discriminate among men, it is simpler to assume their equality than their inequality. This is because the assumption of equality provides some usable guides in deciding subsequently how persons shall be treated. To assume inequality, on the other hand, leaves one in a very awkward position; it is an embarrassingly incomplete assumption in a way the assumption of equality is not. The former principle directs that the humans concerned are not to be treated as equals, but gives no clues about how to make the discriminations it implies must be made. Perhaps this is one reason human equality has often been viewed as "natural," inequality as unnatural.

If these considerations do not suffice to justify the placement of the burden of proof on the inequalitarian, we may at least conclude that there is no good reason to place it upon the equalitarian. In the absence of good reasons to discriminate, it is at least as reasonable to proceed on the assumption of human equality as any other, and the selection of one among equally reasonable alternatives in this sphere becomes a matter of choice. What will govern such a choice may depend upon the temperament and philosophical inclinations of the chooser. If one chooses to proceed upon the assumption of human equality he may accept the justificatory argument presented above, realizing that it is based not upon a certain truth but upon his resolve under the circumstances to treat human beings in that way until there is good reason to do otherwise. When the argument rests upon such conscious resolution it becomes explicitly hypothetical—the supposition of human equality is its *hypo*-thesis, its underlying proposition. So construed the force of the foregoing argument for democracy in the body politic is reduced;

how much reduced it will be depends upon the strength given to the equalitarian resolution to which it is anchored.

One may insist that the force of the argument is reduced very little, if at all, so long as the resolution to treat men as equals (in the sense described earlier) is maintained universally. On this view the principle of human equality will be a rule governing all interpersonal conduct, but one that provides no information regarding the actual conditions or relations of human beings. In Kant's discussion of the transcendental ideas—the ideas of self, world, and of God—he repeatedly insists upon a fundamental distinction of this kind, a distinction between their regulative and constitutive use. Construed constitutively, as though supplying actual concepts of certain objects, these ideas (he argues) are pseudo-rational and lead to intellectual disaster. Employed as regulators of reason the transcendental ideas have an excellent and valuable function; self, world, and God are ideas which focus the efforts of reason, leading thereby to the systematic unity of empirical knowledge in general. Properly employed these ideas regulate the operations of reason, he argues, but cannot supply the intellect with objective knowledge. Kant speaks similarly of that rational principle which bids us to treat every phenomenon in space and time as conditioned by some other and forbids us to treat any such object as absolutely unconditioned. This principle, also, is regulative but not constitutive. It cannot tell us what is or is not conditioned; it serves only as a rule, "postulating what we ought to do" but never saying what is the case beyond or behind experience (*Critique of Pure Reason*, 1789: *(1)* The Antinomy of Pure Reason, Sections 8 and 9; *(2)* Appendix to the Transcendental Dialectic; *(3)* Transcendental Doctrine of Judgment, Chapters II and III).

So, analogously, the idea of human equality may be viewed as having, if not constitutive, then regulative employment. The principle that, having no good grounds to discriminate one should treat all men as equals, may be construed as a regulative principle in the moral and political sphere. If one cannot honestly assert that he knows men to be equal, he may still insist that their being treated as equals (there being no good grounds to do otherwise) be a general rule of political conduct.

What would justify the adoption of such a rule? When Kant faced the need to justify the regulative employment of the transcendental ideas he could point only to the effects of the adoption of these regulators upon the growth of the knowledge thus regulated. When these ideas are so employed, heuristically, he said, ". . . empirical knowledge is more adequately secured within its own limits and more effectively improved than would be possible in the absence of such ideas." So, likewise, the regulative use of the principle of human equality can only be justified by the effects of this use upon the people and societies among whom it is in force. Evaluating these effects obliges one to look, again prospectively, at the consequences of the democracy to which the assumption of equalitarianism leads. With this we are thrown back into the frame of vindicatory arguments in defense of democracy. This outcome should prove no surprise; it is the inescapable consequence of treating the base of the argument as hypothesis. If any defense of democracy is to be wholly free of the need to evaluate its consequences, that defense must rest upon principles quite beyond doubt. In the case of the present justification of democracy such principles would be those asserting the equality of men and their consequent possession of equal rights in the polity. The complete success of this justificatory argument supposes not only the adoption of these principles as regulative, but the knowledge of their truth as constitutive. Whether they be true in that full sense is a question whose definitive answer appears forever elusive.

Chapter 16

The intrinsic values of democracy

16.1 Democracy as autonomy

Democracy may be prized for its own sake, because it has intrinsic value. Exhibiting this intrinsic value does not serve, strictly, as an argument in support of democracy. It does not vindicate democracy by showing its good consequences, nor does it justify democracy by showing it founded upon true principles. It serves only to call attention to certain necessary features of democracy, features worthy of being prized not for their consequences or origins, but for themselves alone.

The essence of democracy is participation in the government of a community by the members of that community; it is *self*-government. No one doubts that in the smaller scale of individual life and conduct self-government is a great and intrinsic value; for its own sake each man prizes his freedom and capacity to govern his own life, to pursue his own ends in his own ways. This experience of personal self-government is writ large in the process of democracy. In the two cases—an individual controlling his own life and a community controlling its own affairs—the same principle is being realized; it is the principle of autonomy.

Autonomy is the expression of self-government as a moral ideal. *Autos*, self; *nomos*, law; auto-nomy is that ideal condition under which any rational agent gives law to itself. Among the ideals of morality it has long been one of the highest. Kant wrote:

> Looking back now on all previous attempts to discover the principle of morality, we need not wonder why they all failed. It was seen that man was bound to laws by duty, but it was not observed that the laws to which he is subject are *only those of his own giving*, though at the same time they are *universal*, and that he is only bound to act in conformity to his own will; a will, however, which is designed by nature to give universal laws. For when one has conceived man only as subject to a law (no matter what), then this law required some interest, either by way of attraction or constraint, since it did not originate as a law from *his own* will, but this will was according to a law obliged by *something else* to act in a certain manner. Now by this necessary consequence all the labor spent in finding a supreme principle of duty was irrevocably

lost. For men never elicited duty, but only a necessity of acting from certain interest. Whether this interest was private or otherwise, in any case the imperative must be conditional, and could not by any means be capable of being a moral command. I will therefore call this the principle of *Autonomy* of the will, in contrast with every other which I accordingly reckon as *Heteronomy*. (*Fundamental Principles of the Metaphysics of Morals*, 1785, Second Section)

Democrats are not necessarily committed to a Kantian position in moral philosophy; but anyone who respects and treasures what Kant called the "supreme principle of morality," the autonomy of the will, will find democracy intrinsically valuable. In it, as in no other system of government, this principle is clearly and fully embodied.

The truly moral agent imposes rules of right conduct upon himself. The proper content of these rules may be a matter of dispute, and the fact that the rules are self-imposed gives no guarantee that the agent has chosen the correct rule, or that he has applied it so as to render his act objectively right. But whatever our judgment of the act, the moral character of the actor depends upon his autonomy; only that man's character is good whose right acts flow from his own will, voluntarily, not from compulsion or constraint. Moral autonomy is the direction and control of action by the agent from within. It is not sufficient, but it is necessary for the most praiseworthy conduct.

Community autonomy—the inter-personal correlate of autonomy in the life of the individual—is fully realized only when the community is democratically governed. Only under democracy do the members of the community at large develop their own rules governing joint affairs, and impose these rules upon themselves. As in the case of individual conduct, the fact that the rules are self-imposed gives no guarantee that the members have acted wisely or justly in choosing their rules or in applying them. However, if the rules governing the members of the community do not arise from their own participation, but are imposed from without or by some despotic element within, the moral character of the community must suffer, even if the decisions imposed are good ones. Individual and community are analogues in this matter; the appraisal of the morality of their conduct depends not only upon what is done, but also upon the source of the decision to do it. Ideally that source of direction and control will be within, autonomous. In the social sphere this autonomy is realizable only when government is carried on through the participation of the governed.

Autonomy is not a consequence of democracy; it does not arise after or because of democracy. In the life of the community autonomy is democracy; from a purely moral perspective the autonomous character of democratic government is its most fundamental and perhaps most important feature. It is an intrinsic value of democracy, a value worthy of being prized directly for its own sake.

16.2 Autonomy and heteronomy in government

The great merit of autonomy in community life is most clearly seen when autonomous and heteronomous governments are contrasted in several fundamental respects. The *first* is their conflicting conceptions of the source of the laws. Heteronomous (*hetero*, other) communities are governed by laws arising from a source other than the members of the community themselves. Authority there rests in some person or body external to the citizens at large, the resultant system properly being called authoritarian. The relation of citizens to governors is that of subordinates to superiors; laws are proclaimed to the people, coming from above and from outside of the people themselves. Government under such systems is necessarily external; even when the laws are good, they must then prove an intrusion into the life of the citizen.

Superficially it may appear that the relation of the citizen to the laws will be external whatever the system of government. The laws command that so-and-so be done; the citizen must obey or be punished. Below the surface, however, the origin of the laws makes a great deal of difference to the citizen commanded. That difference may not be evident in the process of law enforcement—although even on this level there is likely to be more respect shown by the law enforcement officer for the citizen when the former really sees himself as a servant of the public. The great difference lies rather in the convictions of the citizens, their attitudes toward the laws, and in the consequent motivation of their law-abiding conduct.

Where government is autonomous respect for law has a more moral as well as more rational foundation. It is more moral because one's participation in the law-making process commits one to abide by the outcome [14.5]; it is more rational because the laws are the servants of the citizens themselves, serving their own purposes and not those of others [14.2]. If the laws here prove intrusive, or otherwise bad, they do so because of their particular content, not because of their external source. The laws of a democracy may serve the community poorly, but they are necessarily its servants, not its masters.

270

Moreover, the moral quality of the public acts of a citizen—his deliberate obedience or disobedience of the laws—is intensified by his recognition of the autonomy of the community of which he is a participating member. Whatever the sanctions with which obedience might be compelled, it also becomes, because of this recognition, an act of voluntary self-regulation. Not only is the autonomous community itself a moral agent; it elevates the moral agency of its individual members.

Second: with respect to the source of the objectives of the community, the contrast between autonomous and heteronomous systems is fundamental. Here also the basic alternatives are two, however many their variants in practice: the objectives of a community may be selected by its members for themselves, or objectives may be imposed upon them by others, whether by one man or a few.

Heteronomy manifests itself in command relationships, depends essentially upon the recognition by citizens of their subordinate status and of the ruling authority of their superiors. The clearest example of heteronomy in the selection of goals is military organization. The explicit reason for the being of every military unit is the accomplishment of some antecedently determined mission, one that is assigned from above, imposed upon each person or unit by some higher authority in the chain of command [14.8].

Such command relationships are intensely antithetical to democracy. The members of a democracy recognize no superiors in deciding what, as a community, they should do or be. A democratically governed community performs no "mission" assigned by others, but attends to its own business in its own way. Being autonomous government, democracy entails that the choice of goals, as well as the enactment of laws, be determined by the general participation of the membership. Autonomy requires that ends as well as means be developed from within, not imposed from without.

Third: perhaps the deepest antipathy between autonomous and heteronomous systems lies in their opposing conceptions of the nature and proper role of the individual. Community autonomy goes hand in hand with the recognition of dignity in each participating member, a dignity whose universality is central to justificatory arguments in defense of democracy in the body politic [15.4]. No heteronomous government can do justice to this dignity, however wise or benevolent its rule. This is because the citizen, in a heteronomous government, is most fundamentally the instrument of another, a tool for the accomplishment of some higher purpose imposed from without. Every unit in a hierarchical system (excepting only the apex itself) is essentially *subordi-nate*; the role of every person and group is service to superiors, the accomplishment of assigned objectives. The spirit of subordination is exhibited by the language used in its practice. Citizens become, strictly, *subjects*; in the military as in hierarchically organized private businesses human constituents are conceived not as persons but as *personnel*; public pronouncements by leaders are commonly framed in the imperative mood. Where community autonomy is denied, the autonomy of the individual members of the community must also be in good measure denied.

Authoritarian systems will, of course, profess great concern for the welfare of the individual citizen. Even where that concern is genuine, however, the welfare sought is determined not by the citizen but by his rulers, who claim to know better than he what is really best for him. What is benefit in the rulers' eyes may be injury in his; and even if not the subject is necessarily insulted and demeaned by being compelled to do what others believe is right or good for him. In using human beings as means to the ends of others, heteronomous systems cannot recognize or honor in practice the universal possession of human dignity. Such recognition and honor, however, is a necessary feature of democracy, its essence being the participation of persons in decisions that affect their own lives.

Finally: it is autonomous systems only that can do full justice to human rationality. Earlier I argued that democracy presupposes rationality in its members [Chapter 5], and that while it also encourages and supports the development of intellect of all its members, authoritarian systems are often embarrassed by that same development [14.7]. Now, at a deeper level, I submit that autonomy requires of the moral agent—whether individual person or community—a special respect for the power of reason in government. In imposing rules or laws upon itself, the autonomous community presupposes the capacity of its citizens to recognize their need for rules and their understanding of the self-imposed obligation to apply them and obey them consistently. Further, autonomous government presupposes that this rationality will be deep enough and widespread enough to permit the citizens to devise and formulate rules of their own, not merely to adhere to rules set down by others. Human rationality is thus honored in practice by permitting that rationality to be effective in the government of common life. If rationality be a distinctive human characteristic, deserving a central place in the decision-making process of human beings, then democratic, autonomous government is distinctively and deeply human.

16.3 Liberty, equality, fraternity

The three classical ideals closely associated with democracy—liberty, equality, and fraternity—are, like democracy itself, intrinsically valuable. The special relations of these values to democracy, earlier treated in detail [Chapter 10; 4.9; 15.3; 15.6], can now be placed in broadest perspective, a larger framework drawn. Liberty is a condition for the practice of democracy; equality is central to the justification of democracy; fraternity is a presupposition of the existence of any democracy.

Liberty is the most tangible of these, the most easily identified as present or absent in everyday life. Of the three it is liberty that is the dearest, whose absence is most painful, whose limitation is most quickly noted. Liberty is the concrete concern of those who struggle to make democracy a practical reality. The major issues in a democracy therefore frequently concern it, and policy decisions within a democracy will often be defended as extending freedom, or condemned for restricting it. Freedom being the condition of successful self-government it is always likely to be the nub of political argument within a democracy.

Equality has a relation to democracy that is distinctively theoretical, as that between democracy and liberty is distinctively practical. The freedom required is empirically specifiable, freedom to act and speak; the equality required is not specifiable, in concrete terms, but is an underlying theoretical commitment serving as the ground of the right of each to participate. Equality, therefore, though not as likely as freedom to be an issue of practical concern in a democracy, is of the utmost gravity when it does become controversial because the denial of it threatens not only the operation of democracy but its very foundation. The greatest dangers to liberty come from those who, not understanding the operational conditions of self-government, restrict freedoms with the intention of preserving democracy. Equality, on the other hand, is more likely to be attacked by those who do not really want democracy, who do not think it just.

Of the three ideals it is equality that is closest to the theoretical heart of democracy. Where the basic equality of the members is denied or unrecognized the spirit of equal participation by all in their common government is undermined. Whatever the nature of the community, democracy can be justified in it only to the degree that a relevant equality among its members has been established or supposed. If the denial of equality is less tangible, less evident, and perhaps less painful than the denial of liberty, it is, for democracy, injurious at a more profound level. Only with liberty will democracy work, but only with equality is there reason to believe it ought to work, that it is a right and fitting way to organize the public affairs of a community.

Fraternity is the consciousness of community, the recognition by the members of their fundamental, common enterprise. Democracy's need for it is on the deepest level of all, because it provides the context within which equality can be established and freedom can be protected. Of the three ideals, therefore, fraternity must be given temporal and logical priority. There can be no self-government where there is no community recognizing itself as an entity within which self-government might be proposed or realized. Fraternity institutes the democratic community, as equality characterizes it, and liberty safeguards it.

These ideals are not in need of defense. To the extent that each is embedded in democracy—as condition, justification, and presupposition—the realization of them and their intrinsic values go hand in hand with the realization of democracy.

Part Six

THE PROSPECTS OF DEMOCRACY

Chapter 17

Why democracy is not likely to succeed

17.1 A note on political prophecy

It is fitting to conclude this treatise with a look to the future of democracy, partly to assuage our understandable curiosity, partly to help in the guidance of practice. The foregoing account of the nature of democracy, its conditions and presuppositions, gives no ground for prophecy, but does permit reasonable speculation about the prospect before us. The number and kind of human communities being unlimited, democracy is sure to thrive in some, sure to deteriorate (or never develop) in others. In political communities the future of democracy is of special concern. Its success in this sphere will remain always a matter of degree, of course, and its appraisal, or improvement, in any particular community will require much study in the sciences of society. Even now, however, some general observations may be made, some broad tendencies noted, which bear directly upon the realization of the conditions and presuppositions of democracy, and thus affect the probable successs of democracy itself. My conclusion will be that, in bodies politic, the prospects for democracy are not very good.

17.2 The material prospects of democracy

One grave obstacle to the improvement and spread, and perhaps even retention, of democracy throughout the world is the non-realization of its material conditions. Long-range success for democracies in political communities will require the attainment of a standard of living for the masses of the world far higher than that they presently enjoy, and it will require a considerable reduction of the gross economic inequalities that presently divide men. That such material objectives can be achieved, or that they will be achieved before economic pressures explode the present world fabric entirely, appear now to be matters of serious doubt.

The picture is not altogether black. Human productivity constantly rises; old resources are replaced, new ones found. New realms for exploration—new sources of energy from sun or tides, new sources of food from oceans or deserts—leave open the question of what material levels may be reached in time. Spectacular strides in the sciences of communication, moreover, render participation in government by all persons, regardless of condition or residence, possible in the future as it was never dreamed possible in the past.

But if there is some reason to hope that the material conditions of democracy may be improved over the coming decades, there is greater reason to fear that they will not be adequately realized. The outcome, affected by a host of complex factors, will be ultimately decided by the winner of a global race between human productivity on the one hand and human reproductivity on the other. Reproductivity has, and promises to retain, a commanding lead. At the time of the present writing the population of the Earth has just passed three billion; that population continues to grow at terrifying speed. If this growth is not halted or greatly slowed—and it seems now certain that it will not be, unless hundreds of millions are killed by war or famine or both—the fourth billion of humans will arrive by about 1985, the fifth billion by 1995, and sixth billion within another five years, by the end of this century. What will happen from that point is almost beyond the power of present prediction, and probably also beyond the reach of present belief. These estimates are generally agreed to be conservative; some others, from United Nations sources, predict an even more rapid rise in world population. And the history of population predictions reveals that numbers estimated for the future almost invariably prove lower than the actual population when that future arrives.

It is a certainty that the size of the Earth's population must somehow soon be limited. What remains uncertain is the method of that limitation—whether it be accomplished intelligently and justly, or by chance and catastrophe—and the timing of it. The problems posed by population growth may be temporarily met through agricultural or technological ingenuity, but cannot ultimately be solved in this way.

In the realm of the purely arithmetical, it can be shown that if the rate of increase in world population remains the same as it is today, doubling every generation, our present 3.5 billion people will increase in 30 generations (900 years) to 3 sextillion, 758 quintillion, 96 quadrillion, 384 trillion people—4,550 people for each square foot of the Earth's land surface.

In the realm of the possible, careful efforts have been made to determine how many people the Earth could support under the most favorable conditions. Assuming that all the energy in the sun's rays could be captured, and every resource utilized, including even the atomic energy in granite, the most optimistic of reputable estimates is that—if mankind could be satisfied subsisting on the products of algae farms and yeast factories—the Earth might support as many as 50 billion people. At the present rate of population increase there will be 50 billion people on Earth in four more generations, about 120 years.

In the realm of the probable, one should note that in some parts of the world serious famines have already begun; within a decade or two of the present writing, if present trends continue, famine is likely to spread over large portions of the globe, assuming almost indescribably calamitous proportions.

This grim picture has immediate bearing upon the prospects of democracy. Great size is always a problem for a self-governing community; the larger the membership the more difficult it is for each member to have his voice heard, and the more minute must be the contributions of each, relative to the whole. Systems of representation can sometimes maintain effective participation, but the larger the number represented, and the larger the number of representatives, the more indirect and less responsive is the democracy likely to be. These difficulties are already with us. Sheerly numerical difficulties are compounded, however, when the great mass of a political community do not enjoy the material circumstances that render participation in government a practical possibility. The difficulties of achieving such material circumstances are further compounded by the fact that it is precisely among communities already so impoverished that population growth is fastest and promises to become faster. In such communities, already encompassing the majority of the world's population, and soon to encompass its overwhelming majority, the hope for democracy must grow dim. This bleak outlook is more than a speculation; the conditions foreseen are already ugly realities over much of the planet.

In the United States one often hears of the need to eliminate "pockets" of poverty; it is a real need. From a global perspective, however, the two hundred million Americans (some 6% of the present world population) constitute a pocket of wealth, one of very few. Vigorous international efforts now go on to overcome misery and economic destitution, but little progress is being made. As quickly as increased productivity is achieved, rising populations gobble it up. With it they gobble up the savings that need to be reinvested by the community in social overhead (schools, roads, hospitals, etc.) and in productive industry. Poor communities with swelling populations live in a world very much like that of Lewis Carroll's Red Queen: "Now, *here*, you see, it takes all the running *you* can do, to keep in the same place. If you want to get somewhere else you must run at least twice as fast as that."

The unfortunate effects of rapid population growth, and the effects of the generalized poverty that normally accompanies it, are manifold. One could go on to show in detail: (1) how poverty erodes the intellectual conditions of democracy, limiting the funds and efforts that can be devoted to education, both by the individual family and by the community; (2) how material circumstances influence the quality of the lives lived by the citizens of any community, and can affect adversely both constitutional and psychological conditions of democracy; (3) how even the protective capacities of the community are reduced when the standard of living goes down. Democracy is plainly threatened by growing world poverty.

In Europe and North America where, relatively speaking, wealth is the rule and poverty the exception, these threats are commonly ignored or gravely underestimated. Among hungry and miserable masses, on the other hand, the awareness of gross economic inequalities becomes ever more widespread and more acute. How much material deprivation these masses of the Earth will tolerate, and how long, no man can say. But if reproductivity continues to win the race against productivity, the prospects for the realization of the material conditions of democracy, and for democracy itself in the political sphere, will continue to deteriorate.

17.3 The intellectual prospects of democracy

The prospects for the increasing realization of the intellectual conditions of democracy—the maintenance of a well-informed and well-educated citizenry—are somewhat more hopeful than its material prospects, but on the whole are not encouraging.

On the brighter side it is certainly true that the power to acquire and store information, and the power to communicate and manipulate it, now develops with a speed and range never known before. Radio and television are almost universal, and soon will be completely so; new methods of direct communication will be derived. Published research in every sphere swells our libraries at an enormous rate, and new systems of information retrieval are already being created to render this mass of intellectual material usable. New methods of instruction, some employing advanced technology, make basic education a possibility among masses for whom it was once undreamed of. On other fronts, the increased understanding of the human nervous system, continuing experimentation in the conditioning of animals by electrical stimulation of the brain, research into the power of pharmaceuticals in controlling human behavior, research into the nature of human memory, and into the possibility of learning during sleep—all open vistas of possible intensified learning and teaching that are as exciting as they are threatening. What the human mind may master, and the speed at which it may do so, has no clear limits. If these developing powers are quickly put to the service of democracy there is reason for encouragement.

Unfortunately, while the improvement of techniques in education and communication is a challenge that is being met, the command of such techniques presents a further challenge that is not being met—that of developing the principles that ought to guide the employment of this new and powerful technology. Like the sorcerer's apprentice the democracies of the world have set in motion instruments of extraordinary power but do not know how to control them. Several manifestations of this absence of control are worthy of specific notice.

First: without proper guidance the power to instruct becomes the power to inculcate—a term derived from the Latin *inculcare*, to tread upon. Inculcation of doctrine in some areas—in history, or politics, or philosophy—may result in a net reduction in the capacity of the members to make the moral and political evaluations democracy requires of them. Inculcation in matters political or philosophical distorts the educative process, casts it in the role of instrument for partisan ends. So employed, education becomes indoctrination, brainwashing, the very antithesis of what democracy requires. The most impressive command of facts cannot replace the ability to use intellect creatively in judging ends and ideals. If new methods or machines are employed without the concomitant development of that creative ability, such devices may prove to be more the enemies of democracy than its friends.

Second: dangers arising out of advances in techniques of instruction are matched by dangers flowing from the misuse of the media of mass communication, upon which large scale democracy depends. Here again, technical marvels may be used to manipulate the process of participation rather than to serve it. Enormous power lies in the hands of those who control these media; that control already lies in few hands and moves steadily into fewer. There are no easy safeguards against the abuse of this power. Private control may be unscrupulous or naive. Public control, instituted to correct these evils, may result in the greater centralization rather than diffusion of power over the content of what is communicated. I make no brief here for either private or public ownership of the media of mass communication; whatever the forms of their operation, balance in their regulation is fearfully difficult to achieve. Concentration of power in this sphere appears unavoidable, and this growing concentration seems certain to reduce the quality and effectiveness of individual participation. Most national democracies are already afflicted with this deterioration; there is no good reason to suppose that it will cease. With the possibility of growing control over human behavior on the one hand, and the steadily concentrating power over the media of communication on the other hand, it seems unlikely that the intellectual conditions of national democracy will much improve, and very possible that they will go almost wholly unrealized in some communities. Whether, in the government of large bodies politic, participation in depth can long continue, is an issue that for the present remains moot.

Third: from a global perspective there is an ever-increasing gap between the capacities of the well-educated few and those of the ill-educated or uneducated masses, a gap that seems certain to become yet greater over the coming decades. Well intentioned efforts to narrow this gap often have the opposite effect. On the one side the progress of medical science cuts the mortality rate in impoverished lands, resulting in the preservation of masses who have little hope for an education; on the other side vigorous research results in a forward surge on the part of those already educated. An intellectual disparity already threatening is steadily exacerbated.

This split between the educated and the ignorant has direct, adverse effects upon democracy. Knowledge *is* power; great disparity in intellectual development gives inordinate power to the educated few, increasing the likelihood that the masses will be used to the advantage of others. Campaigns by the intellectual elite to "educate" the masses frequently become covert attempts to indoctrinate them, sometimes, but not always, with good intentions. This growing imbalance between the intellectual attainments of the many and of the few renders it increasingly more difficult for the masses to play the proportionate role in government that democracy requires of them.

The most pressing educative task in democracies, therefore, now becomes not to teach more to the few, but to teach enough to the many. The former task is easier, more exciting, more immediately rewarding; so intellectual achievement in the community is often measured by the speed and success with which those already on the frontiers of knowledge advance yet further. The outcome in practice has been continuing support for an intellectual elite who plunge ahead ever more rapidly, while the masses find themselves less and less able to understand or keep up. Even in American society, where universal public education is well-established, the gap between the better educated few and the average many has become unhealthily enlarged; tension between the extremes is aggravated by growing mutual distrust. It is essential, therefore, if democracy is to survive, both within the American nation and on the global scale, to consolidate educational ranks. Advances on intellectual frontiers must not be slowed, of course, but proportionally greater effort must be made to bring to a decent intellectual level those who have been left behind. Mass education, carefully safeguarded against indoctrination, must somehow be instituted successfully in poor lands, by poor people, for themselves. Progress being made in this enterprise is far from encouraging. Over much of the world literacy rates remain essentially stable, or even dip, and the absolute number of illiterates—for whom the role of democratic citizen is practically impossible—steadily rises. Where mass education is vigorously pursued, its dogmatic, doctrinal content is often as antithetical to the spirit of democracy as the ignorance it seeks to erase. Steering a course between the twin threats of mass ignorance and mass indoctrination is the foremost intellectual challenge facing political democracies over the next half century.

Dangers to democracy created by the gap between the well-educated and the ill-educated are increased by the steadily rising intellectual requirements for the operation of political democracy. The intellectual conditions of democracy in any community are functions of its concrete circumstances [11.4]. A tribe of aborigines, totally without formal education, may be able to maintain a democracy if the judgments to be made by the membership do not suppose a level of intellectual attainment higher than that their society makes possible for its members. But it is foolish and even cruel to expect an aboriginal population to govern itself democratically under circumstances demanding judgment and evaluation beyond their intellectual attainments. With the rapidly increasing complexity of human society, with ever more difficult issues to be resolved by community governments, there comes a correlative rise in the minimal level of general intellectual development essential for the success of self-government. Many technical questions can be left in the hands of representatives and hired administrators, but it remains necessary to select such deputies, evaluate their service, and face directly some large questions of general policy. As difficulty heightens, so also does the level of needed sophistication. The moral is clear: continuing success for democracy in large political communities requires what now seems unlikely—that universal intellectual development will keep pace with the complexities of human government. Existing tendencies toward improvement at one end of the intellectual spectrum and deterioration at the other do not present a cheerful prospect for democracy.

17.4 The fraternal prospects of democracy

Recent decades have witnessed a rapid intensification of community consciousness in some parts of the world manifested by the growing nationalism of Asian and African peoples. The drives for "independence" and "freedom"—meaning chiefly independence from colonial supervision, and freedom from external interference—are rooted in strong and spreading feelings of national unity. Political unity and independence is no guarantee of democracy, of course, but there can be no political democracy without it. The movement toward the national independence of people is, in this sense, a step toward their genuine self-determination. This is true whether the nation in question is small and weak, like Senegal or Belize, or large and powerful, like Indonesia or India. Where community consciousness, fraternity, has not developed, democracy cannot even begin.

Sometimes independence comes to a people prematurely, their resulting government taking a form very far from democracy. Community affairs may be free of foreign interference while the masses have as little share in governing themselves as ever they did under colonial rule. Democracy and national independence ought not be confounded; democratic government may be a more distant prospect for the subjects of an absolute, native autocrat than for the citizens of a colony governed by a reasonably enlightened foreign power. Whether the government be colonial or indigenous, however, there is no chance for democracy until a spirit of political community has arisen.

Unfortunately, the nationalistic form in which that spirit has been chiefly manifested has, while furthering democracy in some contexts, rendered it a practical impossibility (for the present, at least) in the most important of all contexts, that of the global community. The effective formation of a genuine world community has been largely stymied by national allegiances and national hatreds. Some faint recognition of a global community there has been, but for the present and near future it appears too weak to sustain any significant democracy.

National communities have been the leading institutional agents in world affairs since the end of the fifteenth century. The state, with all that it stands for both ignominious and noble, has been the focus of men's highest loyalties. This was satisfactory so long as human well-being required a community no larger, and circumstances rendered larger communities virtually impossible. That day is over; men must look now much beyond the interests of their sovereign state. It is a commonplace that the world is one. Instruments of communication and transportation have shrunk the globe; the web of modern industry leaves no significant community isolated or self-sufficient. Global inter-dependence in most spheres of human life has been accompanied by mankind's disheartening refusal to recognize that interdependence in the largest sphere of all, the political. This refusal, whatever its reasons, has serious consequences for democracy.

National democracy is no longer enough. On the one hand the economic interdependence of peoples, and on the other hand the threat posed by future military conflicts of nations, bind the masses of humans into one genuinely global human community encompassing and sur-passing in importance all national communities. Problems of common concern now face the citizens of this global community. Mouths multi-ply, famine has already begun; the nuclear weapons that may destroy us all not only exist but rest in hands often irresponsible; the planetary environment deteriorates. These grave problems affect everyone. They can be dealt with democratically only if the community they create is concretely recognized, and everyone, everywhere, is given opportunity to participate, through representatives, in their resolution. Present ar-rangements in world politics obviously do not permit this.

My purpose here is neither to propose some scheme of world gov-ernment, nor to predict its coming. Mankind has managed to survive for a long time without democracy on the planetary scale, and may be able to do so for a long time yet. But it is on that scale precisely that the most serious problems of men now arise and will continue to arise. Their satisfactory resolution depends upon a concrete recognition of that global community in the form of its intelligent government. For these objectives the growth of new nationalisms, and the irrational dance of national powers in coalitions and confrontations aimed at advancing the interests of some sovereign states at the expense of others, do not augur

285

well. The prospects for democracy on the global scale, where it is perhaps most essential, are not good.

17.5 Realism and world democracy

Global democracy is generally considered an unrealistic ideal, in view of the enormous difficulties standing in the way of its accomplishment. All previous attempts to plan or develop a world government have proved failures; no new schemes appear to offer any greater promise. Moreover, any world democracy would appear to require what seems almost unreasonable to hope for, the sacrifice of national loyalties and national sovereignties. The chances for success in such a venture are not great.

From the fact that the prospects of success are poor, however, it does not follow that efforts to achieve that success are foolish or unrealistic. Even the skeptic must grant that success is not totally out of the question. Repeated failures may have been a necessary prelude to the development of a viable world government; the presence of planetary dangers and destructive potentials unlike any known before may induce remarkable changes in the political attitudes of those threatened with personal catastrophe. Such changes are possible at least.

The refusal to pursue such possibilities may prove criminally shortsighted, because of the dearth of satisfactory alternatives. The absence of such government of the global community may lead to nuclear wars, to the death of tens or hundreds of millions, and even perhaps to the death of all. Even without war, present international anarchy seems perfectly incapable either of avoiding stupendous population growth, or of mitigating the awfulness of its consequences. War or no war, a continuation of the existing state of human government seems likely to render the lives of all or most men impoverished and miserable within decades. Outcomes so grim are not certain, but their probability needs to be weighed honestly in deciding what present sacrifice is justified in the effort to avoid them.

The nation-state has not always been the form of human political government, nor is it likely to remain so forever. Common sense requires that we plan for its replacement before some replacement is thrust upon us by circumstances out of rational control. It is neither wise nor fair to call him who talks of the mutual sacrifice of national sovereignty unrealistic, and him who plans for the demolition of cities and the annihilation of millions a realist. The development of a global democracy need not be utopian, but even supposing that it were, the wildest utopian scheme could not be more clearly and concretely insane than the present conduct of international war.

The citizens of wealthy, Western democracies are now obliged to pass rational judgment upon the wisdom of pressing for the democratic government of a world community. This calls for an honest appraisal of the costs, economic and other, that global democracy might impose upon us, and an honest appraisal, too, of the costs of the other long-range alternatives open to us. What then will emerge as realistic, and what as unrealistic, is a matter that remains for the present undecided.

17.6 A concluding note on the future of democracy

Although the prospects of democracy in many political communities are rather bleak, it is important that these prospects be wisely viewed. Undue pessimism regarding the future of democratic governments can prove self-justifying; excessive optimism may blind us to the difficulties democracy must overcome. Neither pessimism nor optimism is the wisest attitude, but a *meliorism* that calls for our best efforts to see things as they are and, so far as is within our power, make them better. Supporters of democracy have reasons to be gravely concerned about its future, but have some grounds for hope as well. It remains to do what can be done to improve the conditions of democracy; in many communities such efforts may meet with continued, even increasing success.

Finally, whatever may be the world-wide prospects of democracy, it remains true that within those limited contexts in which democracy has been or will be substantially realized, human lives are likely to be lived more wholesomely, more richly, and with more satisfaction than under any other form of human government. Alexis de Tocqueville concluded *Democracy in America* in 1835 "full of apprehensions and of hopes," perceiving "mighty dangers which it is possible to ward off, mighty evils which may be avoided or alleviated." The future of democracy is not so bright now as it was then, but neither should it be foreclosed. What de Tocqueville said then of democratic nations we may hope will prove true of a democratic global community as yet not realized—that for its citizens to be virtuous and prosperous, they require but to will it.

Democracy now excites the imagination and inspires the hopes of all the peoples of the globe. It is a just system of government, rightly prized and defended. But there is no magic power in it. Democracy cannot accomplish for a community what is not within the material or intellectual capacities of its members. Whether democracy, if realized, will lead the peoples of the world to a life of culture and material well-being or to collective poverty and wretched conformity, is a question only answerable by future historians. We help to determine what that answer will be. It is at once the weakness and strength of democracy, its danger and its glory, that the fate of its members lies largely in their own hands. Where government rests ultimately upon the participation of the governed it is their wisdom, collectively formed and expressed, that must determine its failure or success.

Index

Ability, 252
Absolutism: 128–32, 181, 209, 219; conditional, 140–43
Abstention: 189; deliberate, 13; justification of, 14
Abuse of power, 72
Administration, 213, 230
Administrators, 87, 260, 283
Advocacy: 154; incitement and, 143–52
Areopagitica (Milton), 142
Aggression, 192–95, 198
Alien and Sedition Laws of 1798, 136
Aliens, 50–51, 256
American Ethics and Public Policy (Kaplan), 132
Animal Farm (Orwell), 257n
Anti-democratic minorities, 152–55, 198-202
Anti-democrats, 258, 261
Aristocracy, 221
Aristotle, xii, 3, 43, 127, 164, 212, 213, 214, 239, 243–44, 257–59
Arts of conferral, 166–69
Assembly, 149, 232
Athens, 167–68, 189
Attitudes: 102, 105, 170, 191; diversity of, 119
Aurelius, Marcus, 210
Authoritarianism, 237–38
Authority: 223, 230–31, 236, 257, 270–72; concentration of, 198; external, 188; of government, 191; scientific, 129; supernatural, 131
Autocracy: 122–23, 198, 207, 210–11, 220, 230, 232, 235, 284; contrast of democracy and, 181
Autonomy: 6, 193, 268–73; national, 191

Ballot, 67, 108, 124, 165
Barbu, Z., 171
Barker, Ernest, 35, 214
Barzun, Jacques, 168
Belize, 284
Bentham, Jeremy, 179
Bias, xii, 156, 187, 222
Bicameral systems, 81

Bill of Rights, 122, 138–39
Black, Hugo, 137–38, 143, 148
Body politic: 42, 44, 71, 116, 186, 242, 260, 263, 265; justification of democracy in, 248–57
Bonaparte, Napoleon, 227
Boulding, Kenneth, 111, 121
Brandeis, Louis, 151, 185
Burke, Edmund, 90

Caesar, 178
Calculus of Consent, The (Buchanan and Tullock), 78
Calhoun, John C., 72, 120, 183–84
Capitalism, 109
Carrington, Edward, 159
Carroll, Lewis, 112, 280
Censorship, 142–43
Characters and Events (Dewey), 252
Christianity, 46, 103, 193, 210
Churchill, Winston, 227
Cities, 42, 85, 158, 286
Citizens: character of, 170, 172
Citizenship: 15, 42–45, 51, 256; second-class, 51
Classes, 250
Clubs, 42, 168, 239, 247–48, 257
Coalition, 83, 86
Coercion, 125
Collected Legal Papers (Holmes), 181
Commercial organizations, private, 53
Commitment, xii, 45, 47, 54, 64, 140, 155, 184, 186, 224, 258, 273
Common sense, 164
Communication: 55, 107, 253, 278, 280–82; arts of, 166–69, 175
Communion, 46
Communism, 150. *See also* Marx, Marxism
Communist Manifesto, The (Marx), 150
Community: 4–5, 41, 56–57; actual, 29, 31; breakdown of, 48–49; concept of, 6, 41, 54; consciousness of, 45, 47, 274; constitution of, 105, 120, 185, 232; contrast between authoritarian and democratic, 236; fraternal, 42, 45, 168, 248; global, 16, 284–88; great, 43; heterogeneous, 74; heteronomous, 270; hypothetical, 67; ideal expression of, 54; instruments of, 229; internal, 191; international, 42, 184; national, 8, 29, 43–44, 192, 285; nature of, 7; non-political, 45–46, 163; of men, 254; of scientists, 175; overlapping, 25–27; Pan-American, 47; political, 42–44, 51–52, 132, 165, 242, 248–57, 277, 284; primitive, 163; purposes of, 7;

religious, 46, 132; rule of majority and, 46–47; size of, 6, 9, 31, 79–80, 171; special kinds of, 29; structure of, 10; underdeveloped, 75; unrecognized, 16–17; varieties of, 6, 9, 42

Competition: 136; for support, 30–31

Compromise: 47, 64, 69, 82, 84, 180–84, 190, 240; willingness to, 105; disposition to, 226

Conditional absolutism, 140–43

Conditional defense of the freedom of speech, 139–43

Conditions of democracy: constitutional, 102–56, 105, 120, 170; dispositional, 170–91; environmental, 107–8; intellectual, 105, 156–69, 175, 196, 280, 282–83; kinds of, 104–6; material, 104, 275–80; practically necessary, 101–2; protective, 105; psychological, 71, 105, 170–91, 228

Conference: 167; arts of, 156, 166–69

Confidence, 12, 142, 176, 186, 188–89, 191, 211

Confirmation, 46, 54

Conflict of local and larger interests, 93–97

Conformity, 288

Confraternity, 248

Consensus, 75

Consent: 3, 44, 70; of the governed, 31–33

Conservatism, 179, 228

Considerations on Representative Government (Mill), 209, 240

Constituencies, 81–84

Constitution: 36, 61, 141–43, 170, 186; written, 29, 120, 138, 202

Constitution of the United States, 76, 84, 120, 137ff., 153, 185, 217, 255

Constitutional Convention, 138

Constitutional guarantees: 30, 33, 71, 102, 121, 139, 153, 186, 232; limitation of, 141–43

Contributions, 52, 69, 259–60, 279

Courts, 136, 170

Cratylus, 253

Crime: 144–46, 153; non-verbal, 152

Criticism: 240; public, 176–78

Critique of Pure Reason (Kant), 266

Crito (Plato), 258

Cromwell, Oliver, 172

Debate, 214–15

Decision-making: 15, 77, 90, 215, 218, 222, 224, 229, 245, 273; bodies, 23; indirect, 24; participation, 112; processes, 8, 26, 36, 212

Decision-making rules: 61–71, 79, 86; and representative bodies, 80–81; for selecting representatives, 78; protective, 74; varieties of, 70; within the representative body, 78

INDEX

Declaration of Independence, 128
Defense: external and internal, 198; of democracy, 203–74
Delegation, 76, 197–98
Deliberation, 212, 214
Democracy: achievement of, 36; actual, 8; alternative accounts of, 28–33; American, 221; appraisal of, 9, 15, 33–35, 65; appropriateness of, 14; as autonomy, 268–73; Athenian, 162, 189; basic presupposition of, 41; breadth of, 8–18, 27, 199–200, 220; conditions of, xi, 195–96, 206–7, 211, 213, 231, 287; and consent, 31–33; and conditions distinguished, 103–4; consequences of, 28, 205, 267; constitution of, 102ff., 148; constitutional conditions of, 102–55, 215, 233; critics of, 214; defense of, xi, 203–74, 240–67; definition of, 3, 7; depth of, 8, 17–22, 89; deterioration of, 198; difficulties in developing, 75; dimensions of, 8–27, 34, 64; direct, 28, 73, 79, 89; direct and indirect, 76; dispositional conditions of, 11; and distributive justice, 215–24; economic conditions of, 109–19; and economic equality, 118–19; educational, 115; educational systems of, 166; enemies of, 196; essence of, 5–7, 229, 268; existing, 21; formal but superficial, 36–37; forms of, 36–37, 117–18; and freedom, 103; 121–23; and freedom of speech, 127; future of, 275–88; general observations about, 28–37; general theory of, xi–xiii; genuine, 111–18, 219; genius of, 227; global, 286–88; ideal, 18, 30; ideals of, 16; immediate experience of, 49; improvement of, 22, 34–35, 119; index of the health of, 65; instruments, xi, 37, 65, 59–97; intellectual conditions of, 56, 156–69, 233; intellectual skills required by, 164; intrinsic values of, 268–74; justification of, 241–67, 273; kinds of, 3, 116; large, 21, 23–24, 76, 84, 87, 157; laws of, 176; limits of, 227; local, 169; and loyalty, 228–31; Madisonian, 74, 217; majority rule, 68–71; material conditions of, 107–19; mechanical conditions of, 108; models of, 31; national, 19, 21–23, 24, 29–30, 105, 109, 127, 169, 190–91, 193, 195, 228, 282, 285; natural instrument of, 70; nature of, xi, 205; never complete, 36; obligations of, 189; one common criticism of, 213; partial, 52–53; participatory, 29, 115n; political, 116, 228, 242; power of, 75; practicality of, 19; practice of, 206, 236, 273; presuppositions of, xi, 39–57, 277; problems of a given, 163; procedural heart of, 180; processes and forms, 36–37; promotes freedom of speech, 231–33; promotes intellectual growth, 233–38; promotes its psychological conditions, 238–40; prospects of, xi, 275–88; protective conditions of, 75, 192–202; psychological conditions of, 170–91, 238; range of, 8, 22–27, 29, 117, 162; reality of, 37, 108, 208, 210; religious, 115; and representation, 76–97; representative, 24, 73; and secrecy, 161–62; and resolution of disputes, 224–28; small, 77; so-called, 88; sovereign and effective range of, 22–25, 113; spirit of, 36–37, 45, 69, 124; stability of, 15; structural imperfections in, 10–11; subjugation of, 192–93; superiority of, 207; trappings of, 117; values of, 193; western, 19–20, 88, 287; and wise policy, 209–15

Index

"Democracy and Educational Administration" (Dewey), 48
Democracy and Dictatorship (Barbu), 117
Democracy in America (de Tocqueville), 220, 230, 287
Demonstrations, 149
Demosthenes, 188
Despotism, 208–10, 214, 216
de Tocqueville, Alexis, 219–21; 230, 287
Development: economic, 119
Dewey, John, 48–49, 252
Dictatorship, 17, 33, 177
Dignity, 255–56, 262, 264, 271–72
Direct participation, 92
Direct popular control, 24
Direction, 213, 222, 227
Directive decisions, 215
Disarmament, 165
Discipline, 105, 187
Discrimination, 218; racial and religious, 12
Discriminatory selection, 45
Dispositions, 71, 104–5, 191, 192, 238, 240
Disquisition on Government, A (Calhoun), 72, 184
Dissent, 232
Distributive justice, 215–24
Distrust: 211; intelligent, 177

Eccentricity, 185
Echelons, 233, 237
Economic determinism, 114
Economics: and conditions of democracy, 25, 107–19; equality, 119, 222; inequalities, 118–19, 277, 280; interests, 255; justice, 102; power, 259; systems of, 109
Education: 49, 164, 196, 223, 235–36, 280–84; and the arts, 114; basic, 164–65; and books, 126, 142, 168; democracy in, 114; formal, 163; humanities, 164–65, 166; and instruction, 280, 281; literature in, 166; of the citizen, 156, 162–66; schools and, 26, 43, 167, 175, 196, 239, 247; technical, 164–65
Effectiveness: 78–79, 82, 88, 237
Efficiency: 62–64, 65–66ff., 79, 80, 86, 181; degree of, 68
Elections: 11, 13–14, 17, 30, 33, 36, 78, 93, 108, 118, 125, 197, 230, 239, 260; democratic, 78; exigencies of, 176; fake, 117
Electoral College, 69, 87
Electoral districts, 86
Elitism, 223, 283
Enfranchisement, 52, 200, 220–21

Engels, 150
Environmental control, 165
Epistemology, 130
Equality: 103, 112, 243–48, 249–57, 257–67, 273–74; as an hypothesis, 263–67; economic, 109, 118–19
Equilibrium, 74, 90, 217
Espionage Act of 1917, 137
Ethical intuition, 130
Ethics, Christian, 193
Exclusion, 26–27, 48–52
Excommunication, 46
Executives, 87
Experimentalism, 174–75, 208, 228, 281
External threat: protection against, 192–95

Faction, 47, 74, 215, 217
Faculties: rational, 55
Fallibilism, xiii, 105, 172–74, 238–39
Federalist Papers, The (Madison), 73–74, 76–77, 84, 217
Fellowship, 252
Felons, 49, 51–52, 256
First Amendment of the Constitution, 137–39, 141–43, 148, 150, 152–53
Flexibility, 178–79, 190, 228, 238–39
Force: 44, 183–84; military, 192; restraints upon the use of, 186
Foundations: private, 167
Franchise, 220. *See also* Enfranchisement
Fraternal orders, 42, 45, 168, 248
Fraternity: 54, 273–74, 284; and community, 54; system, 45
Free press, 126, 158, 173
Freedom: 103, 112, 193, 231, 268, 284; absolute, 128–32; and rights, 102–22; constitutional guarantees of, 231; defense of, 123; essential for democracy, 123; negative, 121; of elections, 29; of publication, 126; political, 117, 123–24, 151–52, 156; positive, 121; and restriction of travel, 162; religious, 122; to criticize, 196; to oppose, 124–28, 185; to propose, 124–25
Freedom of speech: 103, 117, 123–55, 156, 175, 215, 232; absolutist defense of, 128–32; and the anti-democratic minority, 152–55; conditional defense of, 139–43ff., 155; constitutional protection of, 143, 145–46; guarantees of, 154; restrictions placed on, 128; unrestricted, 136–37, 151; utilitarian defense of, 132–39
Fundamental Principles of the Metaphysics of Morals (Kant), 251, 269

Gerrymandering, 85
God, 46, 172, 180, 209, 226, 250

Government: 43, 71, 76, 111–12, 124, 137–38, 150, 154, 159, 162, 185, 194, 205, 214, 218, 222, 229, 246, 254–56, 270, 287; administrative sense of, 5; American, 142; aristocratic, 222; authoritarian, 239–40; autocratic and oligarchic, 234; autonomous, 273; by consent, 3; by the people, 3–7; by the people and for the people, 223; cares of, 197; constitutional, 143, 155; despotic, 230, 233, 235; directive and administrative, 22; directive function of, 6; directive sense of, 5; imperfect, 179; of the people, 3; representative, 23; Western, 25; with equal rights for all, 3; world, 249, 285–88
Great Britain, 17, 85, 142, 185, 220, 256

Hamilton, Alexander, 212, 217
Handbills, 126, 168
Heraclitus, 253
Heresy, 134, 153
Heterogeneity, 82–85
Heteronomy, 269–73
Hierarchy, 87, 236–38, 239, 258, 271–72
Hitler, 150, 154
Holmes, Oliver Wendell, 135ff., 140, 144–46, 180
Hook, Sidney, 148–49
Human equality: 263–67; principle of, 249–54, 263
Humanity, 254
Hypocrisy, 181
Hypotheses, 174, 208–9, 264; of equality, 263–67

Ideals: 31, 274; democratic, 21; governmental, 33; moral, 268; political, 30, 104; utopian, 56
Illocutionary acts, 145
Impeachment, 177
Impoverishment, 110, 218
Inalienable rights, 128ff.
Incitement: and advocacy, 143–52; criminal, 148; deliberate and specific, 152; generic, 144; illegal specific, 151; specific, 144–52; verbal, 144, 150
Inclusiveness: 62–64, 68; absolute, 63, 66; relative, 63, 66
Inculcation, 281
Independence, 284
Individuality, 184
Individuals, 216, 271
Indoctrination, 281, 283
Inefficiency, 68, 74, 80. *See also* Efficiency
Inequalities: 243–48, 250ff., 258–68; economic, 219–21; of concern, 245–46; of standing, 245–48

Infallibility, 132. *See also* Fallibilism
Information: 105, 233–34; provision of, 156–61
Initiation, 45–46, 54
Initiative, 88–89
Injustice, 53, 154, 218, 224
Instability: 127, 181, 230–31, 237, 253; psychological, 198
Institutions: 36, 101, 104, 112, 151, 158, 170–71, 192, 197; aristocratic, 222; democratic, 222; educational, 170, 175, 236; formal, 167; national, 31; of the past, 179; political, 114, 116; social, 231
Intellect, 236–38, 251–52, 258, 262, 272
Intelligence, 251–52, 258. *See also* Intellect
Intensity; 227; of concern, 70; of interest, 53–54
Internal threats: protection against, 195–98

Jackson, Robert, 153
Jay, John, 217
Jefferson, Thomas, 137, 148, 151, 154–55, 159–60, 166, 169, 226
Judaism, 46
Judicial review, 69
Justice: 76, 78, 182, 218, 223, 247, 255; distributive, 95, 215–24, 242–45; principles of, 262–63
Justification, 205; and vindication, 241–67

Kant, Immanuel, 251, 266, 268
Kaplan, Abraham, 131–32
Kipling, Rudyard, 187
Knowledge: unverifiable kinds of, 130

Language: 272; flexibility of, xi
Latin America, 25
Laws: 55, 121, 135, 137, 146–47, 170, 176, 180, 188, 199, 229–30, 238, 268, 270–72; American, 137; natural, 131–32, 181, 209
Leaders, 35, 177–79, 197
Leadership, 89–90, 227, 230–31; criticism of, 240; power of, 69
Legislation: 4, 81, 166, 199–200, 221, 251; pork-barrel, 93; social welfare, 220
Legislatures: 9, 66, 80, 136, 170, 202; bicameral, 81
Lenin, 134, 175, 227
Libel, 146–47
Liberalism, 187
Liberty, 255, 273–74. *See also* Freedom
Lincoln, Abraham, 3, 146, 227
Lippmann, Walter, 4, 169, 211, 252–53

Literacy: qualification for the franchise, 11, 201; rate 164–65, 283
Locke, John, 44, 70, 154, 264
Loyalty, xii, 44–45, 51, 177, 228–31

Machiavelli, 218–19
Madison, James, 73, 76, 84, 137–38, 217
Madisonian democracy, 217
Majority: 3, 63, 73, 83, 126, 135, 199, 220, 226, 237; absolute control of, 69; fixed, 74; fluctuating, 71–75, 217; misuses of power, 74; numerical 69; permanent, 74; qualified, 66, 70, 80; restrained use of power, 124; simple, 65, 70, 80; tyrannical, 71, 72; will of, 49
Majority rule: 3, 30, 46–47, 71, 86; and its varieties, 64–68; as the instrument of democracy, 68–71; identification of democracy with, 68; interpretations of, 68; stronger variant of, 67
Mao Tse-Tung, 154
Marx, Karl, 150, 154, 175
Marxism, 25, 109, 111–18
Material conditions: of democracy, 107–19
Material well-being, 104, 109–11
Maturity, 50–51, 181, 202, 256
Mechanical conditions of democracy, 107–8
Meiklejohn, Alexander, 150–52
Mein Kampf (Hitler), 150
Meliorism, 180, 287
Members: differentiation of, 54; homogeneity of, 64; rational, 56; voting, 67
Membership: 244, 256–57; active, 45; common, 47; concurrent, 73; degrees of, 52–54; formal recognition of, 46; full, 45; kinds of, 246; marginal, 50; nature of, 52, 247–48; restricted, 51
Men of Destiny (Lippmann), 252
Michels, Robert, 72
Military organization, 219, 237, 271
Mill, John Stuart, 132ff., 155, 184, 206, 209–10, 240
Milton, John, 142–43
Minority: 12, 47–49, 63, 65, 72, 133, 135, 187, 218, 221, 225–26; controlling, 67; intensely affected, 54; large, 68–69; power of, 69, protection of, 84
Mission, 237, 271
Modern Democratic State, The (Lindsay), 216
Monarchy, 177, 208
Morality: 268; supreme principle of, 269
Morris, Governeur, 212

N.Y.U. Law Review, 138, 148

Nation-states, 6, 16, 42–44, 191, 193, 286
National Security Council, 194
Nationalism, 285
Natural law, 131–32, 181, 209
Natural rights, 264
Naturalization, 44–45, 54
Negroes, 12, 51, 218
News Media: broadcasting stations, 158; *Manchester Guardian Weekly*, 17; networks, radio and television, 160; news-wire service, 160; newspapers, 126, 158, 168, 170; publicity, 161–62, 173, 234; radio, 126, 158, 160, 280; television, 126, 158, 160, 280. *See also* Press
Nicomachean Ethics (Aristotle), xii, 239
Nineteenth Century, The, 4
Non-participation: 9–15; as a consequence of social pressure, 12–13; by default, 11; by deliberate choice, 13–15; degrees of, 12
Nowell, John, 159

Objectivity: xii, 187–88, 191; civic, 188
Obligation: 229, 236, 245, 264; to vote, 14–15
Oligarchy, 33, 201, 207–8, 210–11, 216, 220, 232, 236
On Liberty (Mill), 4, 132ff., 185
Opposition: 185–86, 226–27, 238; loyal, 177
Oppression, 49, 72, 140, 218, 224, 259
Order, 103, 127, 149
Ortega y Gassett, José, 187
Orwell, George, 257
Ownership, 111–18

Pan-American relations, 47
Paradox: 61, 130, 187, 201, 251; of self-rule, 5
Paradoxes of Freedom, The (Hook), 148
Parliament, 14, 69–70, 76, 86–88, 90, 92–93, 95–96, 168, 194, 200, 202
Participation: 6–8ff., 195; breadth of, 62–63, 67–69, 189; channels of, 21; character of, 17; complexity of, 28; constitutionally prohibited, 11; depth of, 15, 64, 125–26, 184; direct, 113; effectiveness of, 91, 113, 166, 219; fixed minimum of, 63; forms of, 15, 18; indirect, 89; instruments of, 226; legal, 15; machinery of, 25, 104; measures of, 8; obligatory, 15; perversion of, 162; quality of, 88; range of, 64–65; restrictions upon, 201; spirit of, 183
Parties, 30, 73, 125–26, 150, 166, 215, 226. *See also* Political Parties
Patriotism, 76, 230
Peace, 103, 165, 169
People, the: 3–4, 11, 27, 77, 151, 169, 189, 211–12, 231; distrust of, 87, 142

Index

Pericles, 3, 162, 168

Perlocutionary acts, 145

Pessimism, 287

Philip of Macedon, 188–89

Plato, 211, 258

Plurality rule, 65, 69, 80

Policies: 178, 199, 201, 229, 233, 236, 238, 273; formation, 91–92; implementation, 91–92

Political parties, 20, 29, 33, 69, 72, 117, 185

Political science, xii, 20, 78, 101, 208

Politics, 121, 127, 212–14, 243, 257–58

Population: 165; growth, 278–80; size, 64, 73, 77, 79–80, 279; difficulties created by, 23

Poverty, 110–11, 118, 280, 288

Power: 72, 74, 88, 176, 197, 210, 230–31, 238, 281; abuse of, 72; delegated, 195; economic, 16, 219; governmental, 221; natural lust for, 73; possession of, 72; uncertainty of, 73

Pragmatism, 205ff.

Press: 137, 158–61; private ownership of, 161. *See also* Free Press

Principles: 268; autonomy of the will, 269; general, 55; regulative, 266

Principles of Economic Policy (Boulding), 111, 121

Principles of Social and Political Theory (Barker), 35

Privacy, 185

Private enterprise, 113, 222, 246

Production and distribution: means of, 111–12, 114

Property: 53, 251, 255; ownership of, 26; qualifications, 201–2

Prophecy, political, 277

Prospects of democracy: 275–88; fraternal, 284; intellectual, 280–84; material, 275–80

Proportional representation, 84–87

Prosperity, 110–11, 118

Protection, 44

Protective conditions of democracy, 192–202

Protectiveness: 62–64, 65–66ff., 80–81, 82; degree of, 68

Psychological conditions of democracy, 170–91, 196, 226, 280

Public ownership, 222, 282

Public Philosophy, The (Lippmann), 4, 169

Publication, 157, 232–33

Putney debates, 255

Rank, 251, 255

Rationality, 50, 55–57, 130, 156, 228, 272–73; concept of, 55–57

Reapportionment, legislative, 86

Rebellion, 183, 226. *See also* Revolution

INDEX

Recall, 88–89, 177

Referendum, 88–89

Regulatory agencies, 87

Religion, 52, 131, 137, 199

Representation: 23, 30, 69, 78, 217, 221; as the instrument of democracy, 76–78ff.; bases of, 78, 81–84; between elections, 88–89; degrees of, 78–81, 85, 194; functional, 82–83; geographical and proportional, 84–87; levels of, 87–88, 195; non-functional, 83–84; principle of, 76; systems of, 124, 279

Representative systems: 24, 29, 76–97; basic elements of, 78

Representatives: 24, 179–80, 221, 227, 234, 283, 285; dilemma of, 90–93; integrity of, 93; rule for selecting, 80; tenure of, 89

Republic, 73, 143, 161, 207

Responsiveness, 78, 86

Restraint: 74; self-imposed, 187

Revisionism, 175

Revolt of the Masses (Ortega y Gassett), 187

Revolution, 148, 150, 154–55, 225–26

Rights: civil, 230; constitutional, 140, 151, 196; democratic, 103; God-given, 128; of participation, 245, 260; political, 243, 265; self-evident, 129; to be let alone, 185; to participate, 53, 248, 254, 264; to speak, 105; to vote, 50

Roosevelt, Franklin Delano, 227

Rotten boroughs, 85

Rousseau, 264

Rule: 4; by the majority, 3, 74; by plurality, 65, 69–70; by fluctuating majorities, 71–74; of law, 51

Rulers: 72, 272; absolute, 122–23; and ruled, 4

Rules: 55–56, 61–71, 269; authoritarian, 235, 240

Sabotage, 152, 154

Sanctions, 271

Scientific inquiry, 174–75

Second Treatise of Government (Locke), 44, 70

Secret ballot, 86

Security: 103, 161; internal, 161; of the nation, 143, 152

Sedition, 196

Self-confidence, 189. *See also* Confidence

Self-defense, 232

Self-evidence, 128–31

Self-government: 4–6, 11, 42, 46, 55, 61, 123, 141–43, 152, 170, 181, 188, 197–98, 205, 235, 238, 268, 273–74; defense of, 192; desire for, 202; local, 190–91; representative, 74

Self-interest, 73

Index

Self-realization, 104
Self-restraint, 105, 186
Self-rule, paradox of, 4–5
Senegal, 284
Shaw, George Bernard, 173
Skepticism, 173–74
Social contract, 44
Socialism, 150; guild, 82
Socialism for Millionaires (Shaw), 173
Sociologists, 208
Sovereign range of democracy, 22–25, 113
Sovereignty: 4, 184; national, 285–87; of the people, 3
St. Francis, 252
Stability, 127, 181, 198, 230–31, 237, 253
State and Revolution, The (Lenin), 150
Subordination: spirit of, 272
Subversion, 152
Suffrage, 67–68
Suppression, 132–36, 143, 149, 151–54, 159–60. *See also* Freedom of Speech
Supreme Court Decisions: *Abrams v. U.S.*, 135, 140; *Baker v. Carr*, 86; *Barenblatt v. U.S.*, 142–43; *Feiner v. New York*, 149; *Frohwerk v. U.S.*, 145; *Gitlow v. New York*, 144; *Olmstead v. U.S.*, 185; *Schenk v. U.S.*, 137, and "clear and present danger" doctrine, 137–39; *W. Va. State Board of Education v. Barnette*, 153; *Whitney v. California*, 151

Taxation: 53, 221; property, 26–27; poll, 200–2
Teacher in America (Barzun), 169
Technology: 107–8, 281; questions of, 92–93, 163; skills of, 87, 212–13ff., 251
Theology, 131–32
Threat: external, 193–95; internal, 195–98, 200, 202
Thucydides, 168
Thurber, James, 75, 154
Tolerance, 74, 104, 135, 184–87, 190–91, 238–39
Town meeting, 28, 199–200
Traits: dispositional, 238–39
Transcendental ideas, 266
Truths: 134ff., 147, 159, 172, 182; absolute, xiii; self-evident, 129–30
Two-party system, 80

Unanimity, 63
Undemocratic origins and anti-democratic effects, 198–202
Union, 47–48, 73, 155, 182, 284

INDEX

United Nations, 278

United States: 17, 43–44, 47–48, 69, 73, 84–86, 114, 150–52, 159, 163–66, 218, 220–21, 226, 279, 283; Congress, 66, 137–39, 141–43, 145, 150, 152; Constitution, 150; House of Representatives, 80; president of, 87; Senate, 150; Supreme Court, 86, 137

Universality of suffrage, 18, 22

Universities, 53, 167, 196

Utopia, 287

Values, 206, 251, 273–74

Veto, 169

Vindication of democracy: general remarks about, 205–9; and justification, 241–67

Violence, 149, 151, 154–55, 179, 184, 224–28

Voters: 85, 216; actual, 67, 80; qualified, 67

Voting: 15, 18, 25–27, 63–64, 86, 220; fractional, 52; plural, 52–54

War: 136–37, 169, 182, 184, 192–95, 286; civil, 47

Washington, George, 48

Wealth, 53, 111, 118, 211, 252, 255, 258–59, 260

Whitman, Walt, 252